THE THEORY OF MEANING

Edited by

G. H. R. PARKINSON

OXFORD UNIVERSITY PRESS
1968

Oxford University Press, Ely House, London W.1

GLASGOW NEW YORK TORONTO MELBOURNE WELLINGTON
CAPE TOWN SALISBURY IBADAN NAIROBI LUSAKA ADDIS ABABA
BOMBAY CALCUTTA MADRAS KARACHI LAHORE DACCA
KUALA LUMPUR HONG KONG TOKYO

FILMSET BY ST PAUL'S PRESS, MALTA
PRINTED IN GREAT BRITAIN
AT THE UNIVERSITY PRESS, OXFORD
BY VIVIAN RIDLER
PRINTER TO THE UNIVERSITY

CONTENTS

INTRODUCTION

WE use the words 'mean' and 'meaning' in a variety of senses, and some at least of these give rise to philosophical questions. For example, we say such things as
  (i) 'Football means everything to him'.
  (ii) 'I mean to work this evening'.
  (iii) 'Those black clouds mean rain'.
  (iv) 'The Latin word "pluvia" means "rain"'.
It is clear that the word 'mean' has a different sense in each of these sentences. In the first, it is said that football is all-important to somebody; in the second, someone is stating his intention of doing something. In the third, it is said that black clouds are a sign of something, and for that reason this sense of the word is sometimes called the 'sign' sense of the word 'mean'. In the fourth sentence, the speaker is talking about words; he is not saying that something is important, as in (i), nor is he saying—it would be absurd to say—that a word has certain intentions. Nor, again, is he saying that one word is a sign of the other, as black clouds are a sign of rain; for whereas one can replace (iv) by (iva) 'The Latin word "pluvia" means the same as "rain"' without altering the sense of (iv), it changes the sense of (iii) if one replaces it by (iiia) 'Those black clouds mean the same as rain'. This fourth sense of the word 'mean' is sometimes called the 'symbol' sense of the word, where the word 'symbol' stands for anything that can have meaning in this sense. Usually, symbols of this kind are words, but they can also be, for example, pictures and gestures.

In saying that these are different senses of the words 'mean' it is not implied that there is no overlap between at any rate some of them; and in fact it has been argued that to speak of the meaning of a word (sense iv) is to speak of what people mean by words, and that to speak of what they mean by words is to speak of what they intend ('mean' in sense (ii). Cf. Hart (10)[1] and Grice (12)). It has also been argued that meaning in sense (iv) is a special case of meaning in sense (iii), the 'sign' sense of the word 'mean'. Issues of this sort are not being prejudged by the four-fold classification that has been adopted here; the sole purpose of this classification (for which, incidentally, completeness is not claimed) is to make possible a statement of the problems with which the articles contained in this book are concerned.

[1] Figures in brackets refer to items in the bibliography.

1

These problems concern the 'symbol' sense of the word 'mean', and are two in number. The first concerns the nature of meaning, and may be put in the form of the question, 'When one says that one knows the meaning of a symbol, such as a word, *what* is it that one claims to know?'; or, more briefly, 'What is it for a symbol to have meaning?' The second problem concerns the criteria of meaning, and may be put in the form of the question, 'What requirements must a symbol satisfy if it is to be called meaningful?' It is clear that these two problems are not the same; that to state a criterion of X is not the same as saying what X is. For example, it is a criterion of something's being gold that it has a certain specific gravity, but in stating this, we do not give a full answer to the question, 'What is gold?', for there is more to gold than its specific gravity.

The fact that philosophical articles dealing with this problem have been brought together here under the title of 'The Theory of Meaning' might be thought to suggest that there is among philosophers only one accepted view about the nature and criteria of meaning. This would be far from true, and it would be better to regard these papers as essays *towards* a theory of meaning. There is, however, a further reason for this title. No attempt has been made to give, in these selections, specimens of every theory of meaning; the papers included are such that one can see in them, despite frequent disagreements, at any rate the outlines of a unified theory of meaning. This makes the title 'The Theory of Meaning' more appropriate than, say, 'Theories of Meaning'.

The purpose of this short introduction is to provide a kind of sketch map of theories about the nature and criteria of meaning, to help in the understanding of the articles which follow; this is therefore the place to say something about theories which are not discussed, or are discussed only briefly, in these articles, as well as bringing out the main points of importance in the articles themselves. Before this is done, there are two observations to be made. First, it must be stressed that this is only a rough sketch; it is meant to be a help to finding one's way about, and is not a precise and detailed guide. Second, it has already been said that our concern is with the 'symbol' sense of the words 'mean' and 'meaning'. In what follows, attention will be concentrated on verbal symbols—i.e. words—since these are the most common symbols. We shall be concerned first with the meaning of words or phrases, but to avoid tedious repetition of the words 'or phrases' we shall refer to 'words' simply.

Suppose, then, that one is asked what it is for a word to have meaning. It is perhaps natural to answer that a meaningful word stands for something, whereas a meaningless one does not. The meaning of a word, on this view, is a kind of object, and depending on the presence or absence of an object of this kind a word is meaningful or meaningless. What kind of object, then, is the meaning of a word supposed to be? One answer has been that the meaning of a word is that of which the word is the name; for example, the meaning of the words 'the Parthenon' is the Parthenon, that physical object of which 'the Parthenon' is the name, or, in other words, the 'bearer' of this name. The meaning of a name, then, is the bearer of the name, and since a name is traditionally said to 'denote' its bearer, the theory may be called the 'denotation' theory. Such a theory of meaning was presupposed by Bertrand Russell (cf. Russell (2), and Strawson, No. III below) in his analysis of what he called 'definite descriptions', by which he meant phrases of the form 'the such-and-such', where what is referred to is an individual and not a class—'the present Prime Minister', for example, as opposed to 'the dog' as the words are used in the sentence 'The dog is a friend of man'. The theory is not, and was never claimed to be, applicable to all meaningful words; it is obvious, for example, that there are no ifs and ands for the words 'if' and 'and' to denote. But the theory breaks down even in the case of the words and phrases which it does claim to cover. Frege pointed out that two phrases which differ in meaning or 'sense' (*Sinn*) can stand for the same object—can have, as he put it, the same 'reference' (*Bedeutung*. Cf. Frege (1)). For example, the phrases 'the morning star' and 'the evening star', which differ in meaning, both refer to the planet Venus; but if bearer and meaning are the same, the two phrases should have the same meaning. Conversely, a word may have the same meaning but a different reference in various instances of its use; an example of this is the word 'I', whose reference varies in accordance with the person who uses it, though its meaning—which may be paraphrased as 'the person now speaking or writing these words'—remains the same. There is a further point. It was mentioned above that, according to the denotation theory, the meaning of the words 'the Parthenon' is a certain building. Certainly, a building is the reference of these words, but it is not what they mean. It makes no sense to say that the meaning of the words 'the Parthenon' is made of marble, and was seriously damaged in the seventeenth century; and if, at some future time, the Parthenon is completely destroyed, it will not be correct to say that after this date the words 'the Parthenon' no longer have meaning.

Another answer to the question, 'What kind of object is the meaning of a word?' has been that the meaning of a word is an image (e.g. E. Sapir, *Language* (New York, 1921), Chap. 1; Pei and Gaynor, *A Dictionary of Linguistics* (New York, 1954), p. 133). This 'image theory' of meaning, as it may be called, avoids some of the difficulties that beset the denotation theory, in that it explains how we can talk meaningfully about what no longer exists, or never has existed, and it does not commit us to saying that, for example, the meaning of the words 'the Parthenon' is built of marble. There are, however, overwhelming objections to the theory. On this theory, a word cannot mean the same for all who speak it or hear it, since each person has a different image; we should have to speak, not about the meaning of a word, but about the meaning which this or that person attaches to it. Further, if the theory were true, we could talk about nothing but what is in our own minds. It might be thought that these difficulties can be avoided by modifying the theory so that it states, not that the meaning of a word is an image, but that words have meaning through the medium of images. For example, when Aristotle said (*De Interpretatione*, 16a 3; trans. Ackrill) that 'spoken sounds are symbols of affections in the soul' and that these 'affections' are likenesses of actual things, he may have meant that the meaning of a word is, not an image, but that of which the image associated with the word is the image. However, this modified form of the theory fares no better. It is clear that we can use words meaningfully without having images as we do so; indeed, there are some meaningful words, such as the phrase 'a four-dimensional space', which we cannot interpret in terms of images. More important, however, is the fact that in modifying the theory we have transformed it. For if we say that the meaning of a word is that of which the image associated with it is the image—the Parthenon, say, and not the image of the Parthenon—we are back at the denotation theory, with all its defects.

Some philosophers have tried to improve on the image theory by saying that the meaning of a word is a concept. They would agree that there is, for example, no image of a four-dimensional space, but they would say that the meaning of the words 'four-dimensional space' is the *concept* of such a space. Such a theory, which may be called the 'concept theory', has found its way into textbooks of logic (e.g. H. W. B. Joseph, *Introduction to Logic* (Oxford, 1906), pp. 12 ff.), but is now generally abandoned, for either it falls into some of the difficulties that trouble the image theory, or it says nothing. What is meant is this. If we say that a concept is something in a person's mind, then it seems that there will be as many meanings of a word as there are people who use, hear or read the word; further, it seems that we are doomed to speak only about the contents of our minds. These consequences parallel difficulties in the image theory of meaning; but if we try to avoid these by regarding a concept as something inter-personal, in the sense that we speak of e.g. the concept of law as opposed to this or that person's concept of it, then we explain nothing. For to speak of a concept in this sense is simply to speak of the meaning of a word, so that the concept theory merely says that a word is meaningful in so far as it has meaning.

The theories discussed so far have in common the fact that they concern the meaning of words or phrases; nothing has yet been said about the meaning of the sentences in which these words or phrases may appear. Such an account might seem superfluous, for it might be supposed that the meanings of isolated words are learnt first, and that after learning their meanings we put them together in sentences, the meaning of which is simply the sum of the meanings of their components. To suppose this, however, would be a serious error, the nature of which can best be seen by approaching the theory of meaning not from the word but from the sentence.

There is one theory of the meaning of sentences to which only the briefest reference can be made here, namely the 'picture' theory of meaning stated by Wittgenstein in his *Tractatus Logico-Philosophicus*. The theory is of considerable obscurity, and its exact meaning is still a matter of dispute (compare, e.g., items (15)–(19) in the bibliography); further, although it makes some valuable points, and may also contain a hint of Wittgenstein's later views about meaning (cf. Pitcher (19), p. 249 n. 13), the theory was later abandoned by its creator, and is now chiefly of historical interest. Leaving this aside, therefore, we turn to another theory of meaning—a theory which has a number of adherents, and which will be called here the 'causal theory'. To introduce this theory, it will be convenient to glance back at the various senses of the word 'mean' discussed at the beginning of this introduction. The fourth of these was the 'symbol' sense of the word 'mean'; it is meaning in this sense with which the various theories of meaning are concerned. The third was the 'sign' sense of the word— 'meaning' in the sense in which clouds mean rain. The causal theory of meaning claims that 'meaning' in the fourth sense is related to 'meaning' in the third. The theory may be expounded as follows. When rain falls on human beings, it has certain effects on them;

amongst others, it produces certain characteristic responses, such as the putting-on of raincoats. Now, it also happens that rain is regularly preceded by the appearance of clouds of a certain type, and on the basis of past experience of this fact, the responses to rain are transferred to clouds of this sort. It would, however, be an over-simplification to say that this is what is meant when it is said that clouds mean rain. Someone may see the clouds, and the clouds may mean rain to him, but if he is indoors at the time he is unlikely to put on his raincoat. To this it may be replied that he would do so, if he were to go out; he is ready to do so, or, he has a disposition to do so, and this is part of what is meant when it is said that to him, certain clouds mean rain. If, therefore, one extends the meaning of the word 'response' so that it covers, not only overt behaviour but also dis-positions to behave—for example, not only how a man behaves in the rain, but how he would behave if he were in the rain—then it may be said that to assert that clouds mean rain to somebody is to say that there has been a transference of response from rain to clouds. In the same way, a dog may learn that the ringing of a bell means dinner, and a child may learn the meaning of the sentence 'Dinner's ready'. In each case there is a transference to a sound or sounds (the bell, or the words) of the response or responses normally made to that with which the sound or sounds are regularly associated. The meaning of a sentence, then, is the response, or range of responses, produced by the sentence.

The theory has not received much discussion in the form of articles, and no such article is included in this collection. The items listed in the bibliography under 'Causal Theory' give a detailed discussion of this view of the nature of meaning; here it must be sufficient to mention just one serious defect in the theory, namely, its failure to give due attention to what people intend. Suppose, for example, that I see a man put up his umbrella; this may be a sign to me that rain is falling. But it does not follow that by doing this the man means that rain is falling; for this to be the case, he must intend someone to think that rain is falling. Indeed, he must do more than this. He might perhaps open his umbrella when rain is not falling, but he wants to make someone believe that it is, perhaps with a view to keeping that person indoors. For a man to mean something by his behaviour, then, he must not only intend to induce a belief in his audience, but must also intend the audience to recognize the intention behind the behaviour. What the man with the umbrella really intends is that his audience shall stay indoors, but he does not intend his intention to be recognized; if it is, he may fail in his intention.

In many ways more important than the causal theory of meaning, and certainly more discussed, are those views about meaning which involve the notion of verification. This very general description covers two views, both associated with the so-called 'logical positivists'; the first will be called here 'the verification theory of meaning', and the second 'the verification principle'. The first is a theory about the nature of meaning, and may be stated concisely (though not precisely) in the form of the well-known slogan, 'The meaning of a proposition is the method of its verification' (Schlick (31), p. 148). The second states a criterion of meaning; its precise formulation is still a matter of dispute, but it may be introduced by the following assertion, which does not state a criterion of meaning without qualification, but says what something must be if it is to be meaningful to a given person: 'A sentence is factually significant to a given person if, and only if, he knows how to verify the proposition which it purports to express' (Ayer (20), p. 35). In each case, the verification referred to is verification by means of observations. It is clear that if the first view is true, then the second is true also, but that the converse does not hold. Even if a sentence is factually meaningful to me only if I know the method of verifying the proposition which it purports to express, it does not follow that the method of verification *is* the meaning.

We discuss first what we have called the 'verification principle'; that is, a certain criterion of meaning. Some matters already call for explanation: namely, the presence of the adverb 'factually' in the passage from Ayer quoted above, and the implied distinction between a sentence and a proposition. By a 'proposition' is meant that which is true or false; sentences are the linguistic means by which one expresses what is true or false. (To avoid possible misunderstanding, it must be emphasized that not every sentence expresses what is true or false; many sentences are used to ask questions, or make requests, or give orders. Conversely, what is true or false is not always expressed by a sentence; symbols of other kinds may be used.) The point of saying that truth or falsity is predicated of propositions, but not of sentences, is that the same truth or falsehood can be expressed by a variety of sentences in a language, and is of course expressed in different ways in different languages. Again, it is possible to utter a sentence which in some circumstances expresses a truth or falsehood, but in the circumstances of the utterance does not—e.g. if one speaks the sentence in pronunciation practice, or as a grammatical example. With the distinction between sentence and proposition in mind, consider now the sentence 'God's in his heaven'. This seems grammatically similar to the sentence 'Smith's in his study', and indeed to a whole host of sentences by which propositions may be expressed. Adherents of the verification principle, however, assert that a sentence is the expression of a proposition to a person only if that person knows how to verify by observations the proposition which it might be thought to express, and they would claim that, by this test, it can be seen that 'Smith's in his study' does express a proposition to the person who states or hears it, and 'God's in his heaven' does not. Let us now try to put this in terms of the meaning of what is said. 'God's in his heaven' may have meaning in a sense; for example, it may express a feeling of *joie de vivre* on the part of the person uttering the sentence. As such, it may be said to have *emotive* meaning for that person; but as he will not (it is claimed) be able to verify what the sentence says, it cannot be called *factually* meaningful for him.

The subject of discussion so far has been what is or is not factually significant to a given person, and the criterion stated may be called a restricted form of the verification principle. Clearly, it follows from this that if there is a sentence such that what it says cannot be verified by anyone, then it is factually meaningless, not to a given person only, but simply and without qualification. This criterion will be called the unrestricted form of the verification principle, or the verification principle simply. Here one must add the proviso (as the logical positivists did) that when in this context one speaks of something as 'unverifiable' what is meant is, not what cannot be verified by anyone at a given time, but what is unverifiable *in principle*. If this proviso is not added, then it may be necessary to say that sentences which were factually meaningless at a given time became meaningful later, when the means of verification were more refined. But it would be a very odd use of words if one were to say that the sentence 'There are mountains on the far side of the moon' became factually meaningful only after the invention of long-range rockets and of the means of transmitting pictures by radio.

The view that a sentence is factually meaningful if, and only if, what it says is verifiable in principle is attended with considerable difficulties, which were clearly stated by supporters of this view (e.g. Ayer (20), pp. 37, 93). For example, it would seem absurd to deny that the universal laws of the sciences have factual meaning; yet, if to verify something means to establish or prove its truth, then it is not clear how one can verify an assertion which is about (say) absolutely all particles of matter. The verification of assertions about the past also raises problems; for can one, by means of observations that are made now, or that can be made in future, *prove* the truth of some assertion about what happened in the past, and is no longer observable? Even assertions about physical objects now existing cause problems; for there seems no limit to the number of observations that could be made to test such an assertion, and as long as it is possible that some observation would refute it, so long it seems that one has not established the truth of what is said.

The answer usually suggested to these problems was that the word 'verify' must be taken in a more liberal sense, so that it covers not only the conclusive proof of the truth of propositions, but also the production of evidence which is at any rate relevant to the truth of what is said. In this way, it was thought, one could preserve the difference between 'God's in his heaven' and 'Smith's in his study', the difference being that whereas a good deal of empirical evidence was relevant to the truth of the latter, none was relevant to the truth of the former. But this only shifts the difficulty, for it now has to be explained what is meant in this context by 'relevance'. An early attempt by Ayer to solve this problem is criticized by Berlin in No. 1 of the selections which follow; more elaborate attempts are discussed in the articles listed as (21)–(23), (27) and (29) in the bibliography. These are all attempts to state a criterion of factual significance in terms of entailment; what is said by a sentence is declared to be verifiable if, in certain specified ways, it entails certain observation statements— that is, if certain propositions about what is observed or observable follow with logical necessity from the sentence whose factual meaning is in question. Waismann, however, has argued (and his view has won wide acceptance) that a proposition about a physical object does not in fact entail an observation statement, in the sense that to suppose the first to be true and the second to be false would be self-contradictory (see below, No. 11, p. 42). This does not mean that a satisfactory statement of the verification principle cannot be found; but it seems that, if the principle is stated in a satisfactory way, it will not be in terms of the deductive logician's concepts alone.

An attempt has been made to by-pass the difficulties of the verification principle by taking as a criterion of factual significance, not verifiability, but falsifiability. This criterion has been attributed to Popper, who, however, has said that he did not aim at solving the problem of meaningfulness, but rather at solving the problem of how to draw the line between the statements of the sciences and all other statements

(Popper (26), p. 162). The line is to be drawn, Popper argued, by noting that a statement of the sciences is always falsifiable; if there is a theory which cannot be refuted by any conceivable event, then it is non-scientific. It is easy to generalize from this, and produce what may be called the 'falsifiability criterion' of meaning, by saying that if a sentence is to be factually significant, then what it says must be falsifiable. The attraction of this view is that a universal proposition is falsified if there is even one contrary instance; even if it is granted, then, that a universal law of the sciences can never be verified, the fact that a single contrary instance would falsify it establishes its factual significance. But even if this is true of scientific laws—and incidentally it is by no means certain that such a law would be abandoned on the strength of a single observation: cf. Waismann, No. II, p. 43—yet there are many other sentences of which it seems reasonable to say that they have factual significance, but which are such that they are not falsified by a single observation, or indeed by any finite set of observations. These are sentences which affirm indefinite existential propositions, such as 'There are dodos' (cf. Ayer (20), p. 38).

On the basis of the verification principle, logical positivists declared to be factually meaningless (and sometimes 'meaningless' simply), not only the utterances of theology and metaphysics, but also the language of morals and of aesthetic appraisal. Not surprisingly, this produced a good deal of discussion, and it may indeed be said that the great attention that has been paid to problems of meaning in recent years was partly due to the verification principle. The discussions were often more heated than illuminating, and it can now be seen that the emotively-charged word 'meaningless' tended to obscure a perfectly valid point that lay behind the assertions of the supporters of the verification principle. They were saying in effect that utterances fall into different types; that, for example, there is a fundamental difference between saying 'That was a morally good thing to do' and 'That took a long time to do'. This is true and important, but it was obscured by the assertion that moral utterances are meaningless— which, in a sense, they clearly are not. This may be put in another way by saying that however apt the verification principle may be as a criterion of certain types of meaningful utterance, it does not provide a criterion of all meaningful utterances. What is required, then, is a criterion of meaning, or a theory of meaning, which includes what is sound in the verification principle, but which takes account of meaningful utterances about which the verification principle is silent. Such a theory may be approached through what was called earlier the 'verification theory'.

The verification theory of meaning, it will be remembered, was formulated by Schlick as 'The meaning of a proposition is the method of its verification'. In the commonly accepted sense of the word 'proposition', this is not accurate; a proposition *is* the meaning of a certain type of sentence, and the verification theory was really concerned with the problem of what it is to say that such sentences have meaning. The error, however, is not serious, and is easily rectified by substituting 'sentence' for 'proposition'. Of the verification principle in this slightly revised form one may say at once, as a point in its favour, that it does not assert that the meaning of a sentence is a kind of entity. This, however, is only a negative point; what of the positive side of the theory? Why say that a meaning is a method? It may be helpful here to compare the theory of physical concepts put forward by P. W. Bridgman in *The Logic of Modern Physics* (New York, 1927), and called by him the 'operational' point of view. Take, for example, the word 'length' (Bridgman, op. cit., p. 5); we know what this word means if we can tell what the length of any and every object is, and this involves the performance of certain physical operations. The meaning of the word 'length', indeed, just is that set of operations by which length is determined; or, to put this in terms of verification, the meaning of the word 'length' is the method of verifying what is said by sentences of the form 'The length of x is y units'. But though it may be true that, for example, the meaning of the sentence 'The length of this stick is 24 inches' is the method of its verification, there are many cases in which it is not correct to identify meaning and method of verification. The sentence 'The Prime Minister of Great Britain made a speech yesterday' has factual meaning; but is the meaning of the sentence the method, or methods, of verification? Surely what the sentence means is that yesterday a certain event occurred. The verification theory also suffers from the fact that it applies only to that restricted sense of 'meaning' to which the verification principle applies. But it has already been argued that moral judgements and aesthetic appraisals have meaning, even if the sentences by which they are expressed do not satisfy the verification principle; it follows from this that their meaning is not the method of their verification.

The statement, then, that the meaning of a sentence is the method of its verification is misleading; it is not true of meaningful sentences of every kind, and it is doubtful if it is always true even of those sentences which are factually meaningful. The slogan did, however, express an important idea, namely, that the meaning of an expression is connected with its *use*. Take, again, the word 'length'. If we are to explain this word to someone, it is not enough simply to point to something (for example, a piece of cloth) and say 'That's a length'; for how would the person to whom we are explaining the word know that we meant a length, and not, say, the piece of cloth, or its material, or its colour? To explain the word, we shall have to say such things as 'The length of that is . . . ', or 'That's a length of . . . ', and so on; that is, we explain the *use* of the word 'length', and we explain its use *in sentences*. In short, the meaning of a word is its use in a language (cf. Wittgenstein (35), par. 43). The phrase 'in a language' is important here. An adherent of the denotation theory might perhaps agree that the meaning of a word is its use, but he would add that its use is to denote. This, however, would be a mistake (cf. Haas, No. IV, pp. 93 ff.), for it suggests that a word has meaning in isolation from others, which has just been seen not to be the case. It may be added that this is why it is best to approach the problem of the nature of meaning by first considering the sentence (cf. p. 5 above), since in this way one is less tempted to suppose that words have meaning in isolation from one another.

The view that the meaning of a word is its use in a language may meet with an objection. Granted, it may be said, that to learn the meaning of the word 'length' is to learn its use in the context of sentences, yet this is not all that there is to learning its meaning. We know its meaning fully only when we know how lengths are measured, when we know (as Bridgman would say) the operations by which length is determined. What the objection says is quite correct, but this does not affect the view that the meaning of a word is its use in a language. This is because the word 'language' is used here in a wide sense; a language, in this sense, is not to be regarded as just so many words, but must be seen in the whole context of human behaviour, and to speak of the 'grammar' of such a language is to use the word 'grammar' in such a way that to say how a proposition can be verified is 'a contribution to the grammar of the proposition' (Wittgenstein (35), par. 353; cf. pars. 7 and 23).

It has been objected that the theory just described, commonly called the 'use theory', is too vague: it merely tells us that the meaning of a word is its use in a language, or a role that it is employed to perform, but it gives no indication of what the use *is*, of what particular role it is that constitutes the meaning (Christensen (4), p. 153). The answer is that there are many uses, many roles, but that it is not the business of the use theory to explore these; for example, the question of how words are used in the language of moral discourse is a problem for moral philosophy, the question of how they are used in theological language is a problem for philosophical theology, and so on. What the use theory does in effect is to tell the inquirer into the meaning of words not to think that meanings are a kind of object, but to study the way in which words are used in a language. The latter advice may seem obvious; one might think that anyone who wants, for example, to examine the meaning of metaphysical assertions will not need to be recommended to study what metaphysicians say. There is some point in the recommendation, however, since critics of metaphysics have sometimes argued, on the basis of the verification principle, that no metaphysical sentence can have meaning, and they have quoted only isolated sentences from metaphysicians, which serve as illustrations rather than as topics of inquiry. The use theory is at least a safeguard against brisk dismissals of this sort. At the same time it is not so liberal that it allows everything to have the meaning claimed for it. For example, if a metaphysician claims that what he says has factual meaning, then the use theory requires him to explain what he believes to be the use of words in sentences which have factual meaning, and to show that his metaphysical terms have such a use.

All this does not imply that there are no problems that relate to the use theory in general, as opposed to problems about the use of words in languages of this or that type. A number of such problems are discussed in the last five papers in this book; here they can be mentioned only briefly. The first, discussed in Nos. v (1) and (2) and vi, is a problem about what it is to which the use theory refers. Philosophers have said, not only that the meaning of a word is its use, but also that the meaning of a sentence is its use (e.g. Schlick (31), p. 147). Ryle argues (No. v (1)) that the latter assertion is a mistake; his view has not won universal acceptance (cf. White (40)), though Shwayder (No. vi) argues that the view is sound, and uses it in discussing a problem about the distinction between predicating and referring. In No. v (2), Findlay expresses agreement with Ryle's point of view, and then considers the problem of what is involved in explaining the use of expressions. He attacks the view that a complete account of their use can be given in terms of public operations and circumstances, without reference to operations conducted privately in anyone's head. The final problem discussed in these selections arises out of a development of some of the ideas put forward by J. L. Austin in *How to do things with words* (Oxford, 1962). Put very crudely, Austin's view was that in saying something we not only utter certain words with a certain meaning (perform what Austin called a 'locutionary act'), but we also perform an 'illocutionary act' and may also perform a 'perlocutionary act'. To perform an illocutionary act is, e.g., to order or to warn; it is an act that we do *in* saying something. To perform a perlocutionary act is, e.g., to persuade or to deter; it is something that we achieve *by* saying something. In drawing attention to these uses of words (it would perhaps be more precise to say, to these uses of sentences) it seems to have been Austin's intention to supplement the use theory of meaning rather than to supplant it, and so it might be thought that his views, however important, are not relevant here. However, these views have been used to give an account of meaning, Alston (No. VII) arguing that sameness of meaning 'hangs on' sameness of illocutionary act potential (p. 153). Difficulties in this theory are stated by Holdcroft in No. VIII. It seems likely that the discussion will continue; but this brief introduction to the theory of meaning must end here.

G.H.R.P.

I

VERIFICATION

Sir Isaiah Berlin

This paper is an attempt to estimate how far the principle of verification fulfils the purpose for which it is employed by many
contemporary empiricist philosophers. The general truth of their
doctrines I shall not call into question. The thesis which I shall try
to establish is that the principle of verifiability or verification after
playing a decisive role in the history of modern philosophy, by
clearing up confusions, exposing major errors and indicating what
were and what were not questions proper for philosophers to ask,
which has enabled it to exercise in our day a function not unlike that
which Kant's critical method performed for his generation, cannot,
for all that, be accepted as a final criterion of empirical significance,
since such acceptance leads to wholly untenable consequences. I shall
consequently urge that after due homage has been paid to its thera-
peutic influence, it needs to be abandoned or else considerably revised,
if it is to be prevented from breeding new fallacies in place of those
which it eradicates.

I propose to begin by assuming that what the principle sets out to
do both can and should be done; and to consider whether it can do
this alone and unassisted. I shall seek to show that it cannot, and that
to maintain the opposite entails a view of empirical propositions too
paradoxical to deserve serious notice.

As is well known, its supporters claim that the function which it
fulfils is that of acting as a criterion for determining whether assertions of a certain type mean in fact what they purport to mean. The
pressing need for such a criterion arises out of the view on which much
modern empiricism rests, according to which all truly significant
assertions must be concerned either with the facts of experience, in
the sense in which they are the subject matter of the judgements of
common sense and of empirical science, or else with the verbal means
used to symbolize such facts. The task in question is to find some
infallible criterion by which to distinguish assertions of the first, i.e.

From *Proceedings of the Aristotelian Society*, Vol. 39 (1938–9), pp. 225–48. Reprinted
by courtesy of the author and the Editor of the Aristotelian Society.

experiential type, from all other possible modes of employing symbols. I must begin by making clear my use of certain essential terms: by a sentence I propose to mean any arrangement of words which obeys the rules of grammar; by a statement any sentence which obeys the rules of logic; and finally, by a proposition any sentence which conveys to someone that something is or is not the case. And this seems on the whole to accord with common usage. In addition I propose, at any rate in the first section of the argument, to mean by the term experience only what phenomenalists say they mean by it, that is, only such actual or possible data as are provided by observation and introspection. I do not wish to assert that phenomenalism is self-evidently true. On the contrary, no method yet suggested of translating the propositions about material objects into propositions about observation and introspection data seems wholly satisfactory. But for the purpose of my thesis it will be sufficient to confine myself to the latter, i.e. to propositions concerned solely with objects of immediate acquaintance; since if the verification criterion is inadequate in dealing with them it will *a fortiori* fail to apply to the much more complex case of statements about material objects. If this is true it will tend to show that historical connexion between phenomenalism and 'verificationism' is not a logical one, and that the failure of the latter does not necessarily invalidate the former. This conclusion I should like to believe to be true, since the opposite would prove fatal to the view which seems to me to be true on other grounds, as I shall urge in the last section of this paper, that whereas the phenomenalist analysis of statements of common sense is fundamentally correct, and has not proved convincing more on account of insufficient ingenuity in the formulation of specific analyses, or of the vagueness of the analysandum, than because of some fatal defect in the method itself, the principle of verification, in spite of its undoubted efficacy in the past in detecting and destroying unreal puzzles, has now begun to yield diminishing returns, and even to create new spurious problems of its own. This, I shall argue, is due to the fact that it is not in principle capable of being applied to the whole field of empirical belief and knowledge, but only to a limited portion of it—a fact which is brought out particularly clearly by the examination of that version of it, sometimes called operationalism, according to which the different logical or epistemological categories to which a given proposition may belong are determined by the differences in the kind of tests normally employed to discover its truth or falsity.

The essence of the principle of verification will appear clearly if one considers its progressive modification in the face of difficulties. The bare assertion that all significant statements were concerned either with facts about experience or with the symbolic means of expressing them was too vague and excluded too little. Metaphysicians and theologians could claim that they, too, reported facts of experience, although facts of a very different order from those which were of interest to empirical scientists, arrived at by non-empirical processes of cognition, and thus wholly outside the range of any evidence drawn from the data of observation or introspection. A stricter criterion of significance seemed therefore to be required, at any rate in the case of propositions claiming to describe experience. To supply it (I do not vouch for the historical accuracy of this account) the principle of verification was adopted, a test, which, so it is claimed, made it possible to determine without further ado whether a given collocation of words was or was not significant in the above sense. In its earliest and most uncompromising form it declared that the meaning of a proposition resided in the means of its verification; the questions 'What does the statement p mean?' and 'What must one do to discover whether p is true?' were logically equivalent—the answer to one was the answer to the other. The most obvious objection to this doctrine, which critics were not slow to urge, was that this formulation involved a glaring hysteron proteron; for before I could think of possible ways of verifying a given statement I first must know what the statement means, otherwise there could be nothing for me to verify. How can I ask whether a group of symbols asserts a truth or a falsehood if I am not certain of what it means, or indeed whether it means anything at all? Surely, therefore, understanding what the sentence means—what proposition it expresses—must in some sense be prior to the investigation of its truth, and cannot be defined in terms of the possibility of such an investigation—on the contrary the latter must be defined in terms of it. But this objection is not as formidable as it looks. A supporter of the theory may reply that what he means by the expression 'to know the means of the verification of p' is knowing in what circumstances one would judge the group of symbols 'p' to convey something which was or was not the case; adding that what one means by saying that one understands a given sentence, or that the sentence has meaning, is precisely this, that one can conceive of a state of affairs such that if it is the case—exists—the sentence in question is the proper, conventionally correct description of it, i.e. the proposition expressed by the sentence is true, while if it is not the case, the proposition expressed is false. To understand a sentence—

to certify it as expressing a given proposition—is thus equivalent to knowing how I should set about to look for the state of affairs which, if the state of affairs exists, it correctly describes. To say that a sentence is intelligible, i.e. that it expresses a proposition, without specifying what the proposition is, is to say that I know that I could set about to look for the relevant situation without saying what kind of situation it is. It follows that any sentence such that I can conceive of no experience of which it is the correct description, is for me meaningless. The limits of what I can conceive are set by experience—that is, I can conceive only whatever is either identical with, or else in some respect similar to the kind of situation which I have already met with or imagined; the possible is a logical alternative of, and conceivable only by reference to, the actual; whatever is wholly different from it is wholly inconceivable. The actual, on this view, consists of the data of observation, sensible and introspective, and what can be inferred from them. The logically possible is conceived only by analogy with it; sentences which purport to refer to something outside this are therefore meaningless. If nevertheless I claim that they mean something to me I am using the term 'meaning' ambiguously or loosely: I may wish to say that they suggest, or are evidence for, a situation, without formally describing it, as tears are evidence of distress without being a statement about it; or else that they evoke an emotion in me, convey or induce a mood or an attitude, stimulate behaviour, or even that no more is occurring than that I am acquainted with the normal use of the individual words in the sentences to which I attribute meaning and that they are grouped in accordance with the rules of grammar and of logic, as in certain types of nonsense verse. This seems prima facie plausible enough, and successfully eliminates whole classes of expressions as being meaningless in the strict sense because they seem to describe no conceivable experience, and can therefore, as Hume recommended, be safely rejected as so much metaphysical rubbish. Whatever survives this drastic test can then be classified exhaustively as being either direct statements about possible experience, that is empirical propositions, or second or higher order statements about the relations of types of such statements to each other, i.e. propositions of logic and other formal sciences. And this was as much as the anti-metaphysical party had ever claimed. It was soon seen however that as it stood this position was wholly untenable.

To begin with the conception of 'means of verification' was far too narrow. If it was interpreted literally it always referred to the present or the immediate future in which alone sensible verification of what I was asserting could take place. This gave all statements about the past, and a great many about the present and future, a meaning which was prima facie very different from that which they seemed to have. Such a sentence for example as 'It was raining half an hour ago' had to be regarded as equivalent to one or more of such statements as 'I am now having a moderately fresh memory image of falling rain', 'My shoes look fairly, but not very, wet', 'I am looking at the chart of a recording barometer and observe an undulating line of a certain shape', 'I expect, if I ask you "Was it raining half an hour ago?" to hear the answer "Yes"' and the like. This is unsatisfactory on two grounds both equally fatal. In the first place by translating all propositions about the past (and about the future) into propositions about experience in the present (which alone I can conclusively verify) it gives two senses of the word 'present'; the sense in which it is distinguishable from 'past' and 'future', i.e. the normal sense, and the sense in which it includes them; the second sense, being contrastable with nothing, adds nothing to any statement in which it occurs; to say in this sense that all significant statements refer only to the present is thus to utter a pointless tautology. Yet the sense in which alone it was relevant to say that all conclusively verifiable propositions were concerned only with the present, was the first, not the second, sense; the sense in which to speak of the present state of something is to distinguish it from past and future states. Moreover, the translation feels wrong. One does not usually mean by the sentence 'It rained yesterday' the present empirical evidence for it, not even the total sum of such evidence. For the relation 'being evidence of' not being that of logical implication, the evidential proposition may be true and the proposition which it claims to establish false; the two therefore cannot be equivalent. What I mean to assert is that it was raining yesterday, not that events which are now occurring make it unreasonable to doubt that it did: the rain I speak of is the rain of yesterday, whatever may or may not be happening today. To verify yesterday's rain conclusively (the verificandum being taken in a phenomenalist sense as a logical construction out of observation data), one has to have lived through yesterday and to have observed whether it rained or not. To do this now is in some sense of the word impossible: yet the meaning of the sentence is not seriously in doubt. It follows that either all propositions save those about the immediate present are meaningless: or that meaning cannot depend on conclusive verifiability.

To this the defenders of the theory can answer that in saying that the meaning of p resides in (*liegt in*) the means of its verification they did not literally mean to assert any such equivalence: they meant only that 'p is significant' entails that some means of verifying is possible. The proposition is never equivalent to the sum of evidence for it; but unless one can say that there could be a situation in which an observer could verify it, one cannot say that the sentence has any meaning. Thus 'p is significant' where p is empirical entails and is entailed by 'p is verifiable', but is not equivalent to any specific group of actual propositions cited as evidence for it. Moreover by verifiability what is meant is verifiability not in practice, but in principle; this last being needed to eliminate not only the objection that some propositions e.g. that there are mountains on the other side of the moon are clearly significant and yet cannot be verified on account of technical difficulties which observers with more luck and skill than ourselves might overcome, but to secure plausible analyses of propositions about the past, which we are prevented from verifying by the accident of our position in time as well as space. We *might* have been born earlier than we were, and lived in countries other than those which in fact we inhabit; I cannot now, do what I will, verify the proposition 'Julius Caesar was bald' by direct inspection, but there is no *logical* reason why I should not have been born in ancient Rome in time to have observed Caesar's head; the reason is causal, unless indeed I define myself as having been born in the twentieth century, in which case some other observer could have carried out this observation. For there is no reason why 'p is verifiable' should mean 'p is verifiable by me'.[1] Solipsism even of the so-called methodological variety is a wholly gratuitous assumption. I can conceive of other observers by analogy with my own self, however the notion of a particular self is to be analysed. So much has been pointed out by Berkeley. To verify the proposition that such observers actually exist, and have experiences which are not ours, is of course a very different and much more difficult task. Thus '"p" is significant' has now come to mean 'it is conceivable (i.e. there is no logical contradiction in supposing) that someone should observe or should have observed what is correctly described by "p"'. In this watered-down form the principle does seem to acquire a much wider sphere of application and attempts at 'silly' analyses can be successfully foiled. But the position is still far from secured.

For all that can be accounted for on this hypothesis are such singular categorical propositions as are conclusively verifiable, at any rate in principle, by a suitably situated observer. This leaves three classes

---

[1] *Vide* 'Unverifiability-by-me', by G. Ryle, *Analysis*, 4, 1.

of propositions unaccounted for, and these by far the most commonly used:—(1) Propositions which are not singular:—(2) Propositions which are not categorical:—(3) Propositions which seem to be both singular and categorical, but not to be conclusively verifiable by observation.

(1) General propositions offer the most obvious difficulty. No sentence of the form 'all s is p', whether taken in extension or intension, where s denotes an infinite set (or at any rate does not *explicitly* denote a finite one) can be verified by any finite number of observations. That is to say it is not conclusively verifiable at all. The same applies to all propositions containing 'any' or 'every' as components. The attempt made by Ramsey and those who accept his view to treat them as rules or prescriptions, logical or empirical, and therefore neither true nor false, cannot be defended since, as they are used, they are held to be refutable by a single negative instance, and it is nonsense to say of rules that they have instances or can be refuted. Yet they have clear empirical meaning, particularly when taken in extension, and cannot be left out of account. To meet this difficulty the principle of verification was revised and two types of it distinguished: the first, called verification in the strong sense, was the familiar version. The second, or 'weak' verification was invented to apply to general propositions and to singular-seeming propositions about material objects, in so far as these were thought to entail general propositions about sense data—a view which it has proved far from easy to hold. Two versions of 'weak' verifiability are given by Mr. Ayer[1]: according to the first we ask about a given proposition 'Would any observations be relevant to the determination of its truth or falsehood?' If so the proposition is significant. This may well be true, but as it stands the suggested criterion is far too vague to be of use.[2] Relevance is not a precise logical category, and fantastic metaphysical systems may choose to claim that observation data are 'relevant' to their truth. Such claims cannot be rebutted unless some precise meaning is assigned to the concept of relevance, which, because the word is used to convey an essentially vague idea, cannot be done. Thus 'weak' verification, designed to admit only general, and material object, statements, cannot be prevented from opening the gates for any statement, however meaningless, to enter, provided that someone can be

---

[1] *Language, Truth and Logic*, p. 26.

[2] On this *vide* 'Meaninglessness', by Dr. A. C. Ewing, *Mind*, N.S., Vol. XLVL. No. 183, particularly pp. 352–3.

found to claim that observation is in some sense relevant to it. As a criterion for distinguishing sense from nonsense relevance plainly does not work: indeed to accept it is in effect to abrogate the principle of verification altogether. Mr. Ayer, conscious of this perhaps, attempts to provide another far more rigorous formulation of 'weak' verification, which at first seems to fit our needs more adequately.[1] He says, 'To make our position clearer we may formulate it in another way . . . we may say that it is the mark of a genuine factual proposition . . . that some experiential [i.e. strongly verifiable] propositions can be deduced from it in conjunction with certain other premises without being deducible from those other premises alone. This criterion seems liberal enough.' Unfortunately it is a good deal too liberal, and does not guarantee us against nonsense any better than the previous test. What it appears to assert is this: given three propositions p, q, r, where r is conclusively verifiable in principle, then p is weakly verified, and therefore significant, if r follows from p and q, and does not follow from q alone. Thus 'all men are mortal' is 'weakly' verifiable, because 'Socrates will die' which does not follow from 'Socrates is a man' by itself, follows from the two in conjunction. It may be noted that 'verifiable' seems here to have lost its sense of 'rendered true' or 'established beyond doubt,' and is equivalent to something much looser, like 'made probable' or 'plausible', itself an obscure and unexamined concept. However, even in this diluted form the principle will not do. For if I say

> This logical problem is bright green,
> I dislike all shades of green,
> Therefore I dislike this problem,

I have uttered a valid syllogism whose major premise has satisfied the definition of weak verifiability as well as the rules of logic and of grammar, yet it is plainly meaningless. One cannot reply to this that it is put out of court by the confusion of categories which it contains, or some such answer, since this entails the direct applicability of a criterion of significance other than 'weak' verification, which makes the latter otiose. No criterion which is powerless in the face of such nonsense as the above is fit to survive. 'Weak' verifiability is a suspicious device in any case, inasmuch as it bears the name without fulfilling the original function of verification proper, and appears to suggest that there is more than one sense of empirical

---

[1] Ibid, a few lines later.

truth. The chief argument in its favour seems to be that unless it is valid, any theory which entails it must be false. Since the contrary instance cited above is fatal to it, this consequence must be accepted. Weak verification has thus failed to provide the needed criterion.

By far the most ingenious attempt to solve the difficulty is that made by Dr. Karl Popper[1] who suggests that a proposition is significant if and only if it can be conclusively falsified by the conclusive verification of a singular proposition which contradicts it—as when a law is refuted by the occurrence of one negative instance. But while this may provide a valid criterion of significance for general propositions about observation data, it throws no light on whether the sense in which they are called true is or is not identical with that in which singular propositions are so called. The implication which one may be tempted to draw from this is that propositions of different logical types are true or false, verifiable and falsifiable, each in its own specific fashion: indeed that this is what is meant by saying that they belong to different categories; that is to say that the logical (and epistemological) character of a proposition is determined by the way in which it is verifiable (or falsifiable), the two being alternative ways of saying the same thing about it. This view which if true would solve many difficulties cannot, however, be accepted, as I hope to show in the next section of the argument. It should further be noted that Popper's criterion of falsifiability, while it may deal successfully with general propositions of observation, does not apply equally well to propositions about material objects for whose benefit it was originally introduced. But as we have agreed to accept phenomenalism this is beside the issue, and the criterion may therefore be provisionally accepted.

(2) The second type of proposition not covered by the original 'strong' verifiability criterion consists of those which are not categorical. These are highly relevant to the whole issue, and repay exceptionally close attention. It has too often been assumed by logicians that all hypothetical propositions are general, and all general propositions are hypothetical: 'all s is p' is equivalent to 'if s then p' and vice versa. Nothing could be further from the truth. While some hypothetical propositions are general, others are not. The commonest of all propositions which occur in the writings of contemporary positivists, the propositions indispensable to any discussion of meaning or verification, the familiar 'if I look up I

[1] In his book *Logik der Forschung*.

shall observe a blue patch', are indubitably hypothetical, but in no sense general. To show this one need only point out that they are conclusively verifiable. Indeed it was because an attempt was made to reduce all other statements to verifiable propositions of this type that absurdities resulted. I verify the proposition mentioned above by looking up and observing a blue patch: if conclusive verification ever occurs, it occurs in this case. It must be noted that I have actually proved more than I have asserted: not merely the hypothetical but a conjunctive proposition 'I shall look up and I shall see a blue patch' has been verified. This is unavoidable from the nature of the case. But although the conjunctive proposition entails the hypothetical, it is not entailed by it, and the two are therefore not equivalent. The conjunction is falsified if (a) I do not look up and see a blue patch, (b) I do not look up and do not see a blue patch, (c) I look up and see no blue patch. The hypothetical proposition is falsified by the occurrence of (c) alone. If either (a) or (b) is the case, the hypothetical proposition is rendered neither true nor false, and may be either. It is essential to note firstly that the relation between the protasis 'I shall look up' and the apodosis 'I shall see a blue patch' is not one of material implication, otherwise the whole would be falsified by denying the protasis. Secondly, that it is not one of strict implication, since the antecedent may be affirmed and the consequent denied without a formal contradiction. Thirdly, that it is not necessarily causal: I may, of course, when I declare that if I look up I shall see a blue patch, say this because I believe that there is a causal connexion between the two events, but equally I may not believe this, and decide to bet that this will happen because I am by temperament a passionate gambler, and all the more stimulated if I believe that the weight of inductive evidence is against me; or I may say it because it is an exception which disproves one causal law, without necessarily regarding it as being itself an instance of another law; or I may say it out of sheer contrariness, or any other motive whatever. My *rational* ground for saying what I do would doubtless take the form of a general causal proposition which entails the proposition on whose truth I am betting, but I may choose to behave irrationally, or use the proposition in an *ad absurdum* argument to prove its opposite: the general proposition 'observers in conditions similar to these normally see blue patches if they look up' entails, but is not entailed by, the proposition 'if A looks up he will observe a blue patch': the latter proposition, so far from being equivalent to the former, may be true where the other is false, and, as was said above, may be conclusively verifiable—a condition which the general proposition is logically incapable of attaining. The proposition is therefore both singular and hypothetical, its subject being not a hypothetical variable, but a nameable particular. So far all seems clear. The difficulty arises when the antecedent is not fulfilled: When I assert, for example, that if I look up I shall see a blue patch, and then fail to look up. The proposition appears now to be no longer conclusively verifiable. The opportunity for that has been missed and cannot be recovered. I must now resort to the roundabout method of producing evidence for it, i.e. 'weakly' verifying the general causal proposition of which the proposition to be verified is an instance; nor can the instantial proposition be made more probable than the general proposition which entails it. But clearly the statement 'if I look up I shall see a blue patch', which now becomes 'if I had looked up I should have seen a blue patch', expresses a proposition which is still true or false in precisely the same sense as before, although the means of its verification have altered; yet clearly the statement cannot have changed in meaning because I did not in fact look up. Yet if it were true that the impossibility of strongly verifying a given proposition entailed that it had a logical character different from propositions which can be strongly verified, the proposition in question would alter in character solely because I did or did not choose to act in a certain fashion. This would mean that the kind of meaning possessed by singular hypothetical sentences or statements would depend on the empirical fact that their protases did or did not actually come true, which is patently absurd. It seems to me to follow that neither the meaning, nor the logical character, of a statement can possibly depend on what steps one would naturally take to ascertain its truth: and in so far as operationalists assert this without qualification, they are mistaken.

At this point someone might reply that although an unfulfilled singular hypothetical statement (or for that matter a hypothetical statement whose protasis is not known to be fulfilled) cannot be verified conclusively in actual fact, it can be so verified in principle. I did not in fact look up and so I cannot know for certain what would have happened if I did; but I might have looked up: or rather it is not self-contradictory to assert that an observer could or did look up; and such an observer, possible in principle, is in a position to verify the proposition conclusively. And so such propositions are, after all, no worse off than categorical statements about the vanished past: they too may not in fact have been verified conclusively; but they could have been so verified; and so are verifiable conclusively in principle. This argument, plausible though it is, is ultimately untenable, for the reason that were I situated favourably for verifying these unverified hypotheses, I should *ipso facto* not have been able to verify some of those which I in fact did: and I could not, in the logical sense of 'could not', have done both. An eternal omnisentient being, which is in all places at all times can, if it chooses, verify all categorical propositions about past, present and future phenomena: but even it cannot verify what did not occur; that which might have occurred had not that happened which in fact did. And if it is omniscient as well as omnisentient, and if there is any sense in which it could be said to know this too, it knows it by means other than sensible verification. A simple example will, I hope, make it clear. Suppose that instead of asserting one singular hypothetical proposition, I assert two such propositions in the form of the premises of a dilemma, such that the protasis of each is incompatible with the protasis of the other. For instance: 'if I remain here I shall have a headache. If I do not remain here I shall be bored'. Each of these propositions may itself be verifiable in principle: the conjunction of both cannot be verified conclusively, even in principle, since it involves me in the logical impossibility of being in a certain state and not being in it at the same time. Of course I can adduce the evidence of various observers for what would happen under these two logically incompatible sets of conditions. But such inductive evidence verifies only 'weakly' (whatever meaning may be attached to that unfortunate phrase). 'If I were now at the North Pole I should feel colder than I do' cannot in principle be strongly verified, since I cannot even in principle be simultaneously here and at the North Pole and compare the different temperatures. It is beside the point to say that this arises only if I am defined as capable of being situated here or at the North Pole but not at both; whereas I might have been a giant with one foot on the North Pole and the other in this room, in which case I might have verified the proposition conclusively. I could myself be defined differently, but the same problem would still arise whatever the defined scope of my powers; a proposition asserting an unfulfilled possibility can always be constructed to contradict whatever is the case, and this can be made the protasis of a second singular hypothetical proposition whose verifiability is incompatible with that of the first. To put it semi-formally: given that for every empirical proposition p at least one contradictory *not-p* is constructable; then for every singular hypothetical proposition of the form 'if *p* then *q*' (let us call it *pq*), a second proposition 'if not *p* then *r*' may be constructed (let us call it *pr*), where *r* may or may not be equivalent to *q*. Then it is the case that where *pq* and *pr* are propositions describing the possible data of a given observer, the conclusive verification of *pq* and *pr* is not compossible, and the truth of either is compatible with the falseness of the other. And yet each of the two alternatives of the disjunction is in its own right a proposition which in suitable circumstances could be conclusively verified; either may be true and the other false, either probable and the other improbable; their only logical relation is that of unco-verifiability—they cannot both be conclusively verified even in principle. And this plainly cannot alter the meaning which either has in its own right. If this conclusion is correct it follows that the meaning of a proposition need not be affected—let alone determined—by the fact that a given means of verification is or is not logically possible in its case. I have emphasized the case of singular hypotheticals because they seem to bring out particularly clearly that if meaning depends on the relevant type of verifiability, then in order to know what one of these conjunctions of propositions means one requires to know whether both the protases are true. And this is self-evidently false. Yet these are the very propositions which occur in all philosophical analyses of empirical statements, the stuff of which logical constructions are built, the basic propositions to which propositions about the public world are commonly reduced by phenomenalists of all shades and hues.

Perhaps another example will make this even clearer. Supposing that I have a bet with you that all persons seen entering this room will appear to be wearing black shoes. Let the term 'this room' be defined as anything recognized by both of us as being correctly described as this room in virtue of certain observable characteristics, such that if either of us certifies their disappearance from his sense field, the entity described as this room shall be deemed to have ceased to exist. Under what conditions can such a bet be lost or won? We may begin by affirming the truth of the analytic proposition that the room will last either for a finite time or forever. In either case the set of persons observed to enter it, is similarly either finite or infinite. Only if it is the case that the observed set of visitors is finite, that the room visibly comes to the end of its existence, and that each of the persons who are seen to enter appears to wear black shoes, can I win the bet. When, on the other hand, it is the case either that the room lasts for ever, or that the set of persons seen to enter it is without limit, or both these, but at least one person appears to wear shoes of some other colour than black, or no shoes at all, I lose the bet. There are however further possibilities: when, for example, either the room lasts for ever or the number of persons seen to enter is limitless, or both, and every person entering appears to wear black shoes; in that event the bet is undecided since the proposition on whose truth or falsity it turns, has been neither verified nor falsified conclusively. In all possible cases it could in principle be falsified by seeing the arrival of a person not wearing black shoes. But whereas in some cases it could also be verified conclusively, in others it can not. Yet when we arrange the bet neither of us need know whether I am in principle capable of winning or not. Nevertheless the proposition in terms of which the bet is stated is not in the least ambiguous. It is not the case that the words 'all persons . . . ' must if the proposition is to have a definite meaning be used to refer *either* to a finite set (in which case conclusive verifiability is possible), *or* an infinite set (in which case it may not be, but not to both. Yet if the meaning of a proposition always depended upon the type of verifiability of which it is capable, the above would be systematically ambiguous: we should have to be regarded as having made two separate bets, one on the behaviour of a finite set, the other on that of an infinite one. Yet we are under the impression that only one bet had been made because we attributed to the proposition beginning with the words 'all persons will . . .' not many senses but one, namely, that in which it is equivalent to 'no one person will not . . .'. And we are right.

Like the previous example this tends to show that if one wishes to understand a sentence which purports to express a proposition when it is asserted by someone, while it is doubtless generally useful to discover under what conditions he would consider its truth as established, to regard its meaning as dependent on what kind of conditions these would be, is to hold a false doctrine of what constitutes meaning. Of course I do not wish to deny that in general I can only discover the difference between sentences of different kinds, e.g. between those used to refer to visual data and those concerning auditory ones, or between propositions concerning persons and propositions about physical objects or about sense data, by observing in what kind of experience verification for them is sought. But it does not follow from this that the kind of verification

which a given proposition can in principle obtain, determines the
type of meaning which it possesses, and so can act as a principle of
logical or epistemological classification, such that the propositions
belonging to two different classes defined in this way, cannot for
that reason belong to one and the same logical or epistemological
category, or be answers to questions of the same logical type.
And yet this is the fallacy which seems to me to underlie much that
is said by upholders of theories of verification and operationalism.
That significance is connected with verifiability I have no wish to
deny. But not in this direct fashion, by a kind of one-to-one correspondence.

(3) This brings us to the third type of propositions mentioned
above: the apparently categorical, but not conclusively verifiable
propositions, as for example those about material objects or other
selves. The scope of this paper does not permit an adequate discussion of the merits and defects of phenomenalism; but even if we
conceive it to be in principle correct, however inadequate all existing
formulations of it, we must allow that among the experiential
propositions into which a proposition asserting the existence of
a material object must be analysed, there must inevitably be some
which describe how the object would appear to an observer, were
conditions different from those which in fact obtain; if in other
words he were not observing what he is. The proposition 'I am
holding a brown pencil in my hand' may or may not entail propositions about past and future actual and hypothetical data presented
to me; analysts differ on this point; some hold these to be part of
what is meant by 'this pencil', others maintain them to be only evidence
for the existence of, but not elements in the analysis of it. And this
holds equally of the actual and hypothetical data of observers other
than myself. What is common however to all phenomenalist accounts,
is that part, at any rate, of what I mean by saying that it is an actual
pencil that is now before me, and not the phantom of one, is that the
datum which I am now observing belongs to a group of visual, tactual,
auditory etc. data some of whose members are the subject matter of
hypothetical propositions which describe what I should be exper-
iencing if I were not at this moment in the circumstances in which
in fact I am. These propositions are, as was shown above, not co-
verifiable with the propositions which describe what I am actually
observing, and this fact alone is quite sufficient to make propositions
about physical objects not conclusively verifiable in principle,
whether or not they are held to contain, telescoped within them,

B

various causal and general propositions as, according to some philosophers, they do. Indeed the assertion that general propositions enter into the analysis of prima facie singular propositions about material objects seems to me a good deal more dubious than that these last are not conclusively verifiable; if this seems certain, that is due to the unco-verifiability of some of the singular propositions which are true of the object, not as it is in the past or in the future, but at any given moment. Indeed when anti-phenomenalists maintain that every suggested translation of a given common sense statement into sense datum language, however richly it is equipped with general and hypothetical propositions, fails to render in full the meaning of the original, because material objects possess attributes which necessarily elude observation, when for example, Prof. G. F. Stout[1] in discussing what we mean by the solidity of material objects as conceived by common sense, observes that we think of it not as a permanent possibility but as a permanent impossibility of sensation, what gives such objections apparent plausibility and Prof. Stout's epigram its point, is that there is indeed something which must for logical reasons elude verification by the most exhaustive conceivable series of observations, carried out by any number of possible observers, namely, propositions about what I, or some other given observer, could verify, were we not situated as we are. And this the most thorough going phenomenalism must do justice to, however successfully it may have exorcised the last remaining vestiges of the concept of matter as an invisible, intangible, dimly conceived substratum.

If what I have urged above is true, verification whether 'strong' or 'weak' fails to perform its task even within the framework of pure phenomenalism which must not therefore be so formulated as to entail it as its primary criterion of significance. And to establish this negative conclusion was the main purpose of my thesis. In conclusion I should like to add a few remarks on what this seems to suggest with regard to the question of the proper analysis of physical objects and other selves. If following the view suggested by Prof. C. D. Broad[2] we look upon our concept of a given material object as a finite complex of sensible characteristics (to be referred to as m) selected more or less arbitrarily and unselfconsciously from the wider set of uniformly co-variant characteristics n, then m which is constitutive of the

[1] *Studies in Philosophy and Psychology*, p. 136.
[2] Discussed by Mr. John Wisdom in *Metaphysics and Verification* (1), *Mind* N.S., Vol. XLVII, No. 188, pp. 480–1.

object for a given observer, will differ for different individuals, times and cultures, although a certain minimum of overlapping common reference is needed for the possibility of communication in the present, and of understanding records of the past. The set of characteristics m, if it is affirmed to have an instance, will turn out to render true a finite number of categorical and a potentially infinite number of hypothetical propositions; and the paradoxical fact often urged against phenomenalism that any given proposition or set of propositions recording observations may be false, and yet the relevant proposition about a material object which is 'based' upon them may remain true—that in other words the latter type of proposition cannot be shown either to entail or be entailed by the former—is explained by the fact that m is vague and n (for all we know) infinite, and consequently however much of m you falsify it will never demonstrate that n has been exhausted. But when m, which represents your personal selection out of n, is progressively falsified, a point will arise at which you will probably abandon your belief in the existence of the material object in question, since your experience does not present a sufficient number of characteristics defined as m. But where this point will arise for a given individual is a purely psychological or sociological question; and I, who carve an m which differs from yours, out of the common totality n, will understand you only to the extent to which our respective m's overlap; and therefore what will seem to you evidence adverse to your proposition will seem to weaken mine at the very most only to the extent to which your m overlaps with mine. Even if 'a case of m exists' were far more precisely formulated than it ever is in ordinary life, as a collection of singular propositions, it would still not be conclusively verifiable because some of its components are hypothetical and unco-verifiable; but as words are commonly used it is always fluid and vague, and so cannot be conclusively falsified either. Thus the verification criterion which was intended to eliminate metaphysical propositions in order to save those of science and common sense, cannot deal with these even in its loosest and most enfeebled form.

Other selves are more recalcitrant still. The strict verification principle seems to demand a behaviourist analysis of selves other than that of the observer, introspection data being confined to, because conclusively verifiable by, him alone. Even if, as was argued above, this be rejected and the existence of other selves, conceived by analogy with the given observer's own, be conceded at least the same obscure status as is, in the present state of philosophical discussion, enjoyed by material objects, each self being allowed to verify at any rate its own experience, it still seems difficult to explain, even in terms of the falsifiability criterion, what could show that the sentences 'My toothache is more violent than yours' or 'Smith thinks faster than Jones' are not meaningless. Each observer, we say, can vouch for the occurrence or the non-occurrence only of events in his own experience. Whatever may be said about the meaning of such terms as 'privacy' and 'publicity' as applied to data which are evidence for material objects, introspected states must, as language is ordinarily used, be declared to be private in some sense in which material objects are not: an inter-subjective observer who perceives my thoughts and feelings as well as his own seems a self-contradictory concept: otherwise it would be no more absurd to say that he and I experience the same headache as that we see the same table. Here, once again, the verification principle does not apply in either of its forms; and yet the propositions comparing the experiences of several observers seem at once intelligible, empirical, and as often as not precise and true.

The conclusion which follows if the above account of the matter is correct, is this: that the criterion provided by 'strong' verification at best applies to a very narrow range of observation propositions; while 'weak' verification either fails to act as a criterion of sense altogether or, if made equivalent to 'strong' falsification, and in that form made sole arbiter of meaning, entails a brand of phenomenalism which provides unsatisfactory analyses of propositions about material objects and other selves. It follows a fortiori that the criterion of types of verifiability cannot act as the basis of classification of empirical propositions into logical categories. For it can neither distinguish statements recording observations from other categories of empirical propositions, nor enable us to distinguish different types of observation statements from each other. In view of this complete failure to satisfy our demand for a criterion, are we to abandon our search for a criterion altogether, or even declare the demand itself to be senseless, saying that meaning is meaning—an unanalysable concept—that to understand is an ultimate form of activity like seeing or hearing, that 'empirical' is an ultimate category, and can not be explained or defined otherwise than ostensively, that is by examples? This is perhaps the case. But if so, statements like the above express the fact too baldly and obscurely. What one ought rather to say is that verifiability depends on intelligibility and not vice versa; only sentences which are constructed in accordance with the rules of logic and of grammar, and describe what can logically be conceived as existing, are significant, are empirical statements, express genuinely empirical propositions. The notion of the logically conceivable must not be misunderstood. It must not be confused with the view ultimately derived from Russell, and sometimes offered as a substitute for verification theories, according to which a sentence has empirical meaning when every variable which occurs in it is such that one at least of its values denote an actual or possible object of sensible or introspective knowledge; or, as it is sometimes put, when all the concepts in a judgement are *a posteriori* concepts; or, if a more familiar formulation is preferred, when understanding a proposition entails actual or possible acquaintance with at least one instance of every universal which occurs in it. Even if we ignore the difficulties of the phenomenalism which this entails it can only be a necessary, never a sufficient condition of empirical significance, at most a negative test. For I can formulate a sentence correct by the rules of logic and of grammar and containing as variables only the names of observable characteristics, which yet may turn out to be meaningless, as for example 'red hours are not more passionate than his ambition': this would doubtless involve a glaring confusion of categories, but the criterion, like that of 'weak' verification and for the same reason, is powerless to prevent this. The notion of significance cannot be determined by any such mechanical test: to say of a sentence that it means something, that I and others understand it, in other words that it conveys a proposition, is to say no more and no less than that we can conceive what would be the case if it were true. As for the meaning of 'I can conceive', only that is conceivable by me, which in some respect resembles my actual experience, as it occurs in observation or introspection, memory or imagination, or any other form of direct acquaintance, which can be described only by reference to it, as a determinate however logically distant from its source, of some determinable with at least one of whose determinates I am acquainted; much as a man born blind may understand propositions of visual experience by analogy with the senses which he possesses. The proposition that what is conceivable is necessarily similar to actual experience is analytic, being part of what is meant by the word 'conceivable'. To speak therefore of conceiving an experience dissimilar in all respects, wholly different, from my own, is to advance a self-contradictory concept, suggesting as it does that I both can apply my habitual logical categories to it, inasmuch as it is called experience, and that I cannot do so, inasmuch that it is declared to be wholly and utterly different from it. Statements which are metaphysical in the bad sense are meaningless not because they are unverifiable—but because they purport, in the language which resembles that which we normally use to describe situations which we regard as capable of being empirically experienced, to describe something which is alleged to transcend such experience, and to be incommunicable by any kind of analogy with it. Since, so far as we mean anything by these words, the limits of what can be conceived are set by analogy to what we are acquainted with, to deny such resemblance is tantamount to saying that what the proposition affects to describe is inconceivable; and this is to say that it is not a genuine proposition, but, in the empirical sense of meaning as descriptive, and not, e.g. emotive or evocative, a meaningless statement, linguistically similar to significant ones. Such a statement is unverifiable because, when examined, it turns out to be meaningless and not vice versa, and it is meaningless, because although words are being used in it in accordance with the accepted conventions of logic and of grammar, they represent the result either of genuine confusion, or of a pursuit of obscurity from whatever cause or motive, since they are used in a fashion different from that in which words are used when they are intended to describe the experienced world. And so, while they may resemble genuinely descriptive expressions, whatever else they may or may not be doing, they literally describe nothing.

II

VERIFIABILITY

Friedrich Waismann

MR. MACKINNON's paper raises a number of important questions. In the short time that is at my disposal I can only focus on two or three of them, and this merely in a sketchy way.

I

In the first part of his paper Mr. MacKinnon is concerned with representing and criticizing a thesis which he calls 'evidentialism' and which, in his view, is 'the fundamental presupposition' of empiricism. He formulates it thus:

'There is no more to the content of a statement than the total evidence which would warrant its assertion.'

Well, I don't know whether there is any empiricist who has ever expressed such a view; but it should be said clearly that though it seems to me to be some generalized version of phenomenalism it is not the view of a more advanced type of empiricism, and I would certainly not accept it as such. As the question involves a point of very great importance, I shall try to state the case as clearly and as briefly as I can.

When we reflect on such a sentence as 'The meaning of a statement is the method of its verification', we should, first of all, be quite clear as to what we mean by the term 'method of verification'. From a logical point of view we are not interested in the various activities that are involved in verifying a statement. What, then, is it we have in mind when we talk of such things? Take an example. Suppose there is a metal ball in front of me, and I have the task of finding out whether the ball is charged with electricity. To do that I connect the ball with an electroscope and watch whether the gold leaves diverge. The statement 'The gold leaves of the instrument diverge' (s) describes the verification of the statement 'The ball is charged'

Second paper in a symposium, from *Proceedings of the Aristotelian Society*, Supp. Vol. 19 (1945), pp. 119–50. Reprinted by courtesy of the author and the Editor of the Aristotelian Society.

(p). Now what exactly am I doing when I describe the verification of the statement p? I establish a connexion between two statements by declaring that the one (s) is to follow from the other (p). In other words, I lay down a *rule of inference* which allows me to pass from the statement 'The ball is charged with electricity' to another that describes an observable situation. By doing this I connect the statement with another one, I make it part of a system of operations, I incorporate it into language, in short, *I determine the way it is to be used*. In this sense giving the verification of a statement is an important part of giving its use, or, to put it differently, explaining its verification is a contribution to its grammar.

In everyday life we understand sentences without bothering much as to the way they are verified. We understand them because we understand the single words which occur in them and grasp the grammatical structure of the sentence as a whole. The question of the verification arises only when we come across a new sort of combination of words. If, for instance, someone were to tell us that he owned a dog that was able to think, we should at first not quite understand what he was talking about and ask him some further questions. Suppose he described to us in detail the dog's behaviour in certain circumstances, then we should say 'Ah, now we understand you, that's what you call thinking'. There is no need to inquire into the verification of such sentences as 'The dog barks', 'He runs', 'He is playful', and so on, as the words are then used as we may say in their *normal* way. But when we say 'The dog thinks', we create a new context, we step outside the boundaries of common speech, and then the question arises as to what is meant by such a word series. In such cases explaining the verification is explaining the meaning, and changing the verification is changing the meaning. Obviously meaning and verification *are* connected—so why say they are not?

But when I say that the statement p is connected with the statements $s_1, s_2, \ldots s_n$ which describe evidences for it, I do *not* say that p is *identical* with $s_1, s_2, \ldots s_n$ or their conjunction. To say this would only be true if $s_1, s_2, \ldots s_n$ or their conjunction entailed p. Now is that so? There *may* be statements which are nothing more than abbreviations for all that which is unfolded in their verification. There are, however, other sorts of statements of which this is certainly not true. Recent discussions on phenomenalism, e.g., tend to show that no conjunction or disjunction of sense datum statements, however complex, entails the existence or the non-existence of a certain material object. If that is so, a material object statement, though it *is* connected with

sense datum statements, is not just an abbreviation for them, rather
has it a logical status of its own, and is not equivalent to any truth-
function of the latter ones. I think that the result of these discussions
is essentially right, and I ask for permission, to make my point quite
clear, to add one word more.

The failure of the phenomenalist to translate a material object
statement into terms of sense data is not, as has been suggested, due
to the poverty of our language which lacks the vocabulary for
describing all the minute details of sense experience, nor is it due
to the difficulties inherent in producing an *infinite* combination of
sense datum statements, though all these things may contribute to it.
In the main it is due to a factor which, though it is very important
and really quite obvious, has to my knowledge never been noticed—to
the 'open texture'[1] of most of our empirical concepts. What I mean
is this: Suppose I have to verify a statement such as 'There is a cat
next door'; suppose I go over to the next room, open the door, look
into it and actually see a cat. Is this enough to prove my statement?
Or must I, in addition to it, touch the cat, pat him and induce him
to purr? And supposing that I had done all these things, can I then
be absolutely certain that my statement was true? Instantly we come
up against the well-known battery of sceptical arguments mustered
since ancient times. What, for instance, should I say when that
creature later on grew to a gigantic size? Or if it showed some queer
behaviour usually not to be found with cats, say, if, under certain
conditions, it could be revived from death whereas normal cats could
not? Shall I, in such a case say that a new species has come into
being? Or that it was a cat with extraordinary properties? Again,
suppose I say 'There is my friend over there'. What if on drawing closer
in order to shake hands with him he suddenly disappeared? 'Therefore it was not my friend but some delusion or other'. But suppose a few
seconds later I saw him again, could grasp his hand, etc. What then?
'Therefore your friend was nevertheless there and his disappearance
was some delusion or other'. But imagine after a while he disappeared
again, or seemed to disappear—what shall I say now? Have we rules
ready for all imaginable possibilities?

An example of the first sort tends to show that we can think of
situations in which we couldn't be certain whether something was
a cat or some other animal (or a jinni). An example of the second
sort tends to show that we can consider circumstances in which we

---

[1] I owe this term to Mr. Kneale who suggested it to me as a translation of *Porosität
der Begriffe*, a term coined by me in German.

couldn't be certain whether something was real or a delusion. The
fact that in many cases, there is no such thing as a conclusive
verification is connected with the fact that most of our empirical
concepts are not delimited in all possible directions. Suppose I come
across a being that looks like a man, speaks like a man, behaves like
a man, and is only one span tall—shall I say it *is* a man? Or what
about the case of a person who is so old as to remember King Darius?
Would you say he is an immortal? Is there anything like an exhaustive
definition that, finally and once for all, sets our mind at rest? 'But
are there not exact definitions at least in science?' Let's see. The
notion of gold seems to be defined with absolute precision, say by the
spectrum of gold with its characteristic lines. Now what would you
say if a substance was discovered that looked like gold, satisfied all
the chemical tests for gold, whilst it emitted a new sort of radiation?
'But such things do not happen.' Quite so; but they *might* happen,
and that is enough to show that we can never exclude altogether the
possibility of some unforeseen situation arising in which we shall have
to modify our definition. Try as we may, no concept is limited in such
a way that there is no room for any doubt. We introduce a concept and
limit it in *some* directions; for instance, we define gold in contrast to
some other metals such as alloys. This suffices for our present needs,
and we do not probe any farther. We tend to *overlook* the fact that
there are always other directions in which the concept has not been
defined. And if we did, we could easily imagine conditions which would
necessitate new limitations. In short, it is not possible to define a
concept like gold with absolute precision, i.e. in such a way that every
nook and cranny is blocked against entry of doubt. That is what is
meant by the open texture of a concept.

Vagueness should be distinguished from *open texture*. A word which
is actually used in a fluctuating way (such as 'heap' or 'pink') is
said to be vague; a term like 'gold', though its actual use may not
be vague, is non-exhaustive or of an open texture in that we can never
fill up all the possible gaps through which a doubt may seep in. Open
texture, then, is something like *possibility of vagueness*. Vagueness
can be remedied by giving more accurate rules, open texture cannot.
An alternative way of stating this would be to say that definitions of
open terms are *always* corrigible or emendable.

Open texture is a very fundamental characteristic of most, though
not of all, empirical concepts, and it is this texture which prevents
us from verifying conclusively most of our empirical statements.
Take any material object statement. The terms which occur in it

are non-exhaustive; that means that we cannot foresee completely all possible conditions in which they are to be used; there will always remain a possibility, however faint, that we have not taken into account something or other that may be relevant to their usage; and that means that we cannot foresee completely all the possible circumstances in which the statement is true or in which it is false. There will always remain a margin of uncertainty. Thus the absence of a conclusive verification is directly due to the open texture of the terms concerned.

This has an important consequence. Phenomenalists have tried to translate what we mean by a material object statement into terms of sense experience. Now such a translation would be possible only if the terms of a material object statement were completely definable. For only then could we describe completely all the possible evidences which would make the statement true or false. As this condition is not fulfilled, the programme of phenomenalism falls flat, and in consequence the attempts at analysing chairs and tables into patterns of sense data—which has become something of a national sport in this country—are doomed to fail. Similar remarks apply to certain psychological statements such as 'He is an intelligent person'; here again it is due to the open texture of a term like 'intelligent' that the statement cannot be reduced to a conjunction or disjunction of statements which specify the way a man would behave in such-and-such circumstances.

It may have been a dim awareness of this fact that induced Locke to insist on corporeal, and Berkeley on mental substance. Doing away with their metaphysical fog, we may restate what seems to be the grain of truth in their views by saying that a material object statement or a psychological statement has a logic of its own, and for this reason cannot be reduced to the level of other statements.

But there is a deeper reason for all that, and this consists in what I venture to call the *essential incompleteness* of an empirical description. To explain more fully: If I had to describe the right hand of mine which I am now holding up, I may say different things of it: I may state its size, its shape, its colour, its tissue, the chemical compound of its bones, its cells, and perhaps add some more particulars; but however far I go, I shall never reach a point where my description will be completed: logically speaking, it is always possible to extend the description by adding some detail or other. Every description stretches, as it were, into a horizon of open possibilities: how far I go, I shall always carry this horizon with me. Contrast this case with others in which completeness is attainable. If, in geometry, I describe a triangle, e.g., by giving its three sides, the description is *complete*: nothing can be added to it that is not included in, or at variance with, the data. Again, there is a sense in which it may be said that a melody is described completely in the musical notation (disregarding, for the moment, the question of its interpretation); a figure on a carpet, viewed as an ornament, may be described in some geometrical notation; and in this case, too, there is a sense in which the description may be called complete. (I do not mean the *physical* carpet, but its pattern.) The same applies to a game of chess: it can be described, move by move, from the beginning to the end. Such cases serve merely to set off the nature of an empirical description by the contrast: there is no such thing as a completeness in the case in which I describe my right hand, or the character of a person; I can never exhaust all the details nor foresee all possible circumstances which would make me modify or retract my statement. (This was already seen by Leibniz when he said that anything actual is always inexhaustible in its properties and a true image of the Infinite Mind.)

The situation described has a direct bearing on the open texture of concepts. A term is defined when the sort of situation is described in which it is to be used. Suppose for a moment that we were able to describe situations completely without omitting anything (as in chess), then we could produce an exhaustive list of all the circumstances in which the term is to be used so that nothing is left to doubt; in other words, we could construct a *complete definition*, i.e., a thought model which anticipates and settles once for all every possible question of usage. As, in fact, we can never eliminate the possibility of some unforeseen factor emerging, we can never be quite sure that we have included in our definition everything that should be included, and thus the process of defining and refining an idea will go on without ever reaching a final stage. In other words, every definition stretches into an open horizon. Try as we may, the situation will always remain the same: no definition of an empirical term will cover all possibilities. Thus the result is that the incompleteness of our verification is rooted in the incompleteness of the definition of the terms involved, and the incompleteness of the definition is rooted in the incompleteness of empirical description; that is one of the grounds why a material object statement p can *not* be verified conclusively, nor be resolved into statements s_1, $s_2, \ldots s_n$ which describe evidences for it. (In mathematics such a reduction is often possible: thus a statement about rational numbers *can*, without loss of meaning, be translated into statements about integers; but here you have complete description, complete definition and conclusive proof and refutation.)

Why is it, then, that, as a rule, an experiential statement is not verifiable in a conclusive way? Is it because I can never exhaust the description of a material object or of a situation, since I may always add something to it—something that, in principle, can be foreseen? Or is it because something quite new and unforeseen may occur? In the first case, though I know all the tests, I may still be unable to perform them, say, for lack of time. In the second case I can not even be sure that I know all the tests that may be required; in other words, the difficulty is to state completely what a verification would be like in this case. (Can you foresee all circumstances which would turn a putative fact into a delusion?) Now the answer to the question is that *both factors combine* to prevent a verification from being conclusive. *But they play a very different part*. It is due to the first factor that, in verifying a statement, we can never finish the job. But it is the second that is responsible for the open texture of our terms which is so characteristic of all factual knowledge. To see this more clearly, compare the situation in mathematics: here a theorem, say Goldbach's hypothesis,[1] may be undecidable as we cannot go through all the integers in order to try it out. But this in no way detracts from the *closed* texture of the mathematical concepts. If there was no such thing as the (always present) possibility of the emergence of something new, there could be nothing like the open texture of concepts; and if there was no such thing as the open texture of concepts, verification would be incomplete only in the sense that it could never be finished (just as in the case of Goldbach).

To sum up: An experiential statement is, as a rule, not conclusively verifiable for two different reasons:

(1) because of the existence of an unlimited number of tests;

(2) because of the open texture of the terms involved.

These two reasons correspond to two different senses of 'incompleteness'. The first is related to the fact that I can never conclude the description of a material object, or of a situation. I may, for instance, look at my table from always new points in space without ever exhausting all the possibilities. The second (and more exciting one) is due to the fact that our factual knowledge is incomplete in

[1] [This asserts that every even number is the sum of two primes.—Ed.]

another dimension: there is always a chance that something unforeseen may occur. That again may mean two different things:

(a) that I should get acquainted with some totally new experience, such as at present I cannot even imagine;

(b) that some new discovery was made which would affect our whole interpretation of certain facts.

An illustration of the first sort would be supplied by a man born blind who later obtained the experience of seeing. An illustration of the second sort would be the change brought about by the discovery of a new agent of nature, such as electricity. In this case we perceive that the data of observation are connected in a new and unforeseen way, that, as it were, new lines can now be traced through the field of experience. So we can say more exactly that the open texture of concepts is rooted in that particular incompleteness of our factual knowledge which I have just adumbrated.

What I have said modifies to a more or less extent the account I have given of verification. I said that in giving the method of verification we lay down a rule (or rules) of inference. We should, however, feel grave doubts whether that is so. If a material object statement were to entail a sense datum statement, to entail it in a strictly *logical* sense, then the premise would be cancelled together with the conclusion: or, to put it differently, a single negative instance would suffice to refute the premise. Suppose someone told me, 'Look, there is your friend, he is just crossing the street'. Now if I looked in the direction indicated, but failed to perceive the person who is my friend, would I say that the statement was refuted beyond the shadow of a doubt? There may be cases in which I may say that. But there are others in which I would certainly not think that the statement was refuted on the strength of such a single glance; (for instance, when I was led to expect my friend at this hour, or received a letter from him saying that he will arrive at that time, and the like). A discrepancy between a material object statement and a single sense experience may always be explained away by some accessory assumption: I haven't looked thoroughly, my friend happened in this very second to be behind someone else, he just stepped into a doorway, and so on, not to mention more fanciful theories. I can never exclude the possibility that, though the evidence was against it, the statement may be true.

Whoever considers these facts with unbiassed eyes, will, I trust, assent to the conclusion that a single sense experience, strictly speaking, never excludes a material object statement in the sense in which the negation of p excludes p. That means that no sense datum statement s can ever come into *sharp logical conflict* with a material object statement p; in other words: $p. \sim s$ never represents a *contradiction* in the sense that $p. \sim p$ does. In the light of this we can no longer adhere to the view that p entails s. How, then, should we formulate the 'method of verification'—that is, the connexion between a proposition p and the statements $s_1, s_2, \ldots s_n$ which are evidences for it? I propose to say that the evidences $s_1, s_2, \ldots s_n$ *speak for* or *against* the proposition p, that they *strengthen* or *weaken* it, which does not mean that they prove or disprove it strictly.

There is a striking analogy to that in the relation that holds between a law of nature L and certain observational statements $S_1, s_2, \ldots s_n$, an analogy which may help to clarify the situation. It is often said that the statements of observation *follow* from the law (the latter being regarded as a sort of universal premise). Since an unlimited number of consequences can be derived from a law, the ideal of complete verification is, of course, unattainable; whereas, on the other hand, a single counter observation seems to suffice to overthrow the law. From this it would follow that, while a law cannot be strictly verified, it can be strictly confuted; or that it can be decided only one way.[1] That is unrealistic. What astronomer would abandon Kepler's laws on the strength of a single observation? If, in fact, some anomaly in a planet's behaviour were detected, the most varied attempts at explaining the phenomenon would first be made (such as the presence of unknown heavy masses, friction with rarefied gases, etc.). Only if the edifice of hypotheses thus erected has too little support in experience, if it becomes too complex and artificial, if it no longer satisfies our demand for simplicity, or again if a better hypothesis presents itself to us such as Einstein's theory, would we resolve to drop those laws. And even then the refutation would not be valid finally and once for all: it may still turn out that some circumstance had escaped our notice which, when taken into consideration, would cast a different light upon the whole. Indeed, the history of science exhibits cases (Olaf Römer, Leverrier) in which the apparent defeat of a theory later turned into complete victory. Who can say that such a situation will not repeat itself?

Here again the view suggests itself strongly that the relationship between a statement and what serves to verify it was too crudely represented in the past; that it was a mistake to describe it in logical

[1] See Karl Popper, *Logik der Forschung*.

terms such as 'entailment'; that a law is not a sort of universal statement from which particular statements follow; that its logic is still unexplored, and that it may possibly take the form of rules according to which the law's truth-weight—if I am allowed to use such a term—is increased or lessened by the data of observation. Be that as it may, the mere fact that a single counter observation $\sim s$ can always be reconciled with a general law L by some accessory assumption shows that the true relation between a law and the experiential evidence for it is much more complicated and only superficially in accord with the customary account.

It will be said that this is due to our representing the case in too simple a manner. In reality the observational statement s does not follow from L alone, but from L plus a number of further premises which are often not expressly stated. So that, if the observation s which we expected fails to materialize, we may say that any of the other premises is false.

Now this would be perfectly correct if the system of premises could be stated accurately and completely in every single case. But can it? Can we ever be certain of knowing all, really all the conditions on which the result of even the simplest experiment depends? Plainly not; what is stated is only a *part* of the conditions, viz., those which, e.g., can be isolated in experimental technique and subjected to our will, or which can readily be surveyed, etc. The others merge into one indistinct mass: the vague supposition that 'a normal situation subsists', that 'no disturbing factors are present' or in whatever way we may hint at the possibility of intervention of some unforeseen conditions. The relation between L and s, then, when exactly stated, is this: Given such-and-such laws L_1, L_2, ... L_m, given such-and-such initial and boundary conditions c_1, c_2 ... c_n, and *no other disturbing factors being present*, so-and-so will happen. And here it must be stressed that behind the words italicized a presupposition is concealed which cannot be split up into clear, separate statements. When actually deducing a consequence from a physical law we never make use of this premise: it never forms part of the body of premises; it does not enter the process of deduction. But then it should not be termed a premise at all; what queer sort of premise that is which is never made use of! What is, in fact, conveyed by these words is only that, in case of a conflict between theory and observation, we shall *search* for disturbing factors whilst considering ourselves free to adhere to the theory. The question at issue is *not* whether a certain system of assumptions is sufficiently comprehensive—that is a question of fact which may be left to the expert; the question in which we take an interest is rather whether there is a *criterion* which assures us that a system of premises is complete. To this there is no answer; nay, more, we cannot even form any conception of such a criterion; we cannot think of a situation in which a physicist would tell us, 'Well, I have finished the job; now I have discovered the last law of nature, and no more is to be found'. But if this is devoid of meaning, there is no point in insisting, '*If* all the conditions in the universe, and *if* all the laws governing them were known to us, then—'. As the boundary regions of our knowledge are always enveloped in a dust cloud—out of which something new may emerge—we are left with the fact that s is not a strict logical consequence of L together with the initial conditions. Saying that the class of premises is not 'closed' and that *therefore* the conclusion is lacking in stringency comes, in my view, to the same thing as saying that s is *not* a logical consequence of the premises as far as they are stated. And that is all I wanted to say.

All this tends to suggest that the relation between a law of nature and the evidences for it, or between a material object statement and a sense datum statement, or again between a psychological statement and the evidence concerning a person's behaviour is a looser one than had been hitherto imagined. If that is correct, the application of logic is limited in an important sense. We may say that the known relations of logic can only hold between statements which belong to a *homogeneous* domain; or that the deductive nexus never extends beyond the limits of such a domain.

Accordingly we may set ourselves the task of arranging the statements of our language in distinct strata, grouping in the same stratum all those statements linked by clearly apprehended logical relations. It is in this way, for instance, that the theorems of mechanics are organized in a system the elements of which stand in known logical relations with one another and where it is always possible to decide of two theorems in what logical relation they stand—whether one is a consequence of the other, whether they are equivalent, independent of, or in contradiction with each other. In like manner the statements of a physicist in describing certain data of observation (such as the position of a pointer on his gauges) stand in exactly defined relations to one another. Thus a pointer on a scale cannot possibly be opposite 3 and 5 at the same time: here you have a relation of strict exclusion. On the other hand, no statement of mechanics can ever come into sharp logical conflict with a statement of observation, and this implies that between these two kinds of statements there exist no relations of the sort supplied to us by classical logic. So long as we move only among the statements of a single stratum, all the relations provided by logic remain valid. The real problem arises where two such strata make contact, so to speak; it is the problem of these planes of contact which to-day should claim the attention of the logician. We may, in this context, speak of the *open texture* of the chains of inference (*poröse Schlüsse*) which lead from statements of one stratum to those of another; the connexion is no longer coercive—owing to the incompleteness of all our data.

You will find that it is this fact to which the rise of philosophical troubles often can be traced. (Think of how confusing it is to assert or to dispute the statement, 'The floor is not solid', as it belongs to two quite distinct strata.) The fracture lines of the strata of language are marked by philosophical problems; the problem of perception, of verification, of induction, the problem of the relation between mind and body, and so on.

You will have noticed that I have used the term 'incompleteness' in very different senses. In one sense we may say of a description of a material object that it is incomplete; in another sense we may say that of our knowledge of the boundary conditions in a field of force. There is a sense in which we say that a list of laws of nature is always incomplete, and another sense in which even our knowledge of the agents of nature is so; and you may easily find more senses. They all combine, to a varying degree, to create what I have called the open texture of concepts and the looseness of inferences.

Incompleteness, in the senses referred to, is the mark of empirical knowledge as opposed to *a priori* knowledge such as mathematics. In fact, it is the criterion by which we can distinguish perfectly *formalized* languages constructed by logicians from *natural* languages as used in describing reality. In a formalized system the use of each symbol is governed by a definite finite number of rules, and further, all the rules of inference and procedure are stated completely. In view of the incompleteness which permeates empirical knowledge such a demand cannot be fulfilled by any language we may use to express it.

I have tried to give an account of the method of verification, and this has led me to touch on such subjects as open texture, completeness, language strata and logical relations of an open texture. In this account, though I have nowhere departed from the lines of empiricism, I have arrived at an outlook which is rather different from that which Mr. MacKinnon presents. I am very puzzled why Mr. Mac-Kinnon should think that empiricism is based on the 'fundamental presupposition' that 'there is no more to the content of a statement than the total evidence which would warrant its assertion'. That there is a very close relation between content and verification is an important insight which has been brought to light by empiricists. Only one has to be very careful how to formulate it. Far from identifying the meaning of a statement with the evidences we have for it, the view I tried to sketch leads to a sort of many-level-theory of language in which 'every sort of statement has its own sort of logic'.

Mr. MacKinnon, like so many other philosophers, talks of the 'verification principle'. I will not let pass this occasion without saying how misleading this mode of expression is. It evokes at once the idea that here we have a principle which is the foundation from which a part or the whole of empiricism can be derived. Now a principle is something that serves as a starting point in a deductive theory. It is in this sense that we speak, e.g., of the Principles of Mechanics. Mr. MacKinnon does seem to take it in this sense, for he calls it a 'fundamental presupposition'. It should, however, have become quite clear that empiricism is not a deductive system based on the verification principle or on some other principle. It is, in fact, not a body of propositions at all, but rather a critical attitude, and what is called the 'verification principle' is no more than a maxim devised to guide our philosophical activity in clarifying the content of a statement.

I shall not enter into a discussion on what Mr. MacKinnon says about 'verificatory acts'. I shall confine myself to saying that I entirely fail to see why there should be any difference in kind between a verification made by a physicist in his laboratory and a verification made by an unsophisticated person. Suppose a physicist engaged in directing some intricate experiment is too busy to attend to certain observations; so he trains a young boy to look through a telescope and to tell him in certain intervals whether he sees light or dark. Now when the boy calls out 'Light', why, I ask, is this not as good a verification (or a 'verificatory act') as if Einstein himself had looked through it? We may, indeed, think of the process of verification as divided up amongst different people without impairing in the least the validity of the verification. But perhaps I have not correctly understood Mr. MacKinnon.

II

In the second part of his paper Mr. MacKinnon is anxious to relate the notions of reality and causality by admitting as real only such objects (or events, or processes) which satisfy the conditions of causality. What he says is 'that the manner of discursive thought . . . reveals itself as an obstinate resolve. . . to admit nothing as real that does not manifest some ground of its occurrence'. That is part of Kant's doctrine according to which nothing can ever become object of our knowledge which did not conform to certain *a priori* forms of our intuition and our understanding. Such an attempt, if it succeeded, would be of tremendous importance. Think how miraculous it would be, using this method, to deduce from it causality, premises of induction as well as other enjoyable things—I had almost said to *pro*duce them out of the conjurer's hat called the Transcendental Argument. How comforting would be the belief that we know the nature of space and time through and through so that we are able to enunciate the principles of geometry without fear of ever being defeated by experience. How reassuring it would be to say that nature *must* obey causal laws—and so on, you know the tune. The question is only whether Nature will conform to Kant. You will realize that such over-confidence is no longer permissible to-day, in the age of quantum mechanics. We are told by Mr. MacKinnon that 'we display an unwillingness to admit the completely random' (by the by, what does he mean by that?) 'and discontinuous as objectively real'. But our protest, however strongly worded, would be of no avail if Nature was willing to baffle us. The words Mr. MacKinnon has been using state precisely the sort of situation with which we have come face to face in modern physics: things do happen without ground of their occurrence. May I be allowed to say a few words on this subject?

There are people who think that physicists have just not succeeded in discovering laws which tell us why things happen in the atomic world, in the cheerful hope that someone some day will have a brain-wave which will enable him to fill the gaps in wave mechanics; on this day the latter will turn into a completely deterministic theory. Let these people realize how wide the cleavage is that separates us from the good old days. The hope they cherish is based on an illusion: it has been proved[1] that the structure of quantum mechanics is such that no

---

[1] See; for instance, J. v. Neumann, *Mathematische Grundlagen der Quantenmechanik.*

further laws can be added to it which would make the whole theory deterministic; for if we could, we should, owing to the uncertainty principle, get entangled in contradictions. (The situation is, in fact, more intricate, but this is not the place to go into it.) So we are faced with the dilemma that quantum mechanics is *either* self-consistent *or* deterministic: you can't have it both ways. The crack in the wall of Determinism is definitive, and there is no way out of the situation.

According to Kant causality is an inescapable form which the nature of our understanding imposes on any given material. If this were so, it would be inconceivable—against the conditions of possible experience—ever to come across any events which did not conform to the principle of causality. Quantum phenomena, however, have forced physicists to depart from this principle, or better, to *restrict* it, whilst a torso of it is retained. Though the fate of a single electron is not governed by causal laws, the particle being free to move about, for instance, to 'jump' in a collision with light waves however it pleases, the behaviour of millions of electrons is statistically predictable. Not exactly that quantum mechanics confronts us with a mathematician's dream of chaos come true. For, as I said, there is a causal aspect in the new theory, namely this: there are certain waves connected with the motion of particles, the de Broglie waves, which obey rigorous 'causal' laws. That is, the propagation of these waves is governed by a differential equation of the respectable old type such as you find in the classical physics of fields. Hence we can, given the initial conditions and the values over the boundary of a region during a certain interval of time, predict with absolute precision the propagation of the waves. That is exactly what any causal theory achieves. What is new, however, is the interpretation we must give to these waves: they are a sort of 'probability clouds' the density of which at each point signifies the probability of the occurrence of a particle. So what we can deduce from the theory are only *probability statements* regarding the presence of a particle in a given place at a given time. Such a statement can be tested, not by making a single experiment such as observing a single electron through a microscope, but by repeating the experiment a large number of times, or observing a large number of electrons and forming the mean value of all the data thus obtained. Thus we cannot say where exactly a certain electron will be, but only with what probability, i.e., in what percentage of cases we may expect to find it at a certain place. In other words, the theory can be used only to predict the *average behaviour* of particles. That is the statistical aspect of the theory.

To sum up: quantum mechanics is neither a theory of the causal, deterministic type nor an indeterministic theory, whatever this may be taken to mean. The new physics combines deterministic and indeterministic features. What is deterministic is the law for the propagation of the de Broglie waves. That is, the propagation of these waves is *causally determined* in much the same way as, e.g., the propagation of electromagnetic waves is in the classical theories. What is indeterministic is the *interpretation* of these waves, that is, their connexion with the facts of observation, i.e., with those quantities whose value can be specified exactly. Such an interpretation can only be given in statistical terms, and any attempt at interpreting it differently so as to reinstate causality would lead only to conflict with other well-established parts of the theory. Thus we have the curious result that causality holds for the de Broglie waves which are no more than a purely symbolic and formal representation of certain probabilities whereas the particles themselves obey no causal laws.

To bring home the last point let me add this: If it were possible to repeat exactly the same experiment and to bring about exactly the same conditions, the result would each time be a different one. Therefore the principle 'Like causes—like effects' no longer holds.

But may not quantum mechanics one day be superseded by a better theory that meets our demand for causal explanation? Certainly; no theory is sacrosanct and infallible. This, however, is not the point. What matters is, not whether quantum mechanics draws a true picture of reality, but only whether it draws a *permissible* one. About that there can be little doubt. Kant was of the opinion that if there was no such thing as causality science would simply break down. Now the important thing that has emerged is the *possibility* of constructing a theory along different lines, the *legitimacy* of departing from causality, while science has not died or committed suicide on that account. This suffices to disown any claim on the part of Kant to regard causality as an *indispensable* form of our knowledge of the world. Had he been right, we could not even *entertain* such views as physicists do to-day; to give up causality, even if in part, would mean to rob us of the very condition of gaining knowledge; which could end in one result only, in complete confusion. But that is not so. Though causality has been severely limited, quantum mechanics is a useful tool. Kant did not foresee the possible forms of physical laws; by laying too much stress on the scheme of causality, by claiming for it an *a priori* status, he unduly narrowed the field of research.

The conclusion to be drawn from the preceding seems to me this:

Even if quantum mechanics should one day be found wanting and be superseded by another theory, it still offers a *possible picture* of the material world. This picture is neither self-contradictory nor unintelligible though it may not be the sort of picture to which we are accustomed; anyhow it is a working hypothesis which serves its purpose in that it is fruitful, i.e., that it leads to new discoveries. Whether it contains the ultimate truth we cannot tell (nor can we in the case of the deterministic theories). It's only experience that can bring forward evidence against it. But the very fact that we *can* turn to experience is significant: in doing so we grant that quantum mechanics, and consequently the limits of causality, *can* be tested in experiment. Hence every attempt at raising the principle of causality to the status of a necessary *a priori* truth is irreconcilable with the situation as it has emerged in science. No matter whether quantum mechanics will stand its ground or will have to undergo some modification or other, the mere fact that the construction of such a theory is legitimate should settle the dispute: it proves that Kant's argument is based on a fallacy.

It was an important step when man learnt to ask the question, Why? But it was also a great step when he learnt to drop this question.

But leaving quantum mechanics and turning to the common world of sense, I still fail to see any ground for accepting Kant's position. True, in order to orient ourselves in the world we must presuppose that there is some sort of order in it so that we may anticipate the course of events and act accordingly. What I fail to see, however, is why this order should be a strictly *causal* one. Suppose, for the sake of argument, that the objects around us were, *on the average* to display an orderly behaviour, then the world may still be a liveable place. Suppose for instance, the behaviour of chairs and tables and the support they give us, could be foreseen with much the same accuracy as can the behaviour of Tory and Labour candidates in election times, may we then not make use of them just the same? Or suppose they were to conduct themselves as our best friends do—they won't let us down, no; still you never know—then, as far as I can see, this would be quite enough for all our practical ends. And as to the theoretical ones—well, go to the scientist and you will hear a sorry tale of nature's trickery. I cannot see—nor has Mr. MacKinnon's paper helped me in this point—why such a world should not be possible.

This brings me to the topic in which Mr. MacKinnon is so much interested—are there any *necessary* conditions which must be fulfilled if we are to attain knowledge of the external world? I propose to drop

for the moment the subject of causality and to tackle the problem
from a broader angle. Let me begin with some observations on the
terms 'reality' and 'knowledge'.

Mr. MacKinnon, in his paper, repeatedly speaks of 'the real',
'the reality'; he asks, for instance, whether 'the completely random'
can be admitted as 'objectively real'. He blames Berkeley for having
omitted 'to face the question of the rules whereby the inclusion in or
exclusion from reality was determined; in consequence of which', we
are told, 'his theory of knowledge flags'. In another passage he
speaks of 'the task of compelling the actual to disclose itself'. My
impression is that he talks as if there was a clearly bounded domain
called 'the real' or 'the actual' with the implication that it is one of
the tasks of the philosopher to define it sharply. Unfortunately the
belief that there is such a domain is very slender. Not that I deny
for a minute that a word like 'reality' is a blessing; it definitely is.
Look at such phrases as 'A tautology doesn't say anything about
reality', 'Pure mathematics is not concerned with reality', 'In
reality it was not Smith I saw but his brother'. It would be silly to put
such a word on an *Index Prohibitorum Verborum* as though it were a sin
to use it. It is very handy—if it were not in use, we should have to
invent it. On the other hand, when a philosopher looks closely at it,
tears it from the context and asks himself, 'Now what *is* reality?' he
has successfully manoeuvred himself into a fairly awkward position.
For it is surprisingly easy to ask a number of questions which are
more or less embarrassing; for instance, 'Is the elastic force present
in a spring something real?' I suppose some people would answer Yes,
some No. The fact is that there simply are no fixed rules that govern
the use of the word. To go on—'Is a magnetic field something real?'
'Is energy? and entropy?' 'Are the de Broglie waves (which, in one
aspect, constitute the nature of material particles) real, or mere
symbolic constructions?' Again, I may ask, 'Is the power of my
memory real?', 'Is the genius of a people, is the spirit of an age,
is the beauty of a spring day real?' Now we begin to see how the
idea is lost in indeterminacy. What we must understand is that such
a word is used on many different levels and with many different
shades of meaning. It has a *systematic ambiguity*. At the same time
there is a sort of family likeness between all these uses, and it is
that which makes us denote them by one word.

The same applies to a verb like 'to exist'. We use the word in many
different senses; we may, for instance, say of a memory picture, an
after-image, a mirror image, or again of a material object that it

'exists'; again, we may say of a wave-motion in a space of many dimensions, or of a law of nature, or of a number satisfying certain conditions that it 'exists'; and it is quite obvious that we do use the word in each case according to totally different criteria. So again we have a case of systematic ambiguity.

Next take the term 'knowledge'. Everyone is familiar with the distinction between knowledge by acquaintance and knowledge by description. This division is not fine enough. When I know something by acquaintance, I may know it in very different senses as when I say 'I know sweetness' (meaning 'I am acquainted with this taste'), 'I know misery', 'I know him', 'I know his writings'. In this series we go progressively farther away from simple acquaintance. In a case like 'I know his motives', it is doubtful whether I should say this unless I had experienced some such motive myself. Moreover, there are cases which fall under none of the two groups; so, for instance, when I say 'I know French', 'I know how to deal with that man'. Again, we may speak in different senses of knowledge by description. Compare the case of a reporter who gained knowledge of some hush-hush affair with that of a scientist who claims to possess knowledge of nature. Now ask is this knowledge in the same sense? And mark, in the latter case there are again subtle differences. Compare knowledge of the history of certain birds as based on observation with knowledge of the history of our solar system as based on some hypothesis; again knowledge of a natural law of the causal type with knowledge of a statistical law. Quantum mechanics, though it is based on the assumption of a randomness in the behaviour of electrons (and other particles), leads to a lot of predictions. On this ground physicists do not hesitate to honour the newly discovered laws by awarding them the degree of knowledge; whereas Mr. MacKinnon thinks 'that we do concede the title unintelligible to any field . . . where such [causal] lines have not been traced'. Well, I shall not argue about that; my sole object is to call attention to the fact that the actual usage is unsettled, that there are many different types of knowledge and that, by talking of knowledge *in general*, we are liable to overlook the very important differences between them. Suppose that someone has a vague awareness of the direction in which history moves—shall I or shall I not call this knowledge? Can you draw a clear line to mark where such vague awareness ends and where true knowledge begins? Knowledge as supplied by quantum mechanics was unknown two or three decades ago. Who can tell what forms of knowledge may emerge in the future? Can you anticipate all possible cases in which we may wish to use that term? To say that knowledge is embodied in true propositions does not get you any farther; for there are many different structures that are called 'propositions'—different, because they are verified in different senses of the word and governed by different sets of logical rules. (Incidentally speaking, the failure to draw a clear line between the meaningful and the meaningless is due to the fact that these terms have themselves a systematic ambiguity, and so has the term 'verifiable'.)

There is a group of words such as 'fact', 'event', 'situation', 'case', 'circumstance', which display a queer sort of behaviour. One might say of such words that they serve as pegs: it's marvellous what a lot of things you can put on them ('the fact that—'). So far they are very handy; but as soon as one focuses on them and asks, e.g., 'What *is* a fact?' they betray a tendency of melting away. The peg-aspect is by far the most important of all. It's just as in the case of the word 'reality': in reality, e.g., 'in reality' is an adverb.

Again, there are many different types of fact; there are many different types of statement which are called 'empirical'; there are many different things which are called 'experience'; and there are many different senses of communication and clarity.

Now if I am to contribute to the main subject of this symposium— that is, to the question whether there are any *necessary conditions* for *gaining knowledge of reality*—what am I to reply? Knowledge of reality! Of *what* sort of reality, and *what* sort of knowledge? As a logician I am bound to say that the notions of reality and knowledge have a systematic ambiguity and, moreover, that they are on each level extremely vague and hazy. I am even not quite clear as to what a condition is, let alone a 'necessary condition'. How questionable all these ideas are! How can I be expected to answer a question which consists only of a series of question marks?

III

So far my criticism was mainly negative. In conclusion I should like to offer some constructive suggestions. Before doing so, I must warn you that I can't see any ground whatever for renouncing one of the most fundamental rights of man, the right of talking nonsense. And now I suppose I may go on.

People are inclined to think that there is a world of facts as opposed to a world of words which describe these facts. I am not too happy about that. Consider an example. We are accustomed to see colour as a 'quality' of objects. That is, colour cannot subsist by itself, but must inhere in a thing. This conception springs from the way we express ourselves. When colour is rendered by an adjective, colour is conceived as an attribute of things, i.e., as something that can have no independent existence. That, however, is not the only way of conceiving colour. There are languages such as Russian, German, Italian, which render colour by means of verbs. If we were to imitate this usage in English by allowing some such form as 'The sky blues', we should come face to face with the question, Do I mean the same fact when I say 'The sky blues' as when I say 'The sky is blue'? I don't think so. We say 'The sun shines', 'Jewels glitter', 'The river shimmers', 'Windows gleam', 'Stars twinkle', etc.; that is, in the case of phenomena of lustre we make use of a verbal mode of expression. Now in rendering colour phenomena by verbs we assimilate them more closely to the phenomena of lustre; and in doing so we alter not only our manner of speaking but our entire way of apprehending colour. We *see* the blue differently now—a hint that language affects our whole mode of apprehension. In the word 'blueing' we are clearly aware of an active, verbal element. On that account 'being blue' is not quite equivalent to 'blueing', since it lacks what is peculiar to the verbal mode of expression. The sky which 'blues' is seen as something that continually brings forth blueness—it radiates blueness, so to speak; blue does not inhere in it as a mere quality, rather is it felt as the vital pulse of the sky; there is a faint suggestion of the operating of some force behind the phenomenon. It's hard to get the feel of it in English; perhaps it may help you to liken this mode of expression to the impressionist way of painting which is at bottom a new way of seeing: the impressionist sees in colour an immediate manifestation of reality, a free agent no longer bound up with things.

There are, then, different linguistic means of rendering colour. When this is done by means of adjectives, colour is conceived as an attribute of things. The learning of such a language involves for everyone who speaks it his being habituated to see colour as a 'quality' of objects. This conception becomes thus incorporated into his picture of the world. The verbal mode of expression detaches colour from things: it enables us to see colour as a phenomenon with a life of its own. Adjective and verb thus represent two different worlds of thought.

There is also an adverbial way of rendering colour. Imagine a language with a wealth of expressions for all shades of lustre, but without adjectives for colours; colours, as a rule, are ignored;

when they are expressed, this is done by adding an adverb to the word that specifies the sort of lustre. Thus the people who use this sort of language would say, 'The sea is glittering golden in the sunshine', 'The evening clouds glow redly', 'There in the depth a shadow greenly gleams'. In such phrases colour would lose the last trace of independence and be reduced to a mere modification of lustre. Just as we in our language cannot say 'That's very', but only some such thing as 'That's very brilliant', so in the language considered we could not say 'That's bluish', but only, e.g., 'That's shining bluishly'. There can be little doubt that, owing to this circumstance, the users of such language would find it very hard to see colour as a quality of things. For them it would not be the *things* that are coloured, rather colour would reside in the lustre as it glows and darkens and changes—evidence that they would see the world with different eyes.

'But isn't it still true to say that I have the same experience whenever I look up at the sky?' You would be less happy if you were asked, 'Do you have the same experience when you look at a picture puzzle and see a figure in it as before, when you didn't see it?' You may perhaps say you see the same lines, though each time in a different arrangement. Now what exactly corresponds to this different arrangement in the case when I look up at the sky? One might say: we are aware of the blue, but this awareness is itself tinged and coloured by the whole linguistic background which brings into prominence or weakens and hides certain analogies. In this sense language does affect the whole manner in which we become aware of a fact: the fact articulates itself differently, so to speak. In urging that you *must* have the same experience whenever you look at the sky you forget that the term 'experience' is itself ambiguous: whether it is taken to, e.g., include or to exclude all the various analogies which a certain mode of expression calls up.

Again, consider this case: Suppose there is a number of languages *A*, *B*, *C*, . . . in each of which a proposition is used according to a slightly different logic. Consequently a proposition in the language *A* is not a proposition in exactly the same sense as a proposition in the language *B*, etc. And not only this: what is described by a statement in the language *A*, i.e., if you like, the 'fact', is not a fact in the same sense as a fact described in the language *B*, etc.; which tends to show that what is called a fact depends on the linguistic medium through which we see it.

I have observed that when the clock strikes in the night and I, already half asleep, am too tired to count the strokes, I am seized by an impression that the sequence will never end—as though it would go on, stroke after stroke, in an unending measureless procession. The whole thing vanishes as soon as I *count*. Counting frees me, as it were, from the dark formlessness impending over me. (Is this not a parable of the rational?) It seems to me that one could say here that counting *alters* the quality of the experience. Now is it the same fact which I perceive when counting and when not counting?

Again suppose there is a tribe whose members count 'one, two, three, a few, many'. Suppose a man of this tribe looking at a flock of birds said 'A few birds' whereas I should say 'Five birds,—is it the same fact for him as it is for me? If in such a case I pass to a language of a different structure, I can no longer describe 'the same' fact, but only another one more or less resembling the first. What, then, is the objective reality supposed to be described by language?

What rebels in us against such a suggestion is the feeling that the fact is there objectively no matter in which way we render it. I perceive something that exists and put it into words. From this it seems to follow that fact is something that exists independent of and prior to language; language merely serves the end of communication. What we are liable to overlook here is that the way we see a fact—i.e., what we emphasize and what we disregard—is *our* work. 'The sun-beams trembling on the floating tides' (Pope). Here a fact is something that emerges out from, and takes shape against a background. The background may be, e.g., my visual field; something that rouses my attention detaches itself from this field, is brought into focus and apprehended linguistically; that is what we call a fact. A fact is noticed; and by being noticed it becomes a fact. 'Was it then no fact before you noticed it?' It was, if I *could* have noticed it. In a language in which there is only the number series 'one, two, three, a few, many', a fact such as 'There are five birds' is imperceptible.

To make my meaning still clearer consider a language in which description does not take the form of sentences. Examples of such a description would be supplied by a map, a picture language, a film, the musical notation. A map, for instance, should not be taken as a conjunction of single statements each of which describes a separate fact. For what, would you say, is the contour of a fact? Where does the one end and the other begin? If we think of such types of description, we are no longer tempted to say that a country, or a story told in a film, or a melody must consist of 'facts'. Here we begin to see how confusing the idea is according to which the world is a cluster of facts—just as if it were a sort of mosaic made up of little coloured stones. Reality is undivided. What we may have in mind is perhaps that *language* contains units, viz. *sentences*. In describing reality, describing it in the form of sentences, we draw, as it were, lines through it, limit a part and call what corresponds with such a sentence a fact. In other words, language is the knife with which we cut out facts. (This account is over simplified as it doesn't take notice of *false* statements.) When we pass to a symbolism of language that admits of no sentences, we are no more inclined to speak of facts.

Reality, then, is not made up of facts in the sense in which a plant is made up of cells, a house of bricks, a stone of molecules; rather, if you want a simile, a fact is present in much the same sense in which a character manifests itself in a face. Not that I invent the character and read it into the face; no, the character is somehow written on the face but no one would on that account say that a face is 'made up' of features symbolic of such-and-such traits. Just as we have to interpret a face, so we have to interpret reality. The elements of such an interpretation, without our being aware of it, are already present in language—for instance, in such moulds as the notion of thinghood, of causality, of number, or again in the way we render colour, etc.

Noticing a fact may be likened to seeing a face in a cloud, or a figure in an arrangement of dots, or suddenly becoming aware of the solution of a picture puzzle: one views a complex of elements as one, reads a sort of unity into it, etc. Language supplies us with a means of comprehending and categorizing; and different languages categorize differently.

'But surely noticing a face in a cloud is not inventing it?' Certainly not; only you might not have noticed it unless you had already had the experience of human faces somewhere else. Does this not throw a light on what constitutes the noticing of facts? I would not dream for a moment of saying that I *invent* them; I might, however, be unable to perceive them if I had not certain moulds of comprehension ready at hand. These forms I borrow from language. Language, then, *contributes to the formation and participates in the constitution* of a fact; which, of course, does not mean that it *produces* the fact.

So far I have dealt with perceptual situations only. This, I am afraid, will not satisfy Mr. MacKinnon. What he wants to know is whether there are any *general* conditions of the possibility of factual knowledge. We have seen some of the fallacies involved in putting this question. Still we may ask ourselves whether there are any methodological rules which guide us in gaining knowledge. All I can hope to do here is to throw out some hints.

The empiricist has a let-the-facts-speak-for-themselves attitude. Well, this is his faith; what about his works? Remember, a scientific theory is never a slavish imitation of certain features of reality, a dead, passive replica. It is essentially a *construction* which to a more or less degree reflects our own activity. When, for instance, we represent a number of observations made in laboratory by a corresponding number of dots and connect them by a graph, we assume, as a rule, that the curve is continuous and analytic. Such an assumption goes far beyond any possible experience. There will always be infinitely many other possible curves which accord with the facts equally well; the totality of these curves is included within a certain narrow strip. The ordinary mathematical treatment substitutes an exact law for the blurred data of observation and deduces from such laws strict mathematical conclusions. This shows that there is an element of convention inherent in the formulation of a law. The way we single out one particular law from infinitely many possible ones shows that in our theoretical construction of reality we are guided by certain principles—*regulative principles* as we may call them. If I were asked what these principles are, I should tentatively list the following:

(1) Simplicity or economy—the demand that the laws should be as simple as possible.

(2) Demands suggested by the requirements of the symbolism we use—for instance, that the graph should represent an analytic function so as to lend itself readily to the carrying out of certain mathematical operations such as differentiation.

(3) Aesthetic principles ('mathematical harmony' as envisaged by Pythagoras, Kepler, Einstein) though it is difficult to say what they are.

(4) A principle which so regulates the formation of our concepts that as many alternatives as possible become decidable. This tendency is embodied in the structure of Aristotelian logic, especially in the law of excluded middle.[1]

---

[1] A more detailed account of this will be given in an article *Alternative Logics* which is soon to appear in the *Proceedings*. [See *Proceedings of the Aristotelian Society*, 1945–6, pp. 77 ff.—Ed.]

(5) There is a further factor, elusive and most difficult to pin down: a mere tone of thought which, though not explicitly stated, permeates the air of a historical period and inspires its leading figures. It is a sort of field organizing and directing the ideas of an age. (The time from Descartes to Newton, for instance, was animated by an instinctive belief in an Order of Things accessible to the human mind. Though the thinkers of that time have tried to render this tone of thought into a rationalistic system, they failed: for that which is the living spark of rationalism is itself irrational.)

Such, I think, are some of the regulative principles. The formulation of some of them is very vague, and advisedly so: it wouldn't be good policy to reduce mathematical harmony, consonance with the whole background of an age, etc., to fixed rules. It's better to have them elastic. Principle (5) should perhaps be better described as a condition for making—and missing—discoveries.

Now none of these principles is *indispensable*, imposed on us by the nature of our understanding. Kant has tried to condense the tone of thought of the Newtonian age into strict rules—into *necessary conditions* of factual knowledge; with what success can be seen from the subsequent development: the belief in synthetic *a priori* judgements has soon become something of a brake to research, discouraging such lines of approach as non-Euclidean geometry, and later non-causal laws in physics. Let this be a warning.

Writers on the history of philosophy are inclined to attend too exclusively to one aspect only—to the ideas explicitly stated, canvassing their fabric, but disregarding the tone of thought which gives them their impetus. The deeper significance of rationalism, for instance, lies in the fact that it corresponds to what the scientist *does*, strengthening his belief that, if he only tries hard, he *can* get to the bottom of things. But slowly and gradually the mental climate changes, and then a philosophy may find itself out of tune with its time.

I do not think for a minute that what I have said is a conclusive refutation of Kant. On the other hand—you may confute and kill a scientific theory; a philosophy dies only of old age.

III

ON REFERRING

P. F. Strawson

I

WE very commonly use expressions of certain kinds to mention or refer to some individual person or single object or particular event or place or process, in the course of doing what we should normally describe as making a statement about that person, object, place, event, or process. I shall call this way of using expressions the 'uniquely referring use'. The classes of expressions which are most commonly used in this way are: singular demonstrative pronouns ('this' and 'that'); proper names (e.g. 'Venice', 'Napoleon', 'John'); singular personal and impersonal pronouns ('he', 'she', 'I', 'you', 'it'); and phrases beginning with the definite article followed by a noun, qualified or unqualified, in the singular (e.g. 'the table', 'the old man', 'the king of France'). Any expression of any of these classes can occur as the subject of what would traditionally be regarded as a singular subject-predicate sentence; and would, so occurring, exemplify the use I wish to discuss.

I do not want to say that expressions belonging to these classes never have any other use than the one I want to discuss. On the contrary, it is obvious that they do. It is obvious that anyone who uttered the sentence, 'The whale is a mammal', would be using the expression 'the whale' in a way quite different from the way it would be used by anyone who had occasion seriously to utter the sentence, 'The whale struck the ship'. In the first sentence one is obviously *not* mentioning, and in the second sentence one obviously *is* mentioning, a particular whale. Again if I said, 'Napoleon was the greatest French soldier', I should be using the word 'Napoleon' to mention a certain individual, but I should not be using the phrase, 'the greatest French soldier', to mention an individual, but to say something about an individual I had already mentioned. It would be natural to say that in using this sentence I was talking *about* Napoleon and that what I was *saying* about him was that he was the greatest French

From '*Mind*', Vol. 59 (1950), pp. 320–44. Reprinted by permission of the author and the Editor of *Mind*.

soldier. But of course I *could* use the expression, 'the greatest French soldier', to mention an individual; for example, by saying: 'The greatest French soldier died in exile'. So it is obvious that at least some expressions belonging to the classes I mentioned *can* have uses other than the use I am anxious to discuss. Another thing I do not want to say is that in any given sentence there is never more than one expression used in the way I propose to discuss. On the contrary, it is obvious that there may be more than one. For example, it would be natural to say that, in seriously using the sentence, 'The whale struck the ship', I was saying something about both a certain whale and a certain ship, that I was using each of the expressions 'the whale' and 'the ship' to mention a particular object; or, in other words, that I was using each of these expressions in the uniquely referring way. In general, however, I shall confine my attention to cases where an expression used in this way occurs as the grammatical subject of a sentence.

I think it is true to say that Russell's Theory of Descriptions, which is concerned with the last of the four classes of expressions I mentioned above (i.e. with expressions of the form 'the so-and-so') is still widely accepted among logicians as giving a correct account of the use of such expressions in ordinary language. I want to show, in the first place, that this theory, so regarded, embodies some fundamental mistakes.

What question or questions about phrases of the form 'the so-and-so' was the Theory of Descriptions designed to answer? I think that at least one of the questions may be illustrated as follows. Suppose some one were now to utter the sentence, 'The king of France is wise'. No one would say that the sentence which had been uttered was meaningless. Everyone would agree that it was significant. But everyone knows that there is not at present a king of France. One of the questions the Theory of Descriptions was designed to answer was the question: how can such a sentence as 'The king of France is wise' be significant even when there is nothing which answers to the description it contains, i.e., in this case, nothing which answers to the description 'The king of France'? And one of the reasons why Russell thought it important to give a correct answer to this question was that he thought it important to show that another answer which might be given was wrong. The answer that he thought was wrong, and to which he was anxious to supply an alternative, might be exhibited as the conclusion of either of the following two fallacious arguments. Let us call the sentence 'The king of France is wise' the sentence S. Then the first argument is as follows:

(1) The phrase, 'the king of France', is the subject of the sentence S.

Therefore (2) if S is a significant sentence, S is a sentence *about* the king of France.

But (3) if there in no sense exists a king of France, the sentence is not about anything, and hence not about the king of France.

Therefore (4) since S is significant, there must in some sense (in some world) exist (or subsist) the king of France.

And the second argument is as follows:

(1) If S is significant, it is either true or false.

(2) S is true if the king of France is wise and false if the king of France is not wise.

(3) But the statement that the king of France is wise and the statement that the king of France is not wise are alike true only if there is (in some sense, in some world) something which is the king of France.

Hence (4) since S is significant, there follows the same conclusion as before.

These are fairly obviously bad arguments, and, as we should expect, Russell rejects them. The postulation of a world of strange entities, to which the king of France belongs, offends, he says, against 'that feeling for reality which ought to be preserved even in the most abstract studies'. The fact that Russell rejects these arguments is, however, less interesting than the extent to which, in rejecting their conclusion, he concedes the more important of their principles. Let me refer to the phrase, 'the king of France', as the phrase D. Then I think Russell's reasons for rejecting these two arguments can be summarized as follows. The mistake arises, he says, from thinking that D, which is certainly the *grammatical* subject of S, is also the *logical* subject of S. But D is not the logical subject of S. In fact S, although grammatically it has a singular subject and a predicate, is not logically a subject-predicate sentence at all. The proposition it expresses is a complex kind of *existential* proposition, part of which might be described as a 'uniquely existential' proposition. To exhibit the logical form of the proposition, we should re-write the sentence in a logically appropriate grammatical form; in such a way that the deceptive similarity of S to a sentence expressing a subject-predicate proposition would disappear, and we should be safeguarded against arguments such as the bad ones I outlined above. Before recalling the details of Russell's analysis of S, let us notice what his answer, as I have so far given it, seems to imply. His answer seems to imply that in the case of a sentence which is similar to S in that (1) it is grammatically of the subject-predicate form and (2) its grammatical subject does not refer to anything, then the only alternative to its being meaningless is that it should not really (i.e. logically) be of the subject-predicate form at all, but of some quite different form. And this in its turn seems to imply that if there are any sentences which are genuinely of the subject-predicate form, then the very fact of their being significant, having a meaning, guarantees that there *is* something referred to by the logical (and grammatical) subject. Moreover, Russell's answer seems to imply that there are such sentences. For if it is true that one may be misled by the grammatical similarity of S to other sentences into thinking that it is logically of the subject-predicate form, then surely there must be other sentences grammatically similar to S, which *are* of the subject-predicate form. To show not only that Russell's answer seems to imply these conclusions, but that he accepted at least the first two of them, it is enough to consider what he says about a class of expressions which he calls 'logically proper names' and contrasts with expressions, like D, which he calls 'definite descriptions'. Of logically proper names Russell says or implies the following things:

(1) That they and they alone can occur as subjects of sentences which are genuinely of the subject-predicate form;

(2) that an expression intended to be a logically proper name is *meaningless* unless there is some single object for which it stands: for the *meaning* of such an expression just is the individual object which the expression designates. To be a name at all, therefore, it *must* designate something.

It is easy to see that if anyone believes these two propositions, then the only way for him to save the significance of the sentence S is to deny that it is a logically subject-predicate sentence. Generally, we may say that Russell recognizes only two ways in which sentences which seem, from their grammatical structure, to be about some particular person or individual object or event, can be significant:

(1) The first is that their grammatical form should be misleading as to their logical form, and that they should be analysable, like S, as a special kind of existential sentence;

(2) The second is that their grammatical subject should be a logically proper name, of which the meaning is the individual thing it designates.

I think that Russell is unquestionably wrong in this, and that sentences which are significant, and which begin with an expression used in the uniquely referring way, fall into neither of these two classes. Expressions used in the uniquely referring way are never either logically proper names or descriptions, if what is meant by calling them 'descriptions' is that they are to be analysed in accordance with the model provided by Russell's Theory of Descriptions.

There are no logically proper names and there are no descriptions (in this sense).

Let us now consider the details of Russell's analysis. According to Russell, anyone who asserted S would be asserting that:

(1) There is a king of France.
(2) There is not more than one king of France.
(3) There is nothing which is king of France and is not wise.

It is easy to see both how Russell arrived at this analysis, and how it enables him to answer the question with which we began, viz. the question: How can the sentence S be significant when there is no king of France? The way in which he arrived at the analysis was clearly by asking himself what would be the circumstances in which we would say that anyone who uttered the sentence S had made a true assertion. And it does seem pretty clear, and I have no wish to dispute, that the sentences (1)-(3) above do describe circumstances which are at least *necessary* conditions of anyone making a true assertion by uttering the sentence S. But, as I hope to show, to say this is not at all the same thing as to say that Russell has given a correct account of the use of the sentence S or even that he has given an account which, though incomplete, is correct as far as it goes; and is certainly not at all the same thing as to say that the model translation provided is a correct model for all (or for any) singular sentences beginning with a phrase of the form 'the so-and-so'.

It is also easy to see how this analysis enables Russell to answer the question of how the sentence S can be significant, even when there is no king of France. For, if this analysis is correct, anyone who utters the sentence S to-day would be jointly asserting three propositions, one of which (viz. that there is a king of France) would be false; and since the conjunction of three propositions, of which one is false, is itself false, the assertion as a whole would be significant, but false. So neither of the bad arguments for subsistent entities would apply to such an assertion.

II

As a step towards showing that Russell's solution of his problem is mistaken, and towards providing the correct solution, I want now to draw certain distinctions. For this purpose I shall, for the remainder of this section, refer to an expression which has a uniquely referring use as 'an expression' for short; and to a sentence beginning with such an expression as 'a sentence' for short. The distinctions I shall draw are rather rough and ready, and, no doubt, difficult cases could be produced which would call for their refinement. But I think they will serve my purpose. The distinctions are between:

(A1) a sentence,
(A2) a use of a sentence,
(A3) an utterance of a sentence,

and, correspondingly, between:

(B1) an expression,
(B2) a use of an expression,
(B3) an utterance of an expression.

Consider again the sentence, 'The king of France is wise'. It is easy to imagine that this sentence was uttered at various times from, say, the beginning of the seventeenth century onwards, during the reigns of each successive French monarch; and easy to imagine that it was also uttered during the subsequent periods in which France was not a monarchy. Notice that it was natural for me to speak of 'the sentence' or 'this sentence' being uttered at various times during this period; or, in other words, that it would be natural and correct to speak of *one and the same* sentence being uttered on all these various occasions. It is in the sense in which it would be correct to speak of one and the same sentence being uttered on all these various occasions that I want to use the expression (A1) 'a sentence'. There are, however, obvious differences between different *occasions of the use* of this sentence. For instance, if one man uttered it in the reign of Louis XIV and another man uttered it in the reign of Louis XV, it would be natural to say (to assume) that they were respectively talking about different people; and it might be held that the first man, in using the sentence, made a true assertion, while the second man, in using the same sentence, made a false assertion. If on the other hand two different men simultaneously uttered the sentence (e.g. if one wrote it and the other spoke it) during the reign of Louis XIV, it would be natural to say (assume) that they were both talking about the same person, and, in that case, in using the sentence, they *must* either both have made a true assertion or both have made a false assertion. And this illustrates what I mean by *a use* of a sentence. The two men who uttered the sentence, one in the reign of Louis XV and one in the reign of Louis XIV, each made a different use of the same sentence; whereas the two men who uttered the sentence simultaneously in the reign of Louis XIV, made the same use[1] of the same sentence. Obviously in the case of this sentence, and equally obviously in the case of many others, we cannot talk of *the sentence* being true or false, but only of its being used to make a true or false assertion, or (if this is preferred) to express a true or a false proposition. And equally obviously we cannot talk of *the sentence* being *about* a particular person, for the same sentence may be used at different times to talk about quite different particular persons, but only of *a use* of the sentence to talk about a particular person. Finally it will make sufficiently clear what I mean by an utterance of a sentence if I say that the two men who simultaneously uttered the sentence in the reign of Louis XIV made two different utterances of the same sentence, though they made the same *use* of the sentence.

If we now consider not the whole sentence, 'The king of France is wise', but that part of it which is the expression, 'the king of France', it is obvious that we can make analogous, though not identical distinctions between (1) the expression, (2) a use of the expression and (3) an utterance of the expression. The distinctions will not be identical; we obviously cannot correctly talk of the expression 'the king of France' being used to express a true or false proposition, since in general only sentences can be used truly or falsely; and similarly it is only by using a sentence and not by using an expression alone, that you can talk about a particular person. Instead, we shall say in this case that you *use* the expression to *mention* or *refer to* a particular person in the course of using the sentence to talk about him. But obviously in this case, and a great many others, the *expression*

[1] This usage of 'use' is, of course, different from (*a*) the current usage in which 'use' (of a particular word, phrase, sentence) = (roughly) 'rules for using' = (roughly) 'meaning'; and from (*b*) my own usage in the phrase 'uniquely referring use of expressions' in which 'use' = (roughly) 'way of using'.

(B1) cannot be said to mention, or refer to, anything, any more than the *sentence* can be said to be true or false. The same expression can have different mentioning-uses, as the same sentence can be used to make statements with different truth-values. 'Mentioning', or 'referring', is not something an expression does; it is something that some one can use an expression to do. Mentioning, or referring to, something is a characteristic of *a use* of an expression, just as 'being about' something, and truth-or-falsity, are characteristics of *a use* of a sentence.

A very different example may help to make these distinctions clearer. Consider another case of an expression which has a uniquely referring use, viz. the expression 'I'; and consider the sentence, 'I am hot'. Countless people may use this same sentence; but it is logically impossible for two different people to make *the same use* of this sentence: or, if this is preferred, to use it to express the same proposition. The expression 'I' may correctly be used by (and only by) any one of innumerable people to refer to himself. To say this is to say something about the expression 'I': it is, in a sense, to give its meaning. This is the sort of thing that can be said about *expressions*. But it makes no sense to say of the *expression* 'I' that it refers to a particular person. This is the sort of thing that can be said only of a particular use of the expression.

Let me use 'type' as an abbreviation for 'sentence or expression'. Then I am not saying that there are sentences and expressions (types), *and* uses of them, *and* utterances of them, as there are ships *and* shoes *and* sealing-wax. I am saying that we cannot say *the same things* about types, uses of types, and utterances of types. And the fact is that we do talk about types; and that confusion is apt to result from the failure to notice the differences between what we can say about these and what we can say only about the *uses* of types. We are apt to fancy we are talking about sentences and expressions when we are talking about the uses of sentences and expressions.

This is what Russell does. Generally, as against Russell, I shall say this. Meaning (in at least one important sense) is a function of the sentence or expression; mentioning and referring and truth or falsity, are functions of the use of the sentence or expression. To give the meaning of an expression (in the sense in which I am using the word) is to give *general directions* for its use to refer to or mention particular objects or persons; to give the meaning of a sentence is to give *general directions* for its use in making true or false assertions. It is not to talk about any particular occasion of the use of the sentence or expression. The meaning of an expression cannot be identified with the object it is used, on a particular occasion, to refer to. The meaning of a sentence cannot be identified with the assertion it is used, on a particular occasion, to make. For to talk about the meaning of an expression or sentence is not to talk about its use on a particular occasion, but about the rules, habits, conventions governing its correct use, on all occasions, to refer or to assert So the question of whether a sentence or expression *is significant or not* has nothing whatever to do with the question of whether the sentence, *uttered on a particular occasion*, is, on that occasion, being used to make a true-or-false assertion or not, or of whether the expression is, on that occasion, being used to refer to, or mention, anything at all.

The source of Russell's mistake was that he thought that referring or mentioning, if it occurred at all, must be meaning. He did not distinguish B1 from B2; he confused expressions with their use in a particular context; and so confused meaning with mentioning, with referring. If I talk about my handkerchief, I can, perhaps, produce the object I am referring to out of my pocket. I can't produce the meaning of the expression, 'my handkerchief', out of my pocket. Because Russell confused meaning with mentioning, he thought that if there were any expressions having a uniquely referring use, which were what they seemed (i.e. logical subjects) and not something else in disguise, their meaning must *be* the particular object which they were used to refer to. Hence the troublesome mythology of the logically proper name. But if some one asks me the meaning of the expression 'this'—once Russell's favourite candidate for this status—I do not hand him the object I have just used the expression to refer to, adding at the same time that the meaning of the word changes every time it is used. Nor do I hand him all the objects it ever has been, or might be, used to refer to. I explain and illustrate the conventions governing the use of the expression. This *is* giving the meaning of the expression. It is quite different from giving (in any sense of giving) the object to which it refers; for the expression itself does not refer to anything; though it can be used, on different occasions, to refer to innumerable things. Now as a matter of fact there is, in English, a sense of the word 'mean' in which this word does approximate to 'indicate, mention or refer to'; e.g. when somebody (unpleasantly) says, 'I mean you'; or when I point and say, 'That's the one I mean'. But *the one I meant* is quite different from *the meaning of the expression* I used to talk of it. In this special sense of 'mean', it is people who mean, not expressions. People use expressions to refer to particular things. But the meaning of an expression is not the set of things or the single thing it may correctly be used to refer to: the meaning is the set of rules, habits, conventions for its use in referring.

It is the same with sentences: even more obviously so. Every one knows that the sentence, 'The table is covered with books', is significant, and every one knows what it means. But if I ask, 'What object is that sentence about?' I am asking an absurd question—a question which cannot be asked about the sentence, but only about some use of the sentence: and in this case the sentence hasn't been used, it has only been taken as an example. In knowing what it means, you are knowing how it could correctly be used to talk about things: so knowing the meaning hasn't anything to do with knowing about any particular use of the sentence to talk about anything. Similarly, if I ask: 'Is the sentence true or false?' I am asking an absurd question, which becomes no less absurd if I add, 'It must be one or the other since it's significant'. The question is absurd, because the *sentence* is neither true nor false any more than it's *about* some object. Of course the fact that it's significant is the same as the fact that it *can* correctly be used to talk about something and that, in so using it, some one will be making a true or false assertion. And I will add that it will be used to make a true or false assertion *only* if the person using it *is* talking about something. If, when he utters it, he is not talking about anything, then his use is not a genuine one, but a spurious or pseudo-use: he is not making either a true or a false assertion, though he may think he is. And this points the way to the correct answer to the puzzle to which the Theory of Descriptions gives a fatally incorrect answer. The important point is that the question of whether the sentence is significant or not is quite independent of the question that can be raised about a particular use of it, viz. the question whether it is a genuine or a spurious use, whether it is being used to talk about something, or in make-believe, or as an example in philosophy. The question whether the sentence is significant or not is the question whether there exist such language habits, conventions or rules that the sentence logically could be used to talk about something; and is hence quite independent of the question whether it is being so used on a particular occasion.

III

Consider again the sentence, 'The king of France is wise', and the true and false things Russell says about it.

There are at least two true things which Russell would say about the sentence:

(1) The first is that it is significant; that if anyone were now to utter it, he would be uttering a significant sentence.

(2) The second is that anyone now uttering the sentence would be making a true assertion only if there in fact at present existed one and only one king of France, and if he were wise.

What are the false things which Russell would say about the sentence? They are:

(1) That anyone now uttering it would be making a true assertion or a false assertion;

(2) That part of what he would be asserting would be that there at present existed one and only one king of France.

I have already given some reasons for thinking that these two statements are incorrect. Now suppose some one were in fact to say to you with a perfectly serious air: 'The king of France is wise'. Would you say, 'That's untrue'? I think it's quite certain that you wouldn't. But suppose he went on to *ask* you whether you thought that what he had just said was true, or was false; whether you agreed or disagreed with what he had just said. I think you would be inclined, with some hesitation, to say that you didn't do either; that the question of whether his statement was true or false simply *didn't arise*, because there was no such person as the king of France.[1] You might, if he were obviously serious (had a dazed astray-in-the-centuries look), say something like: 'I'm afraid you must be under a misapprehension. France is not a monarchy. There is no king of France.' And this brings out the point that if a man seriously uttered the sentence, his uttering it would in some sense be *evidence* that he *believed* that there was a king of France. It would not be evidence for his believing this simply in the way in which a man's reaching for his raincoat is evidence for his believing that it is raining. But nor would it be evidence for his believing this in the way in which a man's saying, 'It's raining' is evidence for his believing that it is raining. We might put it as follows. To say, 'The king of France is wise' is, in some sense of 'imply', to *imply* that there is a king of France. But this is a very special and odd sense of 'imply'. 'Implies' in this sense is certainly not equivalent to 'entails' (or 'logically implies'). And this comes out from the fact that when, in response to his statement, we say (as we should) 'There is no king of France', we should certainly

[1] Since this article was written, there has appeared a clear statement of this point by Mr Geach in *Analysis*, Vol. 10, No. 4, March, 1950.

not say we were *contradicting* the statement that the king of France is wise. We are certainly not saying that it's false. We are, rather, giving a reason for saying that the question of whether it's true or false simply doesn't arise.

And this is where the distinction I drew earlier can help us. The sentence, 'The king of France is wise', is certainly significant; but this does not mean that any particular use of it is true or false. We use it truly or falsely when we use it to talk about some one; when, in using the expression, 'The king of France', we are in fact mentioning some one. The fact that the sentence and the expression, respectively, are significant just is the fact that the sentence *could* be used, in certain circumstances, to say something true or false, that the expression *could* be used, in certain circumstances to mention a particular person; and to know their meaning is to know what sort of circumstances these are. So when we utter the sentence without in fact mentioning anybody by the use of the phrase, 'The king of France', the sentence doesn't cease to be significant: we simply *fail* to say anything true or false because we simply fail to mention anybody by this particular use of that perfectly significant phrase. It is, if you like, a spurious use of the sentence, and a spurious use of the expression; though we may (or may not) mistakenly think it a genuine use.

And such spurious uses are very familiar. Sophisticated romancing, sophisticated fiction,[1] depend upon them. If I began, 'The king of France is wise', and went on, 'and he lives in a golden castle and has a hundred wives', and so on, a hearer would understand me perfectly well, without supposing *either* that I was talking about a particular person, *or* that I was making a false statement to the effect that there existed such a person as my words described. (It is worth adding that where the use of sentences and expressions is overtly fictional, the sense of the word 'about' may change. As Moore said, it is perfectly natural and correct to say that some of the statements in *Pickwick Papers* are *about* Mr. Pickwick. But where the use of sentences and expressions is not overtly fictional, this use of 'about' seems less correct; i.e. it would not *in general* be correct to say that a statement was about Mr. X or the so-and-so, unless there were such a person or thing. So it is where the romancing is in danger of being taken seriously that we might answer the question, 'Who is he talking about?' with 'He's not talking about anybody'; but, in saying this, we are not saying that what he is saying is either false or nonsense.)

Overtly fictional uses apart, however, I said just now that to use

[1] The unsophisticated kind begins: 'Once upon time there was . . .'.

such an expression as 'The king of France' at the beginning of a sentence was, in some sense of 'imply', to imply that there was a king of France. When a man uses such an expression, he does not *assert*, nor does what he says *entail*, a uniquely existential proposition. But one of the conventional functions of the definite article is to act as a *signal* that a unique reference is being made—a signal, not a disguised assertion. When we begin a sentence with 'the such-and-such' the use of 'the' shows, but does not state, that we are, or intend to be, referring to one particular individual of the species 'such-and-such'. *Which* particular individual is a matter to be determined from context, time, place and any other features of the situation of utterance. Now, whenever a man uses any expression, the presumption is that he thinks he is using it correctly: so when he uses the expression, 'the such-and-such', in a uniquely referring way, the presumption is that he thinks both that there is *some* individual of that species, and that the context of use will sufficiently determine which one he has in mind. To use the word 'the' in this way is then to imply (in the relevant sense of 'imply') that the existential conditions described by Russell are fulfilled. But to use 'the' in this way is not to *state* that those conditions are fulfilled. If I begin a sentence with an expression of the form, 'the so-and-so', and then am prevented from saying more, I have made no statement of any kind; but I may have succeeded in mentioning some one or something.

The uniquely existential assertion supposed by Russell to be part of any assertion in which a uniquely referring use is made of an expression of the form 'the so-and-so' is, he observes, a compound of two assertions. To say that there is a ϕ is to say something compatible with there being several ϕs; to say there is not more than one ϕ is to say something compatible with there being none. To say there is one ϕ and one only is to compound these two assertions. I have so far been concerned mostly with the alleged assertion of existence and less with the alleged assertion of uniqueness. An example which throws the emphasis on to the latter will serve to bring out more clearly the sense of 'implied' in which a uniquely existential assertion is implied, but not entailed, by the use of expressions in the uniquely referring way. Consider the sentence, 'The table is covered with books'. It is quite certain that in any normal use of this sentence, the expression 'the table' would be used to make a unique reference, i.e. to refer to some one table. It is a quite strict use of the definite article, in the sense in which Russell talks on p. 30 of *Principia Mathematica*, of using the article '*strictly*, so as to imply uniqueness'. On the same page

Russell says that a phrase of the form 'the so-and-so', used strictly, 'will only have an application in the event of there being one so-and-so and no more'. Now it is obviously quite false that the phrase 'the table' in the sentence 'the table is covered with books', used normally, will 'only have an application in the event of there being one table and no more'. It is indeed tautologically true that, in such a use, the phrase will have an application only in the event of there being one table and no more *which is being referred to*, and that it will be understood to have an application only in the event of there being one table and no more which it is understood as being used to refer to. To use the sentence is not to assert, but it is (in the special sense discussed) to imply, that there is only one thing which is *both* of the kind specified (i.e. a table) *and is being referred to* by the speaker. It is obviously not to assert this. To refer is not to say you are referring. To say there is *some table or other* to which you are referring is not the same as referring to a particular table. We should have no use for such phrases as 'the individual I referred to' unless there were something which counted as referring. (It would make no sense to say you had pointed if there were nothing which counted as pointing.) So once more I draw the conclusion that referring to or mentioning a particular thing cannot be dissolved into any kind of assertion. To refer is not to assert, though you refer in order to go on to assert.

Let me now take an example of the uniquely referring use of an expression not of the form, 'the so-and-so'. Suppose I advance my hands, cautiously cupped, towards someone, saying, as I do so, 'This is a fine red one'. He, looking into my hands and seeing nothing there, may say: 'What is? What are you talking about?' Or perhaps, 'But there's nothing in your hands'. Of course it would be absurd to say that in saying 'But you've got nothing in your hands', he was *denying* or *contradicting* what I said. So 'this' is not a disguised description in Russell's sense. Nor is it a logically proper name. For one must know what the sentence means in order to react in that way to the utterance of it. It is precisely because the significance of the word 'this' is independent of any particular reference it may be used to make, though not independent of the way it may be used to refer, that I can, as in this example, use it to *pretend* to be referring to something.

The general moral of all this is that communication is much less a matter of explicit or disguised assertion than logicians used to suppose. The particular application of this general moral in which I am interested is its application to the case of making a unique reference. It is a part of the significance of expressions of the kind

I am discussing that they can be used, in an immense variety of contexts, to make unique references. It is no part of their significance to assert that they are being so used or that the conditions of their being so used are fulfilled. So the wholly important distinction we are required to draw is between:

(1) using an expression to make a unique reference; and

(2) asserting that there is one and only one individual which has certain characteristics (e.g. is of a certain kind, or stands in a certain relation to the speaker, or both).

This is, in other words, the distinction between

(1) sentences containing an expression used to indicate or mention or refer to a particular person or thing; and

(2) uniquely existential sentences.

What Russell does is progressively to assimilate more and more sentences of class (1) to sentences of class (2), and consequently to involve himself in insuperable difficulties about logical subjects, and about values for individual variables generally: difficulties which have led him finally to the logically disastrous theory of names developed in the *Enquiry* and in *Human Knowledge*. That view of the meaning of logical-subject-expressions which provides the whole incentive to the Theory of Descriptions at the same time precludes the possibility of Russell's ever finding any satisfactory substitutes for those expressions which, beginning with substantival phrases, he progressively degrades from the status of logical subjects.[1] It is not simply, as is sometimes said, the fascination of the relation between a name and its bearer, that is the root of the trouble. Not even names come up to the impossible standard set. It is rather the combination of two more radical misconceptions: first, the failure to grasp the importance of the distinction (section II above) between what may be said of an expression and what may be said of a particular use of it; second, a failure to recognize the uniquely referring use of expressions for the harmless, necessary thing it is, distinct from, but complementary to, the predicative or ascriptive use of expressions. The expressions which can in fact occur as singular logical subjects are expressions of the class I listed at the outset (demonstratives, substantival phrases, proper names, pronouns): to say this is to say that these expressions, together with context (in the widest sense) are what one uses to make unique references. The point of the conventions governing the uses of such expressions is, along with the

[1] And this in spite of the danger-signal of that phrase, '*misleading* grammatical form'.

situation of utterance, to secure uniqueness of reference. But to do
this, enough is enough. We do not, and we cannot, while referring,
attain the point of complete explicitness at which the referring
function is no longer performed. The actual unique reference made,
if any, is a matter of the particular use in the particular context;
the significance of the expression used is the set of rules or
conventions which permit such references to be made. Hence we can,
using significant expressions, pretend to refer, in make-believe or
in fiction, or mistakenly think we are referring when we are not
referring to anything.

This shows the need for distinguishing two kinds (among many
others) of linguistic conventions or rules: rules for referring, and
rules for attributing and ascribing; and for an investigation of the
former. If we recognize this distinction of use for what it is, we
are on the way to solving a number of ancient logical and metaphysical
puzzles.

My last two sections are concerned, but only in the barest outline,
with these questions.

IV

One of the main purposes for which we use language is the purpose
of stating facts about things and persons and events. If we want to
fulfil this purpose, we must have some way of forestalling the question,
'What (who, which one) are you talking about?' as well as the question,
'What are you saying about it (him, her)?' The task of forestalling
the first question is the referring (or identifying) task. The task of
forestalling the second is the attributive (or descriptive or classificatory
or ascriptive) task. In the conventional English sentence which is
used to state, or to claim to state, a fact about an individual thing
or person or event, the performance of these two tasks can be roughly
and approximately assigned to separable expressions.[1] And in such
a sentence, this assigning of expressions to their separate roles
corresponds to the conventional grammatical classification of subject
and predicate. There is nothing sacrosanct about the employment of
separable expressions for these two tasks. Other methods could be,
and are, employed. There is, for instance, the method of uttering a
single word or attributive phrase in the conspicuous presence of the
object referred to; or that analogous method exemplified by, e.g. the

[1] I neglect relational sentences; for these require, not a modification in the principle
of what I say, but a complication of the detail.

painting of the words 'unsafe for lorries' on a bridge, or the tying of a label reading 'first prize' on a vegetable marrow. Or one can imagine an elaborate game in which one never used an expression in the uniquely referring way at all, but uttered only uniquely existential sentences, trying to enable the hearer to identify what was being talked of by means of an accumulation of relative clauses. (This description of the purposes of the game shows in what sense it would be a game: this is not the normal use we make of existential sentences.) Two points require emphasis. The first is that the necessity of performing these two tasks in order to state particular facts requires no transcendental explanation: to call attention to it is partly to elucidate the meaning of the phrase, 'stating a fact'. The second is that even this elucidation is made in terms derivative from the grammar of the conventional singular sentence; that even the overtly functional, linguistic distinction between the identifying and attributive roles that words may play in language is prompted by the fact that ordinary speech offers us separable expressions to which the different functions may be plausibly and approximately assigned. And this functional distinction has cast long philosophical shadows. The distinctions between particular and universal, between substance and quality, are such pseudo-material shadows, cast by the grammar of the conventional sentence, in which separable expressions play distinguishable roles.

To use a separate expression to perform the first of these tasks is to use an expression in the uniquely referring way. I want now to say something in general about the conventions of use for expressions used in this way, and to contrast them with conventions of ascriptive use. I then proceed to the brief illustration of these general remarks and to some further applications of them.

What in general is required for making a unique reference is, obviously, some device, or devices, for showing both *that* a unique reference is intended and *what* unique reference it is; some device requiring and enabling the hearer or reader to identify what is being talked about. In securing this result, the context of utterance is of an importance which it is almost impossible to exaggerate; and by 'context' I mean, at least, the time, the place, the situation, the identity of the speaker, the subjects which form the immediate focus of interest, and the personal histories of both the speaker and those he is addressing. Besides context, there is, of course, convention;—linguistic convention. But, except in the case of genuine proper names, of which I shall have more to say later, the fulfilment of more or less precisely stateable contextual conditions is *conventionally* (or, in a wide sense of the word, *logically*) required for the correct referring use of expressions in a sense in which this is not true of correct ascriptive uses. The requirement for the correct application of an expression in its ascriptive use to a certain thing is simply that the thing should be of a certain kind, have certain characteristics. The requirement for the correct application of an expression in its referring use to a certain thing is something over and above any requirement derived from such ascriptive meaning as the expression may have; it is, namely, the requirement that the thing should be in a certain relation to the speaker and to the context of utterance. Let me call this the contextual requirement. Thus, for example, in the limiting case of the word 'I' the contextual requirement is that the thing should be identical with the speaker; but in the case of most expressions which have a referring use this requirement cannot be so precisely specified. A further, and perfectly general, difference between conventions for referring and conventions for describing is one we have already encountered, viz. that the fulfilment of the conditions for a correct ascriptive use of an expression is a part of what is stated by such a use; but the fulfilment of the conditions for a correct referring use of an expression is never part of what is stated, though it is (in the relevant sense of 'implied') implied by such a use.

Conventions for referring have been neglected or misinterpreted by logicians. The reasons for this neglect are not hard to see, though they are hard to state briefly. Two of them are, roughly: (1) the preoccupation of most logicians with definitions; (2) the preoccupation of some logicians with formal systems. (1) A definition, in the most familiar sense, is a specification of the conditions of the correct ascriptive or classificatory use of an expression. Definitions take no account of contextual requirements. So that in so far as the search for the meaning or the search for the analysis of an expression is conceived as the search for a definition, the neglect or misinterpretation of conventions other than ascriptive is inevitable. Perhaps it would be better to say (for I do not wish to legislate about 'meaning' or 'analysis') that logicians have failed to notice that problems of use are wider than problems of analysis and meaning. (2) The influence of the preoccupation with mathematics and formal logic is most clearly seen (to take no more recent examples) in the cases of Leibniz and Russell. The constructor of calculuses, not concerned or required to make factual statements, approaches applied logic with a prejudice. It is natural that he should assume that the types of convention with whose adequacy in one field he is familiar should be really adequate, if only one could see how, in a quite different field—that of statements of fact. Thus we have Leibniz striving desperately to make the uniqueness of unique references a matter of logic in the narrow sense, and Russell striving desperately to do the same thing, in a different way, both for the implication of uniqueness and for that of existence.

It should be clear that the distinction I am trying to draw is primarily one between different roles or parts that expressions may play in language, and not primarily one between different groups of expressions; for some expressions may appear in either role. Some of the kinds of words I shall speak of have predominantly, if not exclusively, a referring role. This is most obviously true of pronouns and ordinary proper names. Some can occur as wholes or parts of expressions which have a predominantly referring use, and as wholes or parts of expressions which have a predominantly ascriptive or classificatory use. The obvious cases are common nouns; or common nouns preceded by adjectives, including participial adjectives; or, less obviously, adjectives or participial adjectives alone. Expressions capable of having a referring use also differ from one another in at least the three following, not mutually independent, ways:

(1) They differ in the extent to which the reference they are used to make is dependent on the context of their utterance. Words like 'I' and 'it' stand at one end of this scale—the end of maximum dependence—and phrases like 'the author of Waverley' and 'the eighteenth king of France' at the other.

(2) They differ in the degree of 'descriptive meaning' they possess: by 'descriptive meaning' I intend 'conventional limitation, in application, to things of a certain general kind, or possessing certain general characteristics'. At one end of this scale stand the proper names we most commonly use in ordinary discourse; men, dogs and motor-bicycles may be called 'Horace'. The pure name has no descriptive meaning (except such as it may acquire *as a result of* some one of its uses as a name). A word like 'he' has minimal descriptive meaning, but has some. Substantival phrases like 'the round table' have the maximum descriptive meaning. An interesting intermediate position is occupied by 'impure' proper names like 'the Round Table'—substantival phrases which have grown capital letters.

(3) Finally, they may be divided into the following two classes: (i) those of which the correct referring use is regulated by some *general*

referring-cum-ascriptive conventions. To this class belong both pronouns, which have the least descriptive meaning, and substantival phrases which have the most; (ii) those of which the correct referring use is regulated by no general conventions, either of the contextual or the ascriptive kind, but by conventions which are *ad hoc* for each particular use (though not for each particular utterance). Roughly speaking, the most familiar kind of proper names belong to this class. Ignorance of a man's name is not ignorance of the language. This is why we do not speak of the meaning of proper names. (But it won't do to say they are meaningless.) Again an intermediate position is occupied by such phrases as 'The Old Pretender'. Only an old pretender may be so referred to; but to know which old pretender is not to know a general, but an *ad hoc*, convention.

In the case of phrases of the form 'the so-and-so' used referringly, the use of 'the' together with the position of the phrase in the sentence (i.e. at the beginning, or following a transitive verb or preposition) acts as a signal *that* a unique reference is being made; and the following noun, or noun and adjective, together with the context of utterance, shows *what* unique reference is being made. In general the functional difference between common nouns and adjectives is that the former are naturally and commonly used referringly, while the latter are not commonly, or so naturally, used in this way, except as qualifying nouns; though they can be, and are, so used alone. And of course this functional difference is not independent of the descriptive force peculiar to each word. In general we should expect the descriptive force of nouns to be such that they are more efficient tools for the job of showing what unique reference is intended when such a reference is signalized; and we should also expect the descriptive force of the words we naturally and commonly use to make unique reference to mirror our interest in the salient, relatively permanent and behavioural characteristics of things. These two expectations are not independent of one another; and, if we look at the difference between the commoner sort of common nouns and the commoner sort of adjectives, we find them both fulfilled. These are differences of the kind that Locke quaintly reports, when he speaks of our ideas of substances being *collections* of simple ideas; when he says that 'powers make up a great part of our ideas of substances'; and when he goes on to contrast the identity of real and nominal essence in the case of simple ideas with their lack of identity and the shiftingness of the nominal essence in the case of substances. 'Substance' itself is the troublesome tribute Locke pays to his dim awareness of the difference in predominant linguistic function that lingered even when the noun had been expanded into a more or less indefinite string of adjectives. Russell repeats Locke's mistake with a difference when, admitting the inference from syntax to reality to the extent of feeling that he can get rid of this metaphysical unknown only if he can purify language of the referring function altogether, he draws up his programme for 'abolishing particulars'; a programme, in fact, for abolishing the distinction of logical use which I am here at pains to emphasize.

The contextual requirement for the referring use of pronouns may be stated with the greatest precision in some cases (e.g. 'I' and 'you') and only with the greatest vagueness in others ('it' and 'this'). I propose to say nothing further about pronouns, except to point to an additional symptom of the failure to recognize the uniquely referring use for what it is; the fact, namely, that certain logicians have actually sought to elucidate the nature of the variable by offering such *sentences* as 'he is sick', 'it is green', as examples of something in ordinary speech like a *sentential function*. Now of course it is true that the word 'he' may be used on different occasions to refer to different people or different animals: so may the word 'John' and the phrase 'the cat'. What deters such logicians from treating these two expressions as quasi-variables is, in the first case, the lingering superstition that a name is logically tied to a single individual, and, in the second case, the descriptive meaning of the word 'cat'. But 'he', which has a wide range of applications and minimal descriptive force, only acquires a use as a referring word. It is this fact, together with the failure to accord to expressions used referringly the place in logic which belongs to them (the place held open for the mythical logically proper name), that accounts for the misleading attempt to elucidate the nature of the variable by reference to such words as 'he', 'she', 'it'.

Of ordinary proper names it is sometimes said that they are essentially words each of which is used to refer to just one individual. This is obviously false. Many ordinary personal names—names par excellence—are correctly used to refer to numbers of people. An ordinary personal name, is, roughly, a word, used referringly, of which the use is *not* dictated by any descriptive meaning the word may have, and is *not* prescribed by any such general rule for use as a referring expression (or a part of a referring expression) as we find in the case of such words as 'I', 'this' and 'the', but is governed by *ad hoc* conventions for each particular set of applications of the word to a given person. The important point is that the correctness of such applications does not follow from any *general* rule or convention for the use of the word as such. (The limit of absurdity and obvious circularity is reached in the attempt to treat names as disguised description in Russell's sense; for what is in the special sense implied, but not entailed, by my now referring to some one by name is simply the existence of some one, *now being referred to*, who is *conventionally referred to* by that name.) Even this feature of names, however, is only a symptom of the purpose for which they are employed. At present our choice of names is partly arbitrary, partly dependent on legal and social observances. It would be perfectly possible to have a thorough-going *system* of names, based e.g. on dates of birth, or on a minute classification of physiological and anatomical differences. But the success of any such system would depend entirely on the convenience of the resulting name-allotments for the purpose of making unique references; and this would depend on the multiplicity of the classifications used and the degree to which they cut haphazard across normal social groupings. Given a sufficient degree of both, the selectivity supplied by context would do the rest; just as is the case with our present naming habits. Had we such a system, we could use name-words descriptively (as we do at present, to a limited extent and in a different way, with some famous names) as well as referringly. But it is by criteria derived from consideration of the requirements of the referring task that we should assess the adequacy of any system of naming. From the naming point of view, no kind of classification would be better or worse than any other simply because of the kind of classification—natal or anatomical—that it was.

I have already mentioned the class of quasi-names, of sub-stantival phrases which grow capital letters, and of which such phrases as 'the Glorious Revolution', 'the Great War', 'the Annunciation', 'the Round Table' are examples. While the descriptive meaning of the words which follow the definite article is still relevant to their referring role, the capital letters are a sign of that extra-logical selectivity in their referring use, which is characteristic of pure names. Such phrases are found in print or in writing when one member of some class of events or things is of quite outstanding interest in a certain society. These phrases are embryonic names. A phrase may, for obvious reasons, pass into, and out of, this class (e.g. 'the Great War').

V

I want to conclude by considering, all too briefly, three further problems about referring uses:

(a) *Indefinite references*. Not all referring uses of singular expressions forestall the question 'What (who, which one) are you talking about?' There are some which either invite this question, or disclaim the intention or ability to answer it. Examples are such sentence-beginnings as 'A man told me that. . .', 'Some one told me that. . . .' The orthodox (Russellian) doctrine is that such sentences are existential, but not uniquely existential. This seems wrong in several ways. It is ludicrous to suggest that part of what is asserted is that the class of men or persons is not empty. Certainly this is *implied* in the by now familiar sense of implication; but the implication is also as much an implication of the *uniqueness* of the particular object of reference as when I begin a sentence with such a phrase as 'the table'. The difference between the use of the definite and indefinite articles is, very roughly, as follows. We use 'the' either when a previous reference has been made, and when 'the' signalizes that the same reference is being made; or when, in the absence of a previous indefinite reference, the context (including the hearer's assumed knowledge) is expected to enable the hearer to tell *what* reference is being made. We use 'a' either when these conditions are not fulfilled, or when, although a definite reference *could* be made, we wish to keep dark the identity of the individual to whom, or to which, we are referring. This is the *arch* use of such a phrase as 'a certain person' or 'some one'; where it could be expanded, not into 'some one, but you wouldn't (or I don't) know who' but into 'some one, but I'm not telling you who.'

(b) *Identification statements*. By this label I intend statements like the following:

(i*a*) That is the man who swam the channel twice on one day.

(ii*a*) Napoleon was the man who ordered the execution of the Duc D'Enghien.

The puzzle about these statements is that their grammatical predicates do not seem to be used in a straightforwardly ascriptive way as are the grammatical predicates of the statements:

(i*b*) That man swam the channel twice in one day.

(ii*b*) Napoleon ordered the execution of the Duc D'Enghien.

But if, in order to avoid blurring the difference between (i*a*) and (i*b*) and (ii*a*) and (ii*b*), one says that the phrases which form the grammatical complements of (i*a*) and (ii*a*) are being used referringly, one becomes puzzled about what is being said in these sentences. We seem then to be referring to the same person twice over and either saying nothing about him and thus making no statement, or identifying him with himself and thus producing a trivial identity.

The bogey of triviality can be dismissed. This only arises for those who think of the object referred to by the use of an expression as its meaning, and thus think of the subject and complement of these sentences as meaning the same because they could be used to refer to the same person.

I think the differences between sentences in the (*a*) group and sentences in the (*b*) group can best be understood by considering the differences between the circumstances in which you would say (i*a*) and the circumstances in which you would say (i*b*). You would say (i*a*) instead of (i*b*) if you knew or believed that your hearer knew or believed that *some one* had swum the channel twice in one day. You say (i*a*) when you take your hearer to be in the position of one who can ask: 'Who swam the channel twice in one day?' (And in asking this, he is not saying that anyone did, though his asking it implies—in the relevant sense—that some one did.) Such sentences are like answers to such questions. They are better called 'identification-statements' than 'identities'. Sentence (i*a*) does not assert more or less than sentence (i*b*). It is just that you say (i*a*) to a man whom you take to know certain things that you take to be unknown to the man to whom you say (i*b*).

This is, in the barest essentials, the solution to Russell's puzzle about 'denoting phrases' joining by 'is'; one of the puzzles which he claims for the Theory of Descriptions the merit of solving.

(*c*) *The logic of subjects and predicates.* Much of what I have said of the uniquely referring use of expressions can be extended, with suitable modifications, to the non-uniquely referring use of expressions; i.e. to some uses of expressions consisting of 'the' 'all the', 'all', 'some', 'some of the', etc. followed by a noun, qualified or unqualified, in the *plural*; to some uses of 'they', 'them', 'those', 'these'; and to conjunctions of names. Expressions of the first kind have a special interest. Roughly speaking, orthodox modern criticism, inspired by mathematical logic, of such traditional doctrines as that of the Square of Opposition and of some of the forms of the syllogism traditionally recognized as valid, rests on the familiar failure to recognize the special sense in which existential assertions may be implied by the referring use of expressions. The universal propositions of the fourfold schedule, it is said, must *either* be given a negatively existential interpretation (e.g., for A, 'there are no Xs which are not Ys') *or* they must be interpreted as conjunctions of negatively and positively existential statements of, e.g., the form (for A) 'there are no Xs which are not Ys, and there are Xs'. The I and O forms are normally given a positively existential interpretation. It is then seen that, whichever of the above alternatives is selected, some of the traditional laws have to be abandoned. The dilemma, however, is a bogus one. If we interpret the propositions of the schedule as neither positively, nor negatively, nor positively *and* negatively, existential, but as sentences such that *the question of whether they are being used to make true or false assertions does not arise except when the existential condition is fulfilled for the subject term*, then all the traditional laws hold good together. And this interpretation is far closer to the most common uses of expressions beginning with 'all' and 'some' than is any Russellian alternative. For these expressions are most commonly used in the referring way. A literal-minded and childless man asked whether all his children are asleep will certainly not answer 'Yes' on the ground that he has none; but nor will he answer 'No' on this ground. Since he has no children, the question does not arise. To say this is not to say that I may not use the sentence, 'All my children are asleep', with the intention of letting some one know that I have children, or of deceiving him into thinking that I have. Nor is it any weakening of my thesis to concede that singular phrases of the form 'the so-and-so' may sometimes be used with a similar purpose. Neither Aristotelian nor Russellian rules give the exact logic of any expression of ordinary language; for ordinary language has no exact logic.

IV

THE THEORY OF TRANSLATION

W. Haas

I

To translate is one thing; to say how we do it, is another. The practice
is familiar enough, and there are familiar theories of it. But when
we try to look more closely, theory tends to obscure rather than explain, and the familiar practice—an ancient practice, without which
Western civilization is unthinkable—appears to be just baffling, its
very possibility a mystery.

To translate, Dr Johnson tells us, is 'to change into another
language, retaining the sense'; and it is easy to agree with him. But
can we think it out? How do we effect this exchange of languages? Is
it like changing horses or carriages? And what, exactly, is it that we
retain? Images are powerful instruments of interpretation. But this
one, the image of something carried across from one vehicle to
another, can it bear the weight we put upon it?

At first sight, this is what we are tempted to make of translation—
an operation with three terms: two expressions, and a meaning
they share. When we translate, we seem to establish a relation of
three distinct entities, each separately apprehended: the two expressions seen on paper or heard in the air, and the meaning in the
translator's mind. The meaning, presumably, we 'retain' and translate; we 'transfer' it from one expression to the other. Strictly, then,
when a sentence or speech or novel is translated, say, from French
into English, what is supposed to be translated or transferred is not
the French sentence or speech or novel at all; it is something utterly
different, something inaudible and invisible—'the meaning' itself,
which is not in French nor in English nor in any language whatever.

This interpretation of translation as a triadic relation does,
of course, accord with some deeply ingrained habits of thought. It
conforms with a model which we are inclined to apply to all conscious
and voluntary manifestations of human life. As a human being might
be thought of as the temporary embodiment of an independent soul,

From *Philosophy*, Vol. 37 (1962), pp. 208–28. Reprinted by permission of the
author and the Editor of *Philosophy*.

so a spoken sentence is regarded as the temporary expression of an independent meaning. The translator might then be said to effect a migration of meanings. Translation is supposed to be possible on account of a twofold relation of an entity, called 'meaning'; two expressions are viewed as 'vehicles' of the same meaning. Thus:

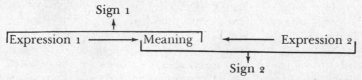

What is cardinal, here, is a theory of meaning, which interprets 'significant expression' ('sign', in linguistic terminology) as constituted by a relation of two distinct entities: an expression and a meaning. The relation itself is mysterious. The vehicle has a ghostly passenger. Inevitably, a 'triadic' theory of translation implies some form of a 'dualist', and therefore mysterious, theory of meaning.

There can be no doubt that we should be hard put to it, if having done some particular piece of translation, we were asked to explain it in terms of this theory. We should only be aware of having operated with expressions, and we could say something about such operations. We should be able to explain the difference between a good and a bad translation in terms of their respective expressions; we should refer to their occurrences among other expressions, and among persons and things. To take an example, we might argue that a famous poem by Goethe about Italy which begins with the line: '*Kennst du das Land, wo die Zitronen blühn?*' has been translated badly, when in English it was made to begin: 'Knowst thou the land . . . '. Our argument would be that '*Kennst du . . .*' is a straight forward piece of colloquial language, as one might say 'Do you know the shop where the sale is on?' (*Kennst du den Laden/ . . . Herrn Schmidt/ . . . meinen Bruder*, etc.), whereas 'knowest thou' would be unusual in corresponding contexts. Again, we should say that '*Land*' occurs in very many contexts ('*Stadt und Land, Ausland, von Land zu Land', die südlichen Länder Europas*', etc.), where the corresponding English word would be 'country' ('town and country, foreign country, from country to country, southern countries', etc.), rather than 'land'.[1] At the same time, we shall reject equally 'Do you know the country': not only because at times German *Land* will also correspond to English *land*, rather than

[1] I borrow the example from Professor L. Forster's 'Translation', in *Aspects of Translation* (Studies in Communication 2, 1958).

country—in contexts such as 'landscape' (*Landschaft*) 'land of promise' (*gelobtes Land*), 'land of dreams' (*Land der Träume*)—but mainly because in such a translation, the important and far from common rhythm of the poem, which is established with this its first line, would be lost. In fact, we should not be able, here, to translate word for word, or even sentence for sentence; the line we have to find will have to be internally very different from the original if it is to preserve a comparable role within the poem as a whole. And having chosen, rejected and accepted, we should explain what makes a better or a worse translation by saying to what extent there is a *correspondence* between (i) the habitual contexts (verbal and situational) of the given original expressions, and (ii) the contextual relations of the expressions used in the translation. But what, in any particular case, could we say, or be expected to say, about operations with *pure ideas*? A triadic theory of the craft of translation, if it were accepted at all—as, for want of a better, it might be—could not be regarded as a working-theory, not as a general account of how we do what we do. We should have to look upon it as some kind of 'ulterior explanation' of the finished work—'mere' theory, 'pure' theory, free from empirical tests, and devoid of technical implications.

It would seem to have fallen to the philosopher to deal with the difficulties of disembodied meanings. If there are such things, where do we find them? How observe them—those naked ideas under their changeable verbal clothing? (Another favourite metaphor, this, besides the 'vehicle of sense'!) Do we ever find them *without* their verbal clothes, just in their natural state?

We are familiar with various attempts to deal with these difficulties. Generally, the dualist scheme of the linguistic sign is preserved, and with it the basic triadic scheme of translation. It is within these limits that the attempt is made to rescue 'pure meanings' from their shadowy existence; generally, by tying them to, or even replacing them by, 'pure' physical facts. Meanings are then said to be 'references' to such facts, 'denotations'; and one expression is supposed to be a translation of another, if both have the same denotation. It is true that this is rarely considered to be quite enough. The two expressions, in addition to their denotation, would be required to share an aptitude for calling forth certain responses, certain 'emotive overtones', and they would have to incorporate a number of purely syntactical operations. There would be a large bag of tricks—some more, some less important—but all of them, mere accessories to communication. They either presuppose 'reference', or, like a sigh or a smile, can dispense with language altogether. The core of meaning is supposed to be denotation, factual reference.

There seem to be two main variants of the reference-theory of meaning. There are, firstly, those following Ogden and Richards[1] who would try to tie 'ideas' or 'meanings' (or, as they call them, 'references') to external things ('referents'), giving us a three-term elaboration of the 'dualist' theory of linguistic signs:

$$\text{Expression} \longrightarrow (\text{Reference} \longrightarrow \text{Referent})$$

Expressions, here, refer indirectly. We may call this the theory of *indirect reference*. It gives us a five-term elaboration of the triadic scheme for translation:

$$\text{Expression 1} \rightarrow \left[\text{Reference 1} \rightarrow \text{Referent} \leftarrow \text{Reference 2} \right] \leftarrow \text{Expression 2}$$

The middle term is presented as being, itself, a relation of three terms: namely, of two 'ideas' or 'meanings' or 'references' (each peculiar to the speakers of a particular language) to the same external things (the same 'referent').[2]

Others have persuaded themselves that—in theory at any rate—we can do away with specifically mental facts; that 'reference' need not involve any 'thing in the mind'. This gives us again a simple dyadic relation for the linguistic sign:

$$\text{Expression} \longrightarrow \text{Referent},$$

the reference of the expression (the arrow) being explained as a physiological disposition or habit we have of using that expression for denoting certain facts. We might call this a theory of *direct reference*. It presents translation as a simple relational scheme of just three physical terms:

$$\text{Expression 1} \longrightarrow \text{Referent} \longleftarrow \text{Expression 2}$$

This, it might seem at first sight, dispels the mystery. We seem to have succeeded in avoiding the puzzle of psycho-physical relations. For we are supposed to operate with ordinary external facts only—with expressions amongst persons and things. On closer examination, however, the puzzles turn out to be still with us. The crucial relation we are said to establish when using or translating an expression is still

---

[1] C. K. Ogden and I. A. Richards, *The Meaning of Meaning*, ch. 1.

[2] Cf. the interesting paper by C. Rabin on 'The Linguistics of Translation' in *Aspects of Translation*, p. 125.

a relation of correspondence between *two distinct orders of thing*, linguistic and extralingual. This is why, even in the case of a theory of direct reference, we may still speak of a dualist view of linguistic signs; and also, why we find that we are still mystified about their meaning, and about translation.

I am not here concerned with the relative merits of different dualist theories of meaning; and I have no interpretation of my own to offer of that opaque and puzzling something which is supposed to 'correspond' to linguistic expressions. I have nothing to say of that extralingual second term of the alleged sign-relation, the middle term of the alleged triadic scheme of translation. Rather, I am concerned to show that the 'of' in 'meaning of' *cannot* be interpreted as a relation of correspondence between two orders of fact, and that translation is *not* an operation with three terms. If there are such entities as are postulated in a dualist theory of sign and a triadic theory of translation—if there are pure meanings or pure external facts, there is certainly nothing we can say about them. We cannot rescue the former from their occult state by tying them to, or replacing them by, the latter. The facts, or referents so-called, if supposed to be grasped independently of any and every language, are themselves as shadowy and nebulous as the naked ideas they are meant to reinforce or to replace.

Expressions 'have meanings', and they are, themselves, external things amongst others. But both external things and meanings dissolve in a dualist interpretation of linguistic signs. They are assigned positions which they cannot occupy; they are placed beyond the reach of the conceptual tools of language.

II

That meanings cannot survive in a dualist theory of signs has been shown—and shown with admirable clarity—by some of the more recent studies in the philosophy of language.[1] 'What an expression means' cannot be found as a separate entity beside the expression. If we insist on having it this way, expression will have nothing to express, and reference nothing to refer to. Meanings, we have learned, are not entities or objects corresponding to expressions; they are the *uses* of expressions; they are the work expressions do. It remains

[1] Cf. L. Wittgenstein. *The Blue and Brown Books, Philosophical Investigations*. G. Ryle, 'Ordinary Language' (*Phil. Review*, 1953). 'The Theory of Meaning' in *British Philosophy in the Mid-Century*. J. R. Firth, *Papers in Linguistics* (chs. 3, 14–16).

true that the meaning of an utterance is not *in* it. But neither is it an object beside it. It includes and transcends the utterance, as my walking includes and transcends my legs. What an expression means, is not an object confronting it, any more than my walking is an object confronting my legs.

The instrumental view of language allows us to discover what is discoverable about meanings, ideas, concepts, propositions; and it delivers us from some very common temptations to pursue chimeras.

It is important, though, to observe, where exactly the line is drawn between fancy and fact. Errors of mistaken identity are not uncommon. Especially, there seems to be some inclination to assume (i) that mental facts are among the chimeras, and (ii) that 'bare facts' confronting expressions are not. I shall try to deal with these two misconceptions.

II (1). First, an instrumental interpretation of meaning does not entail any denial of mental events. On the contrary, it seems to imply that events which we commonly describe as mental, rather than physical, do occur. There must be memories, organized memories. For no *single* use of a word can establish it as significant. The meaning of a word is a collection, an organized recollection, of many individual uses of it, i.e. of various occurrences of it: in verbal and non-verbal contexts, and in positions in which it contrasts with other words. Meaning (like skill) is an 'acquired property'. Whenever a word is being used significantly, another use is added to remembered uses of it; a present context joins the previous ones. Clearly, the organized memories of a word's uses are what would ordinarily be described as *mental events*. So would its present choice from a number of contrasting words. There are relations, even relations of correspondence, between a word's present employment and those other employments which we remember. Moreover, any word I am using now may be abstracted from its context and be treated as a physical fact (for instance, by acousticians or phoneticians or by lexicographers making an entry), while, without its being presently used, its past uses may be 'recalled to mind' (e.g. in a dictionary paraphrase or definition). Signs are souvenirs. When active and actually employed in a new context, they act as reminders of contexts past, or they could mean nothing.

Have we come full circle? Are we back at physical symbols as 'vehicles' of 'bare ideas'? Not quite; and the difference is important. What an inert physical expression may remind us of is not any unverbalized pure idea. What we remember is that same expression in past employments: both *among* other expressions and *in contrast* to other expressions. Our memories or ideas are not extralingual, not 'without language'.

The difference between this articulate account of meaning and the traditional 'vehicle' theory appears most clearly, when we consider translation. Even if '*the* meaning' of an expression is identified with a recollection of its past uses: such a collection of previous occurrences of an expression—in a variety of verbal as well as non-verbal contexts, and in contrast with a variety of other expressions—could not possibly qualify as that kind of 'pure idea', which is supposed to be indifferent to its linguistic setting, and, therefore, transportable from one linguistic vehicle to another. Here, meaning is not an entity beside the expression; it is a particular expression at work, actual work and remembered work. Such work is not a piece of transferable freight. It cannot be transported to another expression in another language, any more than the 'goodwill' of a shop can be transported to another shop in another town. It can be transferred to another user of the same shop in the same town. Another shop in another town can only *parallel* its 'goodwill'. What we have found is no 'bare idea'. We have found expressions which recall expressions in use. All the facts we are dealing with—the expressions and their environments—are on the same plane: they may be actually perceived as external things, and they may be remembered.

Memory is, indeed, a problem. So is choice. But neither is a mere enigma. Our problem—and this is our gain—has become articulated, familiar, and manageable. We are familiar with relating our habits or memories to present experience. We know how to trace acquired skill in the carpenter's use of a hammer; and we know how to trace acquired significance in a man's use of a word. The meaning of a word has a history; we may have records of its past uses. But we cannot know even what it *could* be like to perceive a carpenter's skill, as another thing *beside* his tools, or a word-less idea as a separate thing *beside* a word. We have no way of relating present things (such as hammers being handled, or words being uttered) to objects on 'another plane'. What an expression 'conveys' is not a passenger from another world. Its meaning, a bequest from its past, is related to a given word in some such way as yesterday's walk is related to my legs here and now. To be sure, I may recall it to mind—yesterday's walk or the meaning. But a walk, whether present or remembered, is not a legless affair; and 'what a word means' is not a word-less idea. Nor is it a word-less physical fact. 'Bare facts' are as diaphanous as 'bare ideas': that is my second point about the dividing line between fancy and fact.

II (2). Some, who profess to accept the view that 'the meaning of an expression is its use', seem to claim that they are only making this view more articulate by telling us, more specifically about the 'use' of expressions, that it consists in referring them to extra-lingual facts in our physical environment. Essentially, they say, meaning (or 'the use' of an expression) is *denotation*. In this way, the instrumental approach to language appears to be assimilated to a theory of reference. This appearance of an amalgamation of the two theories seems to me utterly deceptive. Expressions cannot be 'used' for referring to bare and neutral facts.

Denotation has of course been queried recently. It has been argued that though there are *some* expressions which do denote, 'there is not one basic mould, such as the "Fido"—Fido mould, into which all significant expressions are to be forced'. Even such as may be said to 'denote' are found to do a good many other things besides. (This is why, for instance, 'the Morning-Star' would not pass as an adequate translation of 'l'Étoile du Soir', though the two have the same denotation).[1] These denials seem to be wholly justified. But must we not go further? It is hard to see how denotation, as generally understood, can be credited even with so much as a partial explanation of some meanings. Correspondence to bare extralingual facts seems to be a mere fiction. It cannot account even for the meaning of 'Fido', either all or part of it.

I do not deny that there is a genuine operation with expressions which one may choose to describe as 'denoting' or 'referring'. We do use expressions for the purpose of referring to things other than expressions. Our stock of significant expressions may be augmented by this operation; but only by assigning both the new expression and the new thing places among other expressions, never by merely referring one to the other. 'The use of an expression' cannot consist in referring it to 'bare' extralingual things. It is true that, in the present climate of opinion, we might feel safer in attaching expressions to extralingual things in physical space than we would in associating them with extralingual things in a *Geistesraum*.[2] But, we cannot do either.

---

[1] G. Ryle, 'The Theory of Meaning' in *British Philosophy in the Mid-Century*, p 256.
[2] *Geistesraum* being the most serious drawback of some inquiries into 'semantic

I am not trying to advocate some kind of Neo-Berkeleyan meta-physics—some 'to be is to be spoken of'. It would seem to be absurd to deny the *existence* of things 'without' language, whether things physical or things mental—even though, naturally, we could say nothing about such existence. Affinities with Kantian epistemology would appear to be far more plausible. Having persuaded ourselves that conceptual thought, for all we can say about it, consists in 'operating with words',[1] it appears that things outside language—i.e. things unaffected by our operations with words—are something as opaque, and unprofitable to 'refer to', as the Kantian 'thing in itself'. Our world—remembered, imagined, or perceived—is organized by the language we speak.

What are we to make, then, of the notion of 'extralingual reference'?—There is a perfectly sensible interpretation of it. But this cannot tell us how meanings are created in pre- or extra-lingual space, physical or spiritual. We are familiar with the experience of having an idea, image, or concept, as yet lacking a word for it, or the experience of discovering some thing in our physical environment, without having a name for it. We might ask 'What shall we call it?' or 'What is it called?' But such experiences are not enough for extralingual reference. Those things we seek a name for are not extralingual in the required sense. We can always say a great deal about them; indeed, we may be able to describe them quite adequately, and entirely with the help of words already at our disposal. The fact that we may want another word for a thing, besides the many which are already involved with it, is nothing to establish a reference-theory of meaning. The least that such a theory requires is that the thing, which lacks a name, should be *capable* of being singled out for reference, *without there being any other expressions at all*: none except the one by which we want to 'refer' to it. Of this one we should be able to say what Russell says of the words in his 'object-language': that it has 'meaning in isolation', or that it has been learnt 'without its being necessary to have previously learnt other words.'[2] What is it that is being asked for, here? Fact or chimera? What evidence could we possibly have of a word having meaning or having been learnt *in isolation*? There might be just one word that could provide

fields' which are otherwise of considerable interest (cf. J. Trier's works, e.g. 'Deutsche Bedeutungsforschung' in *Germanische Philologie*, 1934).

[1] G. Ryle, 'Ordinary Language' (*Philosophical Review*, 1953), p. 185.

[2] B. Russell, *An Inquiry into Meaning and Truth*, p. 65.

such evidence:—the first word I ever learned. But what a dubious fiction that would be! Could it be a word at all?

The theory of isolated reference is clearly not meant to be put to the test of observation. It is *in principle* unverifiable. Whatever experience we have of referring to external things, or to ideas, is not an experience of isolated reference. So far from *explaining* the meanings of expressions—even of the referring type—reference *presupposes* a language of significant expressions.

Even very young children asking 'What is it called?' do not merely refer to, they can tell us a lot about, 'it'! For this very reason it interests them. They have already rejected a large number of words as inappropriate to the thing, or they would not ask its name. They have prepared a large number of utterance-frames which the new name will fit into; and where it will join, and contrast with, a large number of other words which already fit those frames.—An 'Alsatian'? . . . runs, . . . barks, . . . is big, . . . has a thick fur, I don't like . . .s, etc. The question 'What is it?' or 'What is it called?' is *a request to fill in the blank* in an indefinite number of incomplete expressions; it is a request, we might say, for notational help in giving new values to a number of prepared utterance-functions—help in fixing an organization of utterances about a new focal term. Long before it is named, the new thing has already been placed; and it has been contrasted with other things that run or bark, or are big or have a thick fur, and not liked, etc. It has been so placed and contrasted by the help of expressions which were already dealing with it. When I am looking for a word, 'have it on the tip of my tongue', this is never a case of some 'pure idea' or 'brute fact' begging a name; it is always a case of fragmentary utterances seeking completion. The blank is a variable in a large number of determinate functions; it has a determinate range, and I can already give it many determinate and contrasting values. The variable is the 'unknown' in given expressions. But there is no need to interpret it as an imperceptible 'soul' searching for its body, or a 'thing in itself' wanting a label.

Nobody will deny the existence of extralingual things. But do we ever come across one requiring a name, without there being a large number of expressions already engaged with it?[1] Is it not with such 'mere things' as with Wm. James's 'pure experience'? 'Only new-born babes', he said, 'or men in semi-coma from sleep, drugs, ill-nesses, or blows, may be assumed to have an experience pure in the

[1] Cf. L. Wittgenstein, *Philosophical Investigations* on Ostensive Definition, par. 28 ff., especially par. 30/31.

literal sense of a *that* which is not yet any definite *what*.'[1] Reference to such 'pure experience' is required by a 'reference theory of meaning'. This is what Russell has brought out so clearly. If we wish to explain meaning by 'extralingual reference', then we must insist on a complete and permanent dualism of two orders of thing—linguistic expressions on the one hand, and extralingual things on the other. We must accept the fiction of *isolated references*. This dualism cannot be substantiated in any way; and it makes no difference whether the extralingual things are ideas in the mind or physical facts. For 'reference' to make its sign-producing link, words and other things must be supposed to be permanently divided. My argument is that there is no such division, hence no such link, hence no theory of meaning in terms of such a link.

We can have no conception of what it might be like to confront the general blur of a world that is not already prepared and organized by the use of some signs. Learning a language, or extending it, is not like drawing a map by putting in one line or one colour at a time. This we *can* do; but only because we have another language at our disposal, which tells us where to draw the lines and what colours to put in. The map-maker does not confront a world without language. He is, in fact, a translator—from the language of words into a restricted language of lines and colours.

Those who have tried seriously to construct a language by means of operations of 'reference' have in fact usually proceeded in analogous fashion. Like the cartographer, they worked on the basis of a given language, selecting 'things' already circumscribed. They selected what was suitable for 'reference', as a cartographer selects what is suitable for a map. They picked out what their language allowed them to describe as 'external things', of various kinds. They did not try to refer to 'bare facts'; and the fiction, often upheld, that they *might* have done so, or even that ordinary language might have done so in the first place, is neither here nor there.

The construction of an 'object-language' can be of considerable interest. It may be important to know what *can* be translated into a special language which would restrict the meanings of expressions by rules of reference: e.g. by the rule that the significant use of every accepted expression should be capable of being accompanied by a significant pointing-gesture. In this way, rules of reference can *restrict* the meanings of expressions within a given language, but they cannot, by themselves, *establish* a language. Nothing can come of mere point-

[1] Wm. James, *Essays in Radical Empiricism* ('The Thing and Its Relations'), p. 93 f.

ing into a world of bare 'thats'. For (i) pointing itself, if it is to be of any use as an operation of reference, must have a meaning, which cannot be established by pointing, and (ii) it can have meaning only as part of a language.

(i) If it is of any use, pointing is no mere gesture, any more than a word is a mere noise. Like a word, a pointing finger 'has meaning'; and it is a conventional sign. Some communities point with their chins, others with eyes and brows; we do it with hands and fingers; pointing is clearly not like laughter or tears: it is not a natural physiological symptom. For a dog (and presumably for a child) to learn the meaning of a pointing finger is as difficult as to learn the meaning of an uttered noise. The gesture-language of pointing may include a variety of signs: rigid ('beam') pointing, sweeping ('area') pointing, scanning, pointing at various angles, forward, sideways, upward, etc. Each of these can acquire meaning *only as part of a language*. That is,

(ii) Whatever actual experience we have of the gesture-language of pointing, shows it in the role of an auxiliary language. By itself it would be hopelessly ambiguous. (At a race, how do we point at the track, at a horse, its rider, his number, his cap, his whip, his skill, at the horse's breed, its colour, its speed?) 'Such ambiguity is commonly resolved by accompanying the pointing with . . . words' such as 'this track', 'this horse', 'this colour', etc., assuming that the words 'track', 'horse', etc., are already intelligible.[1] This assumption is made, even when we establish or explain the meaning of a *new* word by pointing. We cannot establish it by *mere* pointing. We might say, for instance, 'This colour is jonquil'. 'The ostensive definition explains the use—the meaning—of the word when the overall role of the word in the language is clear',[2] i.e. when we know it is some individual thing, or a colour, or a shape, etc., that is being pointed at. It appears that I 'must already be master of a language in order to understand an ostensive definition'.[3]

Meanings, then, which are established by ostensive definition cannot be neutral between different languages. Jonquil, for instance, will be definitely a kind of yellow and no kind of red in English; but it need be nothing of the sort for someone like a speaker of Bassa, a language of Liberia, which has only one word to correspond to

[1] W. V. O. Quine, *From a Logical Point of View*, p. 67.
[2] L. Wittgenstein, *Philosophical Investigation*, § 30.
[3] Ibid., § 33.

both 'red' and 'yellow', even if it were defined for him by apparently the same pointing-gesture and in the same situation.[1]

One might, perhaps, try to distinguish between 'what is meant' and 'what is pointed at', by saying that we may 'point at' the same thing, even though 'meaning' different things. 'What we point at' would then be neutral between different languages, though what we mean when pointing might not be. A reference-theory of meaning, and of translation, must insist that this is so. But how could we *know* this? How could we know that 'what we point at' is neutral between different languages, if we can never find it except *within* some language or other? Strictly speaking, even when I say of two persons, as I did, that they appear to be witnessing the same pointing-gesture in the same situation, 'the same' means 'the same in the language in which I describe it'—e.g. when I say, 'Three people together, one of them raising his arm'. Of situations so described, I *can* claim to know that often different things are 'meant' or 'pointed at' by the same gesture, for speakers of different languages. I do not know this by comparing 'what they mean' with something neutral and extra-lingual that is 'just there'—for I have no access to things outside language; I know it by a process of *translation*. I compare the uses of expressions (including pointing-gestures) which belong to different languages. I find, for instance, an Eskimo distributing three different words over the 'same situations' (including the same pointings), in which an Englishman utters the one word 'snow'. The two, I conclude, cannot mean and cannot 'point at' the same thing. There is no puzzle here: each points at facts which are circumscribed by *his* language.

However, the ghost of bare and neutral facts is not an easy one to lay. Reference theories of meaning have made an effort to rescue ostensive definitions from their emplacement in particular languages. A universally valid, 'logical' procedure of generalization seemed capable of replacing the caprice of varying linguistic directives. The operations of 'isolated reference'—pointing, for instance—will be supplemented: but instead of submitting to linguistic guidance, we are to rely on something like Mill's Canons of Induction. No single pointing-gesture or apposite utterance is then supposed to be sufficient for establishing the meaning of an expression; but

---

[1] It is on record that the botanists required two general colour-terms which would correspond to the only two colour words of Bassa. They created, but with reference to their own languages, *xanthic* and *cyanic*. Cf. H. A. Gleason, *An Introduction to Descriptive Linguistics*, p. 4 f.

a number of such would be assumed to accomplish it. Collectively, they would be credited with establishing a 'habitual association' between, on the one hand, a set of similar extralingual facts, and, on the other, a set of similar utterances. In this way, we are supposed to make utterances significant, indeed to construct a whole language— a restricted language of reference, a 'primary' or 'object' language of 'ostensive predicates'.[1]

It is clear at once that we cannot expect to find examples of such a language being developed from scratch; it will always be constructed by someone who is already master of another. This is why it would be better to make clear how a restricted language such as that of reference is *derived from some given ordinary language*, rather than try to do the reverse.[2] However, anyone subscribing to a 'correspondence theory' of meaning has a vested interest in postulating for his object-language 'possible independence' or 'possible priority', whatever that may mean. Otherwise, his referential meanings might be derived from other meanings, when they are supposed to be our original stock—the offspring purely from an intercourse of human utterances with bare and neutral facts.

Reference alone cannot generate meaning. Can it do so with the help of induction? Can the repetition and assembly of isolated references give us the meaning of an expression? This might seem plausible. After all, one might say, was there not a first significant expression? And is it not the point of isolated reference simply to assume of *every* expression of an object-language that it *might* have been the first?

We may well boggle at the pseudo-empiricism of a theory which requires us to view every significant expression as hidden in some mythological pre-history of the language to which it belongs—every expression as capable of having gathered its meaning in that one dramatic moment, long ago and unremembered, when it might have been uttered as the first. However, we need waste no time on these problems of verification, formidable though they are. For even if we assume that, somehow, empirical sense could be made of the notion of isolated reference, we should still have to ask whether any expres-

[1] Cf. e.g. B. Russell, op. cit., pp. 67, 76; W. V. O. Quine, op. cit., p. 68. S. Körner, *Conceptual Thinking*, p. 7.

[2] A special language of reference, constructed for the purposes of logical or epistemological inquiry, may of course be *compared* with ordinary language, without being made its core or source. Of the authors just mentioned, neither Quine nor Körner seems to be interested in 'deriving' ordinary language from the referential. Indeed, Professor Quine seems to repudiate the idea (op. cit., p. 78).

sion, by itself, could possibly be deemed to be significant; and it seems clear that such an expression, even if repeated and applied a hundred times, could never be said to have acquired *meaning*. It could not be viewed as 'having meaning' until, on some occasion, we found it *inappropriate*, and said so: 'This and this and this is a cat. But *that* is *not* a cat. It's a *dog*.'[1] A language, one might say, requires at least two words. Language and meaning take their origin from difference of meaning. A language could conceivably be born with two words: and of as many as two, each refers to a word involved in language. Even a single 'other' word presupposes language, no matter whether this word, like 'not', is classed as belonging to a secondary logical language, or whether, like 'dog', it is considered to belong to the primary one—the 'object-language'.

Similar considerations apply to the presumed 'set of similar expressions'. There can be no such set, in isolation. Modern phonology has made it abundantly clear that we cannot even make up such a set without regard to other and contrasting sets. Unless there are other words, no word could have so much as determinate phonetic shape. We cannot say, for any particular language, what counts as repetition, as occurrence of a 'similar' expression, unless we know what counts as occurrence of a different one. The recurrent shape of 'cat' is determined by contrasts such as '*c*a*t*/*p*a*t*/*m*a*t*; *c*a*t*/*c*o*t*; *c*a*t*/*c*a*p*/*c*a*n*'. For a Japanese, *wrong* is a repetition of *long*, *right* of *light* and *grammar* of *glamour*. This is simply because, in his language, though he does make use of both *l* and *r*, he has no need of their difference for distinguishing meanings. To him, they are in fact indistinguishably 'similar'. The l/r—difference is no more a bare fact, it is as much part of the English language as is the difference between what *light* and *right* 'mean'.

Nor could there be *neutral* facts in that hypothetical language-of-reference. Ostension or reference, when it is supplemented by rules of assembly and classification—no less than when it is supplemented by different languages—is free to generate a variety of different meanings. If we are supposed to refer to what is similar in a number of facts, the question must immediately be: 'Similar in what respect?'

---

[1] Professor Körner would require of ostensive rules that they contain a 'comparing clause': this and this and 'everything like it'. But until we have said: 'That is *not* a cat' or 'That is a *dog*', *everything* is like a cat, in some sense. Professor Körner says that we have understood an ostensive rule, 'when we are competent to give further instances or to give "anti-examples"' (*Conceptual Thinking*, pp. 7, 33). If '*or*', here, were replaced by '*and*', my point would be made. (Professor Körner tells me that he would accept the conjunction.)

'With what degree of similarity?' And the answer to these decisive questions can certainly not be found simply by referring to the facts. Is not what we call 'high' in English similar, *in some respect*, to what we call 'deep'? and therefore deserving of being compassed by just one word, as in Latin, where 'altus' corresponds to both? Is what we call 'blue' similar *enough* to what we call 'green' to allow us to be satisfied with just one word, such as the Celtic 'glas' which corresponds to both English 'blue' and English 'green'? Which things are similar, and which are similar enough, will be decided by our interests, most of which are not imperative even for us; still less for all climates and all communities. Where, then, are the required neutral facts? If we cannot find them in our talk about colours, what can we expect of plants, animals, work, human relations? 'What there is' is different facts, picked out and ordered by different languages—even by different languages-of-reference. If it were possible to establish a language by reference plus induction, the same 'rules of reference' would result in a variety of languages.

It might be suggested of course that, in addition to Mill's Canons of Induction, we should supplement ostension by the whole body of scientific theory; and say, for example, that what colour-words in *any* language 'refer to' is what the language of Optics refers to by 'light-spectrum'. But this unfortunately would merely be to claim a privilege for the particular language of science, and for the 'facts' *within* it (e.g. for a continuous spectrum, without divisions). It would do nothing to establish extralingual, neutral facts.

Of course, there must *be* facts which permit the distinctions we choose to make. And no one will deny that, human lives and interests being what they are, *some* distinctions are all but imperative. We know this by translation. It is also true that we shall find it easier to translate from one language into another, if the two are restricted by similar 'rules of reference' (e.g. if our translation is of scientific texts). But human lives and interests are still so varied, and linguistic instruments so subtle, that, again and again, what appears as one and the same fact in one language, corresponds to a number of different facts in another. The range of permissible choices, *which we have no way of surveying*, must *be* tremendously wide. By switching to different languages, or to different times in the history of the same language, we constantly alter the fact of 'what there is'. Pliant facts far outnumber the stubborn. One has to ignore this great variety and continual change in languages if one is to find plausibility in the familiar assumption of a pervasive extralingual order of 'natural kinds'—this assumption that everything is clearly set out before us, ready to be mapped in more or less uniform fashion, by every language.[1] A doctrine of 'natural kinds' is the last refuge of a denotational theory of meaning. Only within the assumption of such a doctrine can the alleged inductive accumulation of isolated references be supposed to do its work. What this amounts to, on closer examination, is just a naïve belief in the divinity of one's own language; God or Nature is supposed to speak it. The more sophisticated may reserve such divinity for scientific discourse. But whatever the privileged language, it is facts circumscribed by it that are spoken of as extralingual, as bare and neutral.

It will be acknowledged, then, that we can endow expressions with meanings, and even construct languages, by submitting to what we may continue to call 'rules of reference'. We can insist, if we wish, that the significance of every expression be vouched for by some regular concomitance with other things—things other than expressions. But we cannot insist on simply 'finding' them (the expressions or the other things) just 'there' ready to be matched. What expressions there are, and what other things, is determined by what we do with them in developing and speaking a language.

It is of course, ultimately, some relation of linguistic expressions to other things that constitutes their meanings. The question is: What sort of relation? My point is that it is not, and cannot be, a relation between two distinct orders of thing. The alleged confrontation of language with facts, the alleged reference of expressions to things un-involved in language—this we cannot make sense of. If we divide language from other things in this dualist fashion, both are dissolved in a general blur. It is only in their active interplay with one another that either assumes determinate shape; and it is this *interplay*—this active co-operation of utterances with things—that constitutes the meanings of the utterances.

One way of using an expression is to use it as 'a name for a thing'. But before an expression and a thing can be so used, both must have found their places among others. This they cannot do by way of mere 'naming'. Only when it is clear that an expression can be used in many and various ways, and a thing be spoken of in many and various ways, are the two sufficiently established for the one to be used as 'name' for the other.

The generation of meaning is not a naming-ritual. Primary are

[1] See Russell: 'Fortunately, many occurrences fit into natural kinds' (*Inquiry*, p. 76).

the meanings of whole utterances—utterances as part of our active lives. We retain a word as a token, a souvenir, a keepsake of the utterances and situations in which it occurred. The active and organized memory of these constitutes the meaning of the word—the meaning with which it enters new utterances and new situations, adding these in turn to its potential for future use. Every situation, old and new, is organized by the continuous commemorative power of words. Words do not confront situations; they make them what they are.

To be sure, not everything is permitted. But hardly anything is predetermined. Even under restriction of the same rules of reference, we are free to construct different languages, different worlds. There are no rules for a unique matching of mere vocal noises with linguistically neutral facts. Outside a linguistic system, which assigns them their places and roles, there can be neither 'expressions referring' nor 'things referred to'. With an inductively constructed language of reference, as with any other, for a word to 'have meaning' is for it to play a distinctive role, among other words, and among persons and things; our world takes shape in the evolution of our language.

III

It is when we think of translation that we are most liable to become confused about meanings—and tempted to locate them in extra-lingual entities. After all, when we judge different expressions to be *equivalent by translation*, do we not, in fact, abstract *something* from them? And this something which we call 'the same sense', is it not some separate entity—idea or physical fact—which is somehow related to the different linguistic expressions? The answer to the first question is: Yes, something—call it with Dr Johnson 'the same sense'— is abstracted. But the answer to the second question is: No, the same sense is not some separate entity related to the expressions. There are abstractions and abstractions.

I may abstract an apple from its branch. The apple is an object distinct from its branch; I can observe the two in different places and at different times. Again, I may abstract the shape of the apple from its colour. I can feel its shape in the dark, or I can see its colour with some of the shape obscured. Shape and colour may still be regarded as different 'objects' (though of another sort than apples and branches); I can observe them at different times, and by different senses. Furthermore, I may abstract the shape of the apple from its size, though I cannot observe these two in different places or at different times, and I have no sense which could let in the one without the other. There might be things I can do to take in *size* without shape—say, measuring the circumference; but there is nothing I can do to observe the *shape* of anything without its size. When I say of two apples that they are the same round shape, only the one big and the other small, I do not take myself to be distinguishing three distinct objects: one shape and two sizes. The round shape may be *abstracted* from the different sizes, but not as a *third object*. Geometers, when dealing with figures of different sizes, do not define 'similarity' of shape as the recurrence of some object distinct from size. Shape does not accompany size. They abstract 'shape' from size by establishing a *correspondence* between differently sized figures—a correspondence of points, angles and lines. Similarly, we may abstract his dance from a dancer, though we cannot observe it in another place or at a different time, and though we have no special sense to take in the dance without the dancer. The same dance, performed by two different dancers, is not a dancer-less dance recurring. The dance is not *in* the two dancers, but neither is it a third thing related to them. The dance of the two is the same, if there is a correspondence between their two performances. This, also, is how its meaning may be abstracted from an expression. We can examine the expression without attending to its meaning, as we might examine a dancer without attending to a dance. (Phonetics, like anatomy, is a respectable discipline. It deals with expressions in the context, and the language, of physics or physiology.) But we cannot observe the meaning without the expression: it is never in another place or at another time, and we have no special sense which would let it in by itself. (This is why present-day Semantics is so largely a dubious discipline.) The meaning of different expressions is the same if, and only if, there is a correspondence between their uses. What we abstract from different expressions as 'similarity of sense' is a correspondence between their functions. Unless we succeed in thus explaining translation, the mystery of bare and neutral fact will continue to haunt us.

Why—one might ask—are we so strongly inclined to postulate some separate and word-less meaning-entity, in order to account for similarity between the performances of two utterances, while yet we are not so tempted to postulate anything like a third object, a dancer-less dance, in order to explain similarity between the performances of two dancers? Does not this point to an important difference between the two cases? It does. The difference is that it is more difficult to establish correspondence of performances in the case of two utterances than it is in the case of two dancers. We tend to evade the greater difficulty by taking refuge in a myth. Yet, we don't do so always. It depends on the degree of difficulty. This seems worth examining.

When a speaker of what is described as Standard English and a speaker of Cockney English converse with one another, they perform some kind of translation. They establish certain correspondences: e.g. 'a good bay' (for bathing) corresponds in Cockney to something that sounds much like Standard English 'a good buy'; Standard 'a good buy', on the other hand, corresponds very nearly to Cockney 'a good boy'; and Standard 'a good boy' to something with a vowel (a closer one) which is unfamiliar to Standard English—'a good bo·y'. Translation here is easy: the correspondences concern generally a few recurrent sounds. Though the expressions are different in the two systems, we soon discover that on the whole there is a one-to-one correspondence between their constituent elements: /ei—ai, ai—oi, oi—o·i/. Translation then appears to be sufficiently explained by this similarity of structure, and we have little inclination to postulate a half-way house of pure meanings.

The situation is similar when we translate from speech into writing or print, especially when the writing or print is phonetically regular. Marks on paper share nothing with sounds in the air; but the expressions in the two media are of similar structure. We say that they have the same meaning. With modern English spelling, and even more so with, say, Chinese logograms, the difficulties of such translation between writing and speech are greater. But there is no difference of principle. The complication arises simply from the fact that the items which correspond to one another in the two systems are so numerous. Assume that they are words, and there are thousands of them. Nevertheless, since the number of words, though large, is limited, we should still find it natural here to explain translation by similarity of structure, i.e. by a broad one-to-one correspondence between words in the written utterances with words in the spoken. Also, if we discovered two communities actually speaking languages which were related in this way, we should say that they spoke closely related languages, though we should not go so far as to describe these as dialects of the same language.[1] Difference of language is a matter

[1] In fact, the Chinese logographic script is even less closely related to the spoken languages of those who use it. Such spoken utterances as might accompany the

of degree; and the degree of difficulty we find in translation (and in explaining translation) is a measure of the difference.

Two linguistic systems are said to be different languages, i.e. not just different dialects of the same language, if the sounds they employ, though possibly identical, do not on the whole, utterance for utterance, occur in a relation of one-to-one correspondence. Commonly, difference of structure will extend further. It is a common experience of translators that they cannot even rely on being able to match words with words. Generally, the only kind of unit which on the whole permits interlingual matching is the whole sentence. But sentences are unlimited in number. There are no finite classes of them, to be mapped on one another, in the way in which two alphabets or two dictionaries might be. It is here that we tend to despair of the task of explaining the actual operation of translation, and are inclined to fall back upon the intervention of mythological entities and processes to help us out.

But what of the translator himself? He is well aware of having no list of correspondences to refer to; but his task remains to establish correspondences between expressions of the different languages. He can do nothing else. He operates with expressions, nor with wordless ideas.

He will try to reduce his difficulties by limiting his range of choice. He will, first of all, determine the required 'style of speech', i.e. confine his range to a type of context: scientific description, reportage, love-story, advertisement, religious tract, poetry, conversation, etc. Within such a style, he may admit units smaller than the sentence for his one-to-one mapping operation—for instance, technical terms; or he may have to choose units larger than the sentence—for instance, the stanzas of a poem, or even a whole poem.[1] But whatever he does he will work on the assumption that there is *some* type of unit which permits a fair measure of one-to-one correspondence between utterances in the two languages. In other words, he will assume that, if chosen correctly, such units will show comparable possibilities of combination (comparable 'mutual expectancies', as the ancient Indian grammarians would have said) as well as comparable contrasts

reading of the written words are rarely intelligible to anybody by ear alone. The script is a visual language on its own: to have learned to write and read it is to have made oneself bilingual. It is not surprising then that speakers of different languages can understand one another by means of this script: they have learned the same third language.

[1] Cf. L. Forster, 'Translation', pp. 11 ff. in *Aspects of Translation*.

in the two languages.[1] Essential about the chosen units will be only these powers of combination and contrast; what happens *within* any such unit will be less important (much as in translating from speech into alphabetic writing, the shape of a letter is less important than its 'distribution' and its contrasts).

The discipline of translation consists very largely in choosing the smallest possible unit that will admit of adequate matching. But it may well be impossible even to find a normal sentence in one of the two languages to match a normal sentence in the other. In that case, a difficult and unusual sentence will have to do the new job. It *must* be difficult and unusual, or else it would do what is in that language an old and normal job, instead of the new. In the Kikuyu Bible, for instance, 'the Holy Ghost' is rendered by words which, *if* they were matched with English words, would correspond to something like 'white liver'.[2] But they are *not* so matched. There is no bilingual dictionary of metaphors. If the powers of combination and contrast of the Kikuyu metaphor, in its Kikuyu context, are parallel to those of the English expression 'the Holy Ghost', in its place amongst other English expressions, then the internal difficulty of the corresponding Kikuyu phrase stands to be resolved in the required way by those who hear it. The language will have been *made* to provide the required correspondences, as Old English once was, when missionaries introduced the strange expression 'haleg gast' into *their* sentences. They, and the translators of the Kikuyu Bible, might have done worse. Instead of constructing a metaphor or a 'loan translation', they might have left a virtual blank in their difficult sentence; i.e. they might have put a new 'borrowed' word, relying on the rest of their text to determine its role.[3]

We should say, then—the translator chooses *what* units to translate, and he chooses such units as correspond or can be *made* to correspond to one another. He tries to keep the size of his translation units to a minimum. But he cannot, generally, avoid having to deal with units larger than the word. It follows that he will operate with open classes and have no ready map to follow. But he has a compensating advant-

[1] Cf. p. 87, above.

[2] C. Rabin, op. cit., p. 136.

[3] A functional or instrumental theory of meaning, when fully worked out, should be able to explain in detail how this happens: i.e. how expressions acquire their meanings from their contexts, and how their meanings continually and continuously change. This is a task for linguistic studies. The present discussion can do no more than try to discern the general direction which such studies would take.

age which alone makes his task feasible: the classes of matching units being open, he is able to *create* expressions for his one-to-one mapping. This is how languages are fashioned and re-fashioned by translation. The translator, dealing with 'free constructions', constructs freely. He is not changing vehicles or clothing. He is not transferring wine from one bottle to another. Language is no receptacle, and there is nothing to transfer. To produce a likeness is to follow a model's lines. The language he works in is the translator's clay.

V

USE, USAGE AND MEANING

(1) GILBERT RYLE

IN 1932 Mr. (now Sir) Alan H. Gardiner published *The Theory of Speech and Language* (Clarendon Press). A central theme of his book was what, with some acknowledged verbal artificiality, he labelled the distinction between 'Language' and 'Speech'. I shall draw, develop and apply this distinction in my own way.

A Language, such as the French language, is a stock, fund or deposit of words, constructions, intonations, *cliché* phrases and so on. 'Speech', on the other hand, or 'discourse' can be conscripted to denote the activity or rather the clan of activities of saying things, saying them in French, it may be, or English or some other language. A stock of language-pieces is not a lot of activities, but the fairly lasting wherewithal to conduct them; somewhat as a stock of coins is not a momentary transaction or set of momentary transactions of buying, lending, investing, etc., but is the lasting wherewithal to conduct such transactions. Roughly, as Capital stands to Trade, so Language stands to Speech.

A Language is something to be known, and we get to know it by learning it. We learn it partly by being taught it, and partly by picking it up. For any given part of a language, a learner may not yet have learned that part; or he may have learned it and not forgotten it, or he may have learned it and forgotten it, or he may have half-learned it; or he may have half-forgotten it. A Language is a corpus of teachable things. It is not, of course, a static corpus until it is a dead language. Nor would two teachers of it always agree whether something should be taught as a part of that language. Is French literary style to be taught by teachers of the French Language or by teachers of French Literature? Just when does an acceptable turn of phrase become an idiom? How old can a neologism be? What about slang?

Saying something in a language involves but does not reduce to knowing the requisite pieces of that language. The speaker is here

Symposium by Gilbert Ryle and J. N. Findlay, from *Proceedings of the Aristotelian Society*, Supp. Vol. 35 (1961), pp. 223–42. Reprinted by courtesy of the authors and the Editor of the Aristotelian Society.

and now employing what he had previously acquired and still possesses. He is now in the act of operating with things of which he has, perhaps for years, been the possessor. The words, constructions, intonations, etc., that he employs in saying what he says in these words, constructions, etc., is not another part of that language. It is a momentary operation *with* parts of that language, just as the buying or lending that I do with part of my capital is not itself a part of that capital, but a momentary operation with a part of it. That, indeed, is what my capital is for, namely, to enable me to make purchases, benefactions, loans, etc., with parts of it whenever I wish to do so. It is a set of moderately permanent possibilities of making particular momentary transactions.

If I say something in French, then, even though what I say has never been said before, I do not thereby enlarge the French language, i.e., increase the amount to be learned by a student of the French language. The fact that he does not know what I said does not entail that there is a bit of the French language that he has still to learn. Dicta made in French are not parts of the French language. They are things done with parts of the French language. You might utilize the same parts in saying something identical with or quite different from what I said. Your act of saying it is not mine, and neither is a part of the fund on which we both draw. But dicta can notoriously fossilize into *clichés*. '*Je ne sais quoi*' can now be used as a noun; and '*Rest and be Thankful*' can be a proper name.

We are tempted to treat the relation between sentences and words as akin to the relation between faggots and sticks. But this is entirely wrong. Words, constructions, etc., are the atoms of a Language; sentences are the units of Speech. Words, constructions, etc., are what we have to learn in mastering a language; sentences are what we produce when we say things. Words have histories; sentences do not, though their authors do. I must have learned the words that I utter when I say something with them. I need not, and, with reservations, cannot have learned the sentence that I come out with when I say something. It is something that I compose, not something that I have acquired. I am its author, not its employer. Sentences are not things of which I have a stock or fund. Nor are my buyings and lendings things of which I have a hoard or purseful.

In daily life we do not often mention as such the sentences that people produce. We speak instead of their allegations, complaints, promises, verdicts, requests, witticisms, confessions and commands. It is, in the main, people like grammarians, compositors, translators, amanuenses and editors who need to refer to the things that people say as 'sentences', since they are *ex officio* concerned with such matters as page-space, punctuation, syntax, plagiarisation, and so on. None the less, what they are interested in are instances of someone, actual or imagined, alleging, complaining, warning, joking, etc., though their special concern is with the punctuation of them and not with their humorousness; with their length and not with their truth; with their moods and tenses and not with their relevance or rudeness.

When Caesar said '*Veni; vidi; vici*', he said three things, though he used only three Latin words. Then is '*Vici*' a word or a sentence? The queerness of this disjunctive question is revealing. What Caesar produced, orally or in writing, on a certain day, was a laconic sentence, if a sentence is an instance of someone saying something. In this instance Caesar said something which was true. But he said it using only one Latin word, a word which had long been there for anyone to use anywhen in saying all sorts of considerably different things. The word was not true, or, of course, false either. Caesar boasted '*Vici*', but the dictionary's explanation of the verb '*Vici*' need say nothing about Caesar boasting. What it describes was, perhaps, also used by, *inter alios*, some concussed gladiator asking anxiously '*Vici?*'. The boast '*vici*' was a different sentence from the question '*vici?*', though the authors of both used the same Latin word, of which neither was the inventor. The word '*vici*' was there, in their common fund, to be employed, misemployed or left unemployed by anyone anywhen. The boast '*vici*' and the query '*vici?*' were two momentary speech-acts in which this one word was utilized for saying different things. Our question 'Is "*vici*" a word or a sentence?' was queer because its subject was ambiguous. Was it about a speech-episode, like a boast or a query, or was it about an inflected Latin verb? It was queer also because '... a word or a sentence?' was a disjunction between predicates of quite different categories, on a par with '... a bat or a stroke?'

Is the interrogative sentence '*vici?*' a part of the Latin language? Well, would a student still have some Latin to learn who had never met it? Surely not. What he had learned is enough to enable him to construe it if he should ever meet it. What he construes are employments of Latin words, constructions, etc.; what he must know in order to construe or understand these employments, are the Latin words, inflections, constructions, etc. He must know the word in order to understand the one-word boast or question; but that knowing is not

this understanding; what he had long since known is not what he has
just understood or misunderstood. As we employ coins to make loans,
but do not employ lendings, so we employ words, etc., in order to
say things, but we do not employ the sayings of things—or misemploy
them or leave them unemployed either. Dictions and dicta belong to
different categories. So do roads and journeys; so do gallows and
executions.

Sometimes a person tries to say something and fails through
ignorance of the language. Perhaps he stops short because he does not
know or cannot think of the required words or constructions. Perhaps
he does not stop, but produces the wrong word or construction,
thinking it to be the right one, and so commits a solecism. Perhaps
his failure is of lesser magnitude; he says something unidiomatically
or ungrammatically; or he gets the wrong intonation or he mis-
pronounces. Such failures show that he has not completely mastered,
say, the French language. In the extended sense of 'rule' in which a
rule is anything against which faults are adjudged to be at fault,
solecisms, mispronunciations, malapropisms, and unidiomatic and
ungrammatical constructions are breaches of the rules of, e.g., the
French language. For our purposes we do not need to consider the
sources or the status of rules of this kind, or the authorities whose
censures our French instructor dreads. Solecisms are in general philosophically uninteresting. Nor, for obvious reasons, do we often
commit solecisms, save when young, ill-schooled, abroad or out of our
intellectual depth.

The reproof 'You cannot say that and speak good French' is
generically different from the reproof 'You cannot say that without
absurdity'. The latter is not a comment on the quality of the speaker's
French, since it could be true though the speaker had spoken in
flawless French, or had not been speaking in French at all, but in
English or Greek instead. The comment, if true, would be true of what
was said whatever language it was said in, and whether it was said in
barbarous or impeccable French or English. A mis-pronunciation or
a wrong gender may be a bit of faulty French, but a self-contradiction
is not a fault-in-French. Cicero's *non sequiturs* were not lapses
from good Latin into bad Latin. His carelessness or incompetence was
not linguistic carelessness or incompetence, if we tether the adjective
'linguistic' to the noun 'Language' as this is here being contrasted
with 'Speech'.

There is an enormous variety of disparate kinds of faults that
we can find or claim to find with things that people say. I can complain,

justly or else unjustly, that what you said was tactless, irrelevant, repetitious, false, inaccurate, insubordinate, trite, fallacious, ill-timed, blasphemous, malicious, vapid, uninformative, over-informative, prejudiced, pedantic, obscure, prudish, provocative, self-contradictory, tautologous, circular or nonsensical and so on indefinitely. Some of these epithets can be appropriate also to behaviour which is not speech-behaviour; some of them cannot. Not one of them could be asserted or denied of any item in an English or French dictionary or Grammar. I can stigmatize what you said with any one of these epithets without even hinting that what you said was faulty in its French or whatever other language you said it in. I grumble at your dictum but not at your mastery of the language that it was made in. There are countless heterogeneous disciplines and corrections which are meant to train people not to commit these Speech-faults. Not one of them belongs to the relatively homogeneous discipline of teaching, say, the French language. Speech-faults are not to be equated with Language-faults. Nothing need be wrong with the paints, brushes and canvas with which a portrait is bungled. Painting badly is not a pot of bad paint.

Logicians and philosophers are, *ex officio*, much concerned with kinds of things that people say or might be tempted to say. Only where there can be fallacies can there be valid inferences, namely in arguments; and only where there can be absurdities can there be non-absurdities, namely in dicta. We are presented with *aporiai* not by the telescope or the trawling-net, but by passages in books or by ripostes in debates. A fallacy or an impossible consequence may indeed have to be presented to us in French or English, etc. But it does not follow from this that what is wrong with it is anything faulty in the French or English in which it is presented. It was no part of the business of our French or English instructors to teach us that if most men wear coats and most men wear waistcoats it does not follow that most men wear both. This is a different sort of lesson and one which we cannot begin until we have already learned to use without solecism 'most', 'and', 'if', etc. There are no French implications or non-implications, so though 'p' may be said in French and 'q' may be said in French, it is nonsense to say 'q does not follow from p in the best French'. Similarly, what is impossible in 'The Cheshire Cat vanished, leaving only her grin behind her' is not any piece of intolerably barbarous English. Carroll's wording of the impossible story could not be improved, and the impossibility of his narrated incident survives translation into any language into which it can be translated. Something was amusingly wrong with what he said, but not with what he said it in.

I have a special reason for harking on this point that what someone says may be fallacious or absurd without being in any measure solecistic; i.e., that some Speech-faults, including some of those which matter to logicians and philosophers, are not and do not carry with them any Language-faults. Some philosophers, oblivious of the distinction between Language and Speech, or between having words, etc., to say things with and saying things with them, give to sentences the kind of treatment that they give to words, and, in particular, assimilate their accounts of what a sentence means to their accounts of what a word means. Equating the notion of the meaning of a word with the notion of the use of that word, they go on without apparent qualms to talking as if the meaning of a sentence could equally well be spoken of as the use of that sentence. We hear, for example, that nonsensical English sentences are sentences that have no use in English; as if sentences could *be* solecisms. Should we expect to hear that a certain argument is henceforth to contain an Undistributed Middle in B.B.C. English?

My last sentence but three, say, is not something with which I once learned how to say things. It *is* my saying something. Nor is an execution something erected to hang people on. It *is* the hanging of somebody. Part of what we learn, in learning the words of a language, is indeed how to employ them. But the act of exercising this acquired competence, i.e., the saying something with them is not in its turn an acquired wherewithal to say things. It neither has nor lacks a use, or, therefore, a use in English.

The famous saying: 'Don't ask for the meaning; ask for the use', might have been and I hope was a piece of advice to philosophers, and not to lexicographers or translators. It advised philosophers, I hope, when wrestling with some *aporia*, to switch their attention from the trouble-giving words in their dormancy as language-pieces or dictionary-items to their utilisations in the actual sayings of things; from their general promises when on the shelf to their particular performances when at work; from their permanent purchasing-power while in the bank to the concrete marketing done yesterday morning with them; in short, from these words *quâ* units of a Language to live sentences in which they are being actively employed.

More than this; the famous saying, in association with the idea of Rules of Use, could and I think should have been intended to advise philosophers, when surveying the kinds of live dicta that are or might be made with these trouble-giving words, to consider especially some of the kinds of non-solecistic Speech-faults against which the producer of such live dicta ought to take precautions, e.g., what sorts of dicta could not be significantly made with them, and why; what patterns of argument pivoting on these live dicta would be fallacious, and why; what kinds of verification-procedures would be impertinent, and why; to what kinds of questions such live dicta would be irrelevant, and why; and so on. To be clear about the 'how' of the employment of something we need to be clear also about its 'how not to', and about the reasons for both.

Early in this century Husserl and later Wittgenstein used the illuminating metaphors of 'logical syntax' and 'logical grammar'. Somewhat as, say, indicative verbs used instead of subjunctive verbs render some would-be Latin sentences bad Latin, so certain category-skids and logical howlers render dicta, said in no matter which tongue, nonsensical or absurd. A so-called Rule of Logical Syntax is what a nonsensical dictum is in breach of. But the analogy must not be pressed very far. The rules of Latin syntax are part of what we must learn if we are to be able to produce or construe Latin dicta. They are parts of the equipment to be employed by someone if he is to say either sensible or silly things in decent Latin. The Rules of Logical Syntax, on the other hand, belong not to a Language or to Languages, but to Speech. A person who says something senseless or illogical betrays not ignorance but silliness, muddle-headedness or, in some of the interesting cases, over-cleverness. We find fault not with his schooling in years gone by but with his thinking here and now. He has not forgotten or misremembered any of his lessons; he has operated unwarily or over-ingeniously in his execution of his momentary task. In retrospect he will reproach not his teachers, but himself; and he will reproach himself not for never having known something but for not having been thinking what he was saying yesterday.

The vogue of using 'Language' and 'linguistic' ambivalently both for dictions and for dicta, i.e., both for the words, etc., that we say things in and for what we say in them, helps to blind us to the wholesale inappropriateness of the epithets which fit pieces of language to the sayings of things with those pieces; and to the wholesale and hetero-geneous inappropriatenesses of the variegated epithets which fit things said to the language-pieces and language-patterns that they are said in.

It remains true that philosophers and logicians do have to talk about talk or, to put it in a more Victorian way, to discourse about discourse. But it is not true that they are *ex officio* concerned with what language-teachers are *ex officio* concerned with.

(2) J. N. FINDLAY

I AM in great agreement with what I regard as the substantial points in Professor Ryle's paper. His definition of language I think rather arbitrarily narrow: for him it is a 'stock, fund or deposit of words, constructions, *cliché* phrases and so on'. I should have thought it would be wrong not to include in a language the various syntactical and other *rules* which restrict our employment of the capital of expressions mentioned by Professor Ryle, though perhaps I am wrong in thinking he meant to exclude them. That adjectives must agree with the gender of their substantives in certain cases would certainly be held to be part of the French language, as it is not part of the English. There is also, I think, a further arbitrariness in excluding sentences from *language*, and in making them the units of *speech* which are produced when we say things. I think we can and should distinguish between the sentence *Je ne sais quoi* as a mere possibility permitted by the French language, and the same sentence as used or produced by someone to say something. I can in fact see no good reason why one should not have a narrower and a wider conception of a language. On the narrower conception, a language includes a vocabulary and rules, whereas on the wider conception it includes also *all* the possible sentences that could be framed out of the vocabulary in accordance with the rules. In this sense French or English would include all the permissible sentences that could be framed in it, whether anyone ever uttered or wrote or thought them or not. If this conception of a language makes it absurdly wide, the conception of it as a vocabulary plus rules makes it unduly narrow. Certainly, however, I think we want to distinguish between a sentence as a grammatically permissible word-combination, and the utterance or writing down or silent thinking of that sentence by someone on some occasion to make an allegation, raise a query, express a doubt, etc., etc., and in the latter case I find a language of *use* or *employment* more natural than Professor Ryle's language of *production*. I think therefore that Professor Ryle is legislating rather vexatiously in forbidding us to speak of sentences as parts of language, or to say that such sentences can be *used* by speakers. I do not, however, think that this vexatious piece of legislation is in the forefront of Professor Ryle's intentions.

What Professor Ryle is mainly concerned to do seems to me to be to distinguish between grammatical faults in the use of words in constructing sentences, and faults in what may be called 'logical syntax' or 'logical grammar', which involve the use of words to construct perfectly grammatical sentences, but which none the less violate a deeper set of rules, the rules of sense, the rules of logic, the rules regulating the mutual relations of categories, etc., etc. With all this I am deeply in agreement, because it involves precisely the recognition that different sorts of words, as it were, make different sorts of abstract *cuts* in their subject-matter, or help to execute different sorts of abstract *cuts*—some, as Aristotle might say, tell us *what* things are, others *how* they are, others *how many* they are, others *conjoin*, others *emphasize*, others *bracket*, etc., etc.—and that in making such quite different types of cross-section they become subject to the relations necessarily obtaining among such cross-sections, so that some verbal combinations which are smooth and pretty grammatically none the less make hideous nonsense. Professor Ryle, it seems to me, is here suggesting that it is the relations of different sorts of *meanings* to one another which determine the depth-grammar of words, and that these meanings and their relations are matters that must be *independently* considered if we are to study logical as well as grammatical syntax. If this suggestion is not implicit in his words, perhaps he will explain what sort of abuse of words it is that is logical or depth-grammatical as opposed to merely surface-grammatical abuse. Incidentally, I feel in the contexts invoked by Ryle that it is doubly tempting to talk of the *use* and *abuse* of grammatical sentences. The sentence is there, a fully-fashioned grammatical entity, and it is its use to express a categorially possible combination of meanings which is at times possible and legitimate, whereas at other times there is really only an abuse.

Having expressed my agreement and disagreement with Ryle, I may perhaps allow myself to dwell a little on the famous dictum which he quotes and which has dominated philosophical discussion for the past twenty years: 'Don't ask for the meaning: ask for the use.' I wish to make against it the not often raised objection that the use for which it bids us ask, is of all things the most obscure, the most veiled in philosophical mists, the most remote from detailed determination or application, in the wide range of philosophical concepts. There is, I think, a use of 'use' which is humdrum and ordinary, but in which a study of the use of expressions is of only limited philosophical importance and interest. There is also a use of 'use' characteristic of the later writings of Wittgenstein which is utterly remote from the humdrum and ordinary, and which has won its way into the acceptance of philosophers largely because it has *seemed* to have the clearness and the straightforwardness of the ordinary use. We are all proof against the glozing deceits of words like 'substance', 'being', 'nothingness', 'consciousness', etc., etc.: we at once see that some occasions of their employment are really only abuses—but we are not yet proof against the fascinations exerted by the singular abuses of so ordinary a term as 'use'. When these abuses are exposed, the whole attitude represented by the slogan quoted by Ryle reveals itself as completely without significant basis, which unfortunately puts an end to all but a limited emphasis on 'use' and 'usage' by philosophers. Since the suggestion that use and usage—in some acceptable sense— *are* philosophically very important, certainly underlies Ryle's paper, I need not apologize for irrelevance in proceeding to demolish this suggestion.

The reason why it is absurd to tell us *not* to attend to the meaning of expressions but to concentrate on their use, is perfectly simple: it is that the notion of use, as it ordinarily exists and is used, presupposes the notion of meaning (in its central and paradigmatic sense), and that it cannot therefore be used to elucidate the latter, and much less to replace or to do duty for it. The notion of use is a *wider* notion than the paradigmatic notion of meaning: it covers many *other* things beside the meaning of an expression, but the meaning-function in its paradigmatic sense is certainly *one* of the things it covers, and it is not possible to give a clear account of use without presupposing this function. What I am saying is simply that we cannot fully say, in a great many cases, how an expression is used, without saying what sort of things it is intended to refer to, or to bring to mind, and just how, or in what angle or light, it purports to refer to them, or to bring them to mind. And in cases where it would be wrong and absurd to say that an expression *independently* brought something to mind, or presented it in a certain light, it would none the less be uncontestably right to say that it *helped* to do such things in some definite manner, so that what was brought to mind would be *different*, or *differently presented*, if the expression were not part of our total utterance. Thus if I make use of the word 'dragon' in a large number of contexts, I use it to refer to a human being or beings, generally mature and female, and I use it also to represent such a human being or beings as being restrictive, uncompromising and somewhat terrifying. And if I *apply* the term in a certain context I see that to which I apply it in the light connoted by my words. And if I use the words 'such a' before uttering the word 'dragon', these words certainly help to suggest that what I am describing is *very* restrictive, *very* uncompromising and *very* terrifying, i.e., they contribute to the force of my description without playing an independent part of it. In saying what the use of my expressions is, I therefore have to say what, in the ordinary diction of logicians, they denote and connote, what their precise reference is or what their general scope, or how they contribute to connotation or denotation, and it is not thought possible to say how many expressions are *used*, without bringing in such connotative and denotative particulars.

The notion of use of course goes far *beyond* that of connotation and denotation, and it is one of the extremely important discoveries of modern semantics that there are *some* expressions whose use, in certain contexts, is *not* to connote or denote anything, nor even to help to do either, but to do such things as give voice to feelings and wishes, evoke certain attitudes in others, or *perform* certain formal social acts, e.g., promises, which have certain definite social consequences, etc., etc. That *not* all expressions, on all occasions of their *use*, perform the functions of reference or characterization, or assist in such performance, is certainly a discovery not to be underestimated, which has cleared the deck of much tangled tackle and many stumbling-blocks. But this kind of *non*-referential, *non*-connotative use is parasitic upon a connotative, referential one, and could hardly exist without it. It is one of Wittgenstein's more irresponsible fancies that there could be a language composed *only* of commands, or *only* of curses, or *only* of greetings. The concept of use also certainly covers all the hidden *implications* and *suggestions* which attach to the writing or utterance of a word or a sentence, but which are not strictly part of what it means or says: thus when I say 'He did not commit this murder' I may use this sentence to imply that he committed certain other murders, that I absolutely believe him to be no murderer, that we live under laws forbidding the taking of life, etc., etc. But all such implications and suggestions are likewise dependent upon the function of directly connoting or denoting something, and are in fact an extension of the same.

Use also obviously covers the mere requirements of accidence and syntax, though these, as Ryle has shown, are mere instrumentalities in the task of significant diction.

What is implicit, however, in the slogan 'Don't ask for the meaning: ask for the use' is not that use covers much *more* than the connotative and denotative functions of language, but that it somehow resumes and completely explains the latter, that we can completely see around and see through talk about the reference and connotation of expressions by taking note of the way people operate with such expressions, how they combine them with other expressions to form sentences, and the varying *circumstances* in which producing such sentences is reckoned appropriate or fully justifiable. This study of verbal manoeuvres, and of appropriate and justifying circumstances, must not, however, be confined to the single instant of utterance: it must point *backwards* to the all-important situations in which use was *learnt* or *taught*, and it must point *forwards* to the innumerable situations in which the utterance in question will again be found *appropriate*, or will be found to be more and more abundantly *justified*. The study of use therefore includes a genealogy and a prognosis of the most indefinite and complex kind, much more extensive than any that occurs in a merely grammatical or philological study. In another respect, however, the slogan gives 'use' an extraordinarily restricted interpretation. The operations involved in use are not to be operations conducted privately in anyone's head, or at least such operations can only be brought into consideration in so far as they can be narrowly tied up with other non-private operations, and the *circumstances* in which such operations are conducted must all be circumstances belonging to what may be called the common public environment, circumstances in which bricks are being assembled into buildings, apples taken from drawers and handed over to customers, railway-signals altered, or hunting expeditions conducted. The sort of change which is a mere change in perspective or in conscious 'light' is *not* among the circumstances mentionable in describing use.

And there is yet another most extraordinary restriction placed upon our account of the *circumstances* in which a word is correctly used: we must not employ the word or its equivalent to explain those circumstances. We must not, e.g., say, that when a man is confronted by three apples in a drawer, or by an apple and another apple and yet another apple, he is then justified in employing the word 'three' in connexion with such apples. The word 'three' may be employed in describing the circumstances justifying countless *other* sorts of utterance, but not the circumstances justifying its *own* employment. In the same way we must never say that it is when a man is confronted by a red object, or has learnt to discriminate its colour, that he is justified in calling it 'red'. Such accounts are held to be wholly trivial and unilluminating, and are moreover held to suggest various deep philosophical fallacies: the belief that meanings exist 'out there' in the things we deal with *before* we find the appropriate words to 'pick them out', or that they exist 'in the mind' or the understanding before we find words to express them. Whatever we suggest by our accounts of use, we must never suggest that there are *pre-existent meanings*. Words enjoy meaning and reference in and by our use of them, and our use cannot be explained in terms of any meaning that antedates the use of words. And since understanding and thinking are defined in terms of the operation with signs, we must never speak as if we could understand or think anything before we dispose of appropriate verbal expressions and have been taught to employ them. The programme of this extreme 'utilitarianism'—as one may perhaps call the use-doctrine—is impressive: it resembles nothing so much as the brave empiricist programme of Locke and Hume, in which no idea was to be admitted into the charmed circle of thought and knowledge without producing a genealogy purer than any required by the Nuremberg laws, exhibiting a proper origin in sensation and reflection, and a derivation from these by approved processes. But, like that brave programme, it faces the crucial objection that it cannot be carried out completely, and that no comprehensive account of use and usage can be given which does not contain some members of impure origin. That the brave programme was hopeless Wittgenstein himself perhaps obscurely realized, when he wrongly said of the *Brown Book*, the most profound and wonderful of his writings, that it was *nichts wert*. But if success, rather than stimulus and provocation, is the criterion of philosophical value, his judgement was entirely justified.

I need not range far nor cite many instances to make plain the totally unilluminating, indeed deeply obfuscating character of attempts to give a complete account of the use of expressions in terms of merely public operations and circumstances. The very conception of a *rule*, central to the 'utilitarianism' in question, abounds in difficulty. For we are expressly told that to follow a rule is not necessarily to be guided by a spoken or written formula, since each such formula admits of interpretation in terms of another formula, and this in terms of another, and so on indefinitely. Nor is the following of a rule to be identified with any sort of inner personal understanding of that rule which can guide one's subsequent performance, since to hold this would be to accept pre-existent meanings resident in the queer medium of the mind. Nor can the following of a rule be identified with one's actual performance up to a point, since this is always compatible with an infinity of rules. In the end it would seem that following a rule must be an ineffable sort of affair: it must be something that can be accomplished in one's *doing* (in this case, speaking), but not effectively spoken *about*. It is something that one can know how *to do* without being able to know how what one does is done. The conception of a linguistic rule has, in fact, all the irretrievable obscurity of the structural resemblance constitutive of meaning in the *Tractatus*, which cannot be expressed but only *shown*. If it is at least *possible* that a rule should at times be understood or grasped in thought, we can understand what it is like to follow it without thought, but if grasping is a function of following, the whole activity of following dissolves in mystery. I do not myself know how it differs from the most arbitrary irregularity except that it mysteriously *feels* right at every stage, and that others, standing at my side, mysteriously agree in such feelings. And if it is hard to throw light on the following of rules in terms of outward circumstances and performances, how much harder it is to say in what lies conformity to an *open* rule, one which is to be applied over and over *indefinitely*. While the *thought* expressed by the phrase 'and so on indefinitely' is most absolutely simple and easy to entertain, it is a thought *logically* impossible to evince adequately in one's performance. Much has been written, from the standpoint of the use-doctrine, about the difference between closed and open games, but the discussion ends up with very much what it started from, that it is a difference in the *spirit* with which the respective games are played. A man, e.g., using an open arithmetic simply has a system or general rule for constructing numerals *indefinitely*. That a spirit is operative in this case I should not care to deny, but that it consorts well with the use-doctrine, or establishes its superiority, I cannot conceive.

Similar difficulties confront us if we consider the use-account of the use of descriptive adjectives like those of colour. We are forbidden to talk of prior colour-differences in objects, or prior colour-discriminations in persons, as this would involve the grave error of positing pre-existent meanings. We are introduced to imaginary tribal activities which involve the picturesque carrying about of charts of colour samples and their comparison with, or imposition on objects, but these it would seem explain little or nothing, since the charts are dispensable and admit moreover of a wrong use. From the use of charts the tribe progresses to the use of colour samples carried somehow in the mind's eye, and ultimately to the mere unhesitant pronouncement, after sufficient training, of certain colourwords in the presence of certain objects. With this pronouncement others as unhesitatingly agree. From the Scylla of holding that 'blue' stands for a discriminable blueness in objects, or expresses an awareness of blueness in one's mind, one proceeds to the Charybdis of saying that those things are blue which we and others agree, and have been trained, to call so. It is plain, of course, that one must have ultimates somewhere, and it is plain also that there are different possibilities of colour-discrimination corresponding to different possibilities of usage: what is *not* plain is why one should prefer such a strange, secondary ultimate as a *use* to the more obvious, understandable ultimates of discriminating thoughts in the mind, or discriminable features in things.

The most superb example of the problem-increasing character of the use-semantics is, however, to be found in its treatment of cases where men use expressions without obvious reference to any palpable feature of the public environment, when they give voice, e.g., to recollections or anticipations, or describe their personal feelings or impressions, or report their fantasies or their dreams. Here the course is followed of attempting to account for such uses by supposing men to be such as *spontaneously* to want to use expressions taught in certain contexts in contexts where their normal justification is absent, and that these non-normal needs, so strangely universal among us, constitute the basis for a new *secondary* set of linguistic usages, where the sole fact that we agree in feeling certain linguistic urges is the sole criterion of their correctness. Thus children perhaps spontaneously run over the names of objects recently presented to them, or can be encouraged to do so without difficulty: meaning can then be given to the *past tense*, and they can learn to say that they *had* a ball, a stick, a rattle, etc. To 'refer to the past' is merely to learn to employ the past tense in such circumstances, an account as amusingly free in presupposing pastness and temporal passage in the *circumstances* of the learning, as it is firm in denying any non-verbal *understanding* of them. Men then spontaneously begin to use the past tense where there is no such recent provocation: we then give a use to talk about 'remembering', particularly if others agree in such spontaneous inclinations. The reference to the past in memory is therefore not the ultimate, mysterious thing that Husserl, Broad and others have supposed it to be: it merely reflects the strange tendency of men to talk preteritively beyond the limits of recency, and the further linkage of this fact with the readings of instruments, the reports of others, and many other observed matters. It may now happen that men waking from sleep spontaneously talk in the past tense *as if* recalling happenings which no one remembers, and which do not fit in with the observable contemporary state, or with the memory-inclinations of others. The concept of 'dreaming' now makes its *debut* to take care of these extraordinary performances. Malcolm, the admirable exponent of a preposterous analysis, admits[1] that on it dream-language is very odd: it is *as if* one is faithfully recalling something, but one cannot explain this fact by saying that one *did* experience what one is disposed to report, since this would involve an unintelligible hypothesis, one excluded by the guiding assumptions of the doctrine of use. What these queer-nesses surely show is the profound mistakenness somewhere of these guiding assumptions. To make use of a gnostic principle used by Moore in other contexts: we *know* certain facts about meaning much more absolutely than we can be sure of the premises, or the inferential rules, of semantic arguments designed either to establish them, or to explain them away. Obviously we cannot make straight sense of many linguistic usages without postulating just those pre-existent understandings (not confined to matters in the public fore-front) and the possibility of communicating such understandings to others, which it is the whole aim of the use-doctrine to exclude.

The use-doctrine may further be objected to for its profoundly circular, question-begging character. This is a point ably made by Mr. Gellner in a book[2] where some of the most profound criticisms of the use-doctrine and its consequences lie hidden under a some-what popular exterior. To have seen an unacceptable, unargued naturalism behind Wittgenstein's brilliant façade of exposition, is no mean insight. By describing the functioning of linguistic expression exclusively in public and social terms, we at once go *too far* in assuming such approaches to be wholly justified and clear, and we also *do not go far enough* in refusing to recognize aspects of language not fitting an approach of this sort, or in 'proving'

---

[1] [The reference is to N. Malcolm, *Dreaming* (London, 1959). Ed.]

[2] [E. Gellner, *Words and Things* (London, 1959). Ed.]

them to be misguided or senseless. These two lines of objection really coincide, since it is by turning away from aspects of language it cannot readily accommodate that the use-doctrine is unable to see its own difficulties and obscurities. The use-theorists have dwelt much on the profound subtlety of ordinary language, but they have been far from recognizing *how* subtle it actually is. For it not only uses expressions to point to, or to throw light on, ordinary objects, but it also uses them *reflexly*, in the manner studied in Husserl's *Logische Untersuchungen*, to point to or throw light on its own *meanings*, thereby setting up an order of objects as clear-edged and partial as its normal objects are fuzzy and full, and as delicate in their abstraction as they are indispensable for the higher flights of thought. That a phrase like 'the third door on the right' can be used both straightforwardly to refer to a door, and reflexly to refer to its own meaning, is a truth plain to babes, but occasioning head-aches to the semantically over-wise and prudent. Ordinary speech further, provides us with an instrument for communicating with others about matters public and common, which is also an instrument for purely personal use, in which different observations, different views, different judgements provide much the same complementary parallax, and the same corrective or confirmatory testing as in the interpersonal case. But not only is it thus double in its use, it also manages to incorporate the personal in the public use, and the public in the personal, in a regress pursuable as far as even we choose. Thus we all understand other people's first-person talk by analogy with our own, and its imperfect public intelligibility is also perfectly and publicly intelligible, since everyone makes just such first-person statements in his own case. The manner in which we smoothly swing over from another man's perfectly understood use of the first-person pronoun 'I', and replace it with 'he' in reporting the content of his statement, and expect the other man to do the same in regard to us, as well as the children's games in which these proprieties are amusingly violated: all these show an understanding of the antithesis of contrasted privacies, and of their overcoming in a wider publicity, of which the use-semantics betrays no inkling. In the same manner, ordinary speech has in it the germs of what may be called the Cartesian or the Lockean inversion, the reversal of the ordinary approach from outward things to the mind, into an approach to outer things from the facts of our subjective life. Though the language in which we talk of and to ourselves—the best subject-matter and audience—may have had its *source* in contexts

E

of public ostensibility, it can, by a profitable ingratitude, use the personal language thus painfully acquired to cast doubt upon, or to throw light on, its own origin. We may illuminate our understanding and knowledge of public matters in terms of just those personal experiences and pre-existent understandings which talk about public matters first renders possible. And this personal Cartesian or Lockean story can then achieve the widest publicity, since to have back rooms continuous with those opening on the public square is the most universal, most inescapable of predicaments. It is no doubt by a creative transformation that the rumour of the square penetrates backwards, and is re-echoed in the small back rooms, and it is likewise by a creative transformation that these transformed echoes rejoin the rumour of the square. All this, however, unquestionably happens, and it is the task of a philosophical semantics to make sense of it, and not to declare it unintelligible.

Nothing that has been said in the foregoing is meant to reflect on the painstaking, detailed study of linguistic usage, or the actual manner of its teaching, if used to show how we actually come to mean what we undoubtedly do mean, or to throw light on the complexity and subtlety of our meanings, or to show how we come to be misled into supposing we mean what really conflicts with the 'depth-grammar' of our meanings. Our criticisms are only of a radical use-theory carried to extremes, which constructs fables as to how we might have been taught the meanings of words in order to buttress *a priori* doctrines as to what we *must* or *cannot* mean. If anyone thinks such doctrines archaic and superseded, and so not requiring rebuttal, he is wide of the truth. Wittgenstein's accounts of language-games are so arresting, so novel, so subtle in their detailed development, so daring in their frank embrace of the unplausible, so imbued with intellectual seriousness and earnestness, and so great, finally, in their aesthetic appeal, that it is hard to see through them or around them. They fascinate the philosopher in the same way that Wittgenstein claimed that philosophers were fascinated by the forms of ordinary language, and against such fascination determined steps are necessary. The steps I have taken in this paper may not have been sufficiently subtle, and may have involved certain misunderstandings of detail: I shall hope, at least, to have incited others to do better.

All this should not, of course, be taken as reflecting on the philosophical greatness of Wittgenstein. Wittgenstein is the author of three wholly differing accounts of meaning, all of which merit entire rejection: meaning is *not* reduplication of structure, it is *not* verification or verifiability, it is plainly *not* what he meant by 'use'. It is not these things, though it is of course intimately connected with them all, but it will be best illuminated by construing further the old humdrum notions of connotation and denotation, and by seeking painfully to throw light on the 'thought behind our words', for which, on account of the peculiar categories it involves, it would seem that no adequate surrogate has been, or can be, offered. It is, I surmise, in the 'intentional nature of thought' that the true solution of the problems of meaning is to be found. But by formulating these three inadequate accounts, Wittgenstein has given the semantic problem the central place it deserves in philosophy, and has contributed vastly to its solution. Through his inability to account satisfactorily for certain linguistic performances, he has indicated the precise nodes where language makes its various creative leaps and has thereby given philosophical semantics its opportunity and its task. Moreover, each of Wittgenstein's frequent rhetorical questions is such that, if answered in the sense *not* intended by the question, it will lead to an illuminating result: they are practically all arrows which, if read in the reverse direction, point unerringly to some truth. A philosophy of meaning so valuably wrong does not differ profoundly from one that is systematically right.

USES OF LANGUAGE AND USES OF WORDS
With Application to a Problem of Frege*

D. S. SHWAYDER

I

CONTEMPORARY philosophers have come more and more to put questions about language in terms of 'use'. The effect has, on the whole, been salutary, for reasons I do not here aim to discuss. But it is worth pointing out that there is a rather far-reaching ambiguity on 'use'. This ambiguity, while easily resolved, poses a question over the relationship between the two uses of 'use'.

The ambiguity is indicated, on the one side, by the phrase 'the fact-stating (or statement-making) *use of language*', and, on the other side, by the phrase 'the referring *use of words*'. I thus distinguish these two ideas by calling the first 'use of *language*' and the second 'use of *words*', where any kind of expression, and not words alone, may be given the same word-use.

A use of language is a category of what we can call language acts. It is a classification according to what the agent aims to produce and will produce if his act succeeds. Stating is a kind of use of language. It comprises all those acts in which the agent aims to produce a statement. The statement, which might have been made via and identified in any number of language acts—call them 'assertions' if you wish—, is what a competent observer could identify in the agent's act, if that act is successful.

*Success and the possibility of failure are crucial ideas. I maintain that any kind of action can be theoretically defined by listing conditions that must be satisfied if acts of that kind are to succeed. Language acts have the additional feature of indicating in them-

From *Theoria*, Vol. 26 (1960), pp. 31–43. Reprinted, with revisions and additions, by permission of the author.

This paper was read before the 32nd annual meeting of the Pacific Division of the American Philosophical Association, at Eugene, Oregon, December 30, 1958, and was revised for publication in this volume. Passages which contain or constitute major revisions are marked with asterisks at the beginning and end, as in this note.

selves what those conditions are. In doing a language act one thus shows what he means to do, and must adopt means calculated to achieve that result. Thus the speaker conforms to conventions according to which the occurrence of expressions employed by him indicate that particular conditions must obtain if the act is to succeed. The occurrence of a so-called referring expression indicates, for example, that an object identified in a certain way should exist. Any package of conditions which can thus be indicated by the employment of some expression defines a *use of words*. If the language in question actually has an expression which can be employed to indicate just those conditions, I say that the use of words is available to the speakers of that language. Different languages make different word-uses available, though it appears with a substantial general overlap. When a speaker actually employs an expression whose occurrence would in the circumstances indicate the conditions which define a use of words, I say that the speaker *realizes* that use in his language act. Each such realization of a use of words is an element of the act. I shall then also elliptically speak of the use being present in the act. I assume that any language act may be semantically parsed into such elements, and that every semantically interesting feature of the act is due to the presence of one or more such elements. The presence of a particular use is itself a semantical feature of the language act.

In what follows, I restrict my attention to language acts and neglect the products or effect which result if the act is successful, e.g. I restrict myself to acts of promising and stating (assertions) and do not discuss the promises or statements which are produced in such acts.

Promising and stating are representative instances of what I call *uses of language*, and others are ordering, contracting, counting, baptizing, marrying, swearing, cheering, pronouncing criminal sentence, requesting, questioning, conjecturing, predicting, postulating, defining. Uses of language are enormously numerous. I can't imagine where a listing would end.*

Uses of words are as various as uses of language are numerous. Words are used to refer, to distinguish, to relate, to qualify; they may be used as conjunctions, forming assertions by connecting sentences, or marking off the conclusions of arguments; they may be used to indicate that a certain kind of statement is to be made, where statements may variously be classified, or that a certain use of language is being attempted; they may be used to hold open gaps, signal cross references; to indicate the mode of utterances and where they start and

stop, and how definitively are to be taken. Observe too that there are
as many referring and distinguishing uses as there are classifiable
forms of reference and kinds of property. Demonstrative referring
uses differ from proper name referring uses, and predicables in the
category of second substance differ from predicables in the category
of quality.

My main thesis is that uses of words are not uses of language.

In what follows I shall for purposes of convenience mostly restrict
myself, on the one side, to the referring use of words, and I hurry to
grant that what I say about referring will not hold generally of all
uses of words, though I hope that something comparable could always
be said.

On the other side, I restrict myself mostly to the statement making
use of language, and, in particular, to what I shall call 'predicating'.
One predicates when one aims to make a singular subject-predicate
statement. In English, we frequently do that by uttering or inscribing
upon an appropriate occasion a sentence of the form ' . . . is [a] ***',
where ' . . . ' is to be replaced by a referring expression, and '***' is to
be replaced by a suitable common-noun or adjective. Thus when
talking about material objects we may put in place of '***' size, shape
and colour adjectives, among others.

To predicate successfully *is* to make a subject-predicate statement;
predicating is a sub-use of language, a species of language act. In
order to predicate successfully we must somehow or other contrive
to refer to an object and say something about it, without having to
refer to any other object; otherwise we fail at the task.

Referring is not a use of language, but a use of words, one of
the subsidiary elements present in language acts falling within
different uses of language; while predicating is fact-stating, referring
is neither fact-stating, command-giving, nor anything else comparable.

This may be seen by observing that a referring expression may be
used in one and the same way now to make a statement, now to ask a
question and now to forward the success of acts of other kinds.
Though not all language acts contain referring elements (the assertion that all men are mortal does not), the same referring element may
occur in language acts of innumerable different kinds.

Presently I shall attempt to show we refer *only* when doing some
language act falling under a use of language. Granting this, what we
see is that, if referring were a use of language, it would also always
involve the performance of some *other* use of language. But these other

uses of language are not related among themselves in any way at all like that. Asking a question is not also making a statement, nor anything else. This begins to indicate that referring is not itself a proper use of language.

We do not make a statement, or accomplish anything else comparable to making a statement, merely by calling off a list of names. When we merely refer, and nothing else, we are not yet doing anything. Only that is a misleading way of putting it: in fact there is no such thing as 'mere referring'.[1] *Referring is that part of the act of saying something about a referent by which the referent is made available for discussion. Elements of any kind are identified in complexes, in complementary connexion with other elements. Ordered pairs of numbers represent points on the plane, but (in this application) single numbers represent nothing. Similarly, the realization of a referring use by which the referent is made available requires complementation with other uses.* We fail even to refer with a referring expression unless we put it into the context of a sentence or by some other means say something about the referent as identified—order it, welcome it, etc., etc. Take, for example, a referring expression, a surname like 'Wittgenstein'. If I pronounce the word 'Wittgenstein' that might be construed as a summons or as an answer to the question, 'Who is the greatest modern philosopher?' But if I simply say, 'Wittgenstein', not intending to do anything with the word except to refer to Wittgenstein, then I fail to do even that; I am not referring to Wittgenstein, although the word 'Wittgenstein' is made for the job. If, however, I say, 'Wittgenstein is Viennese', then I do indeed refer to Wittgenstein, and at the same time I say something about him. An important fact, then, about referring is that a word is not yet used to refer unless it is used to contribute an element to a language act. Generally, to have a use of words is to know how to employ a conventionally appointed expression in language acts falling within various uses of language. When an expression is employed with a certain use, it actually contributes to the sense of a language act. There can be no such performance as 'mere referring' or 'mere full stopping'. We refer always in the act of saying something; we can full stop only if there is a language act to stop. Clearly, different language acts of different kinds can have elements hence word-uses in common. The question whether Johnnie is coming and the statement that Johnnie is coming may both contain a diminutive

[1] I mean as a use of *words*; there is a use of *language* we might call 'giving references' towards the success of which we must use words to refer, and in other ways as well

proper name referring use to a person familiarly known to those present as 'Johnnie'.

Observe, finally, that single words may be employed to perform language acts, e.g., 'Yes', 'No', and even 'Johnnie', but then 'Johnnie' does not have simply a referring use but must also indicate that other conditions are satisfied, e.g., that an identifiable question has just been asked.

The thesis I am arguing for was long ago anticipated by Wittgenstein's application of Frege's dictum, 'nur im Zusammenhang des Satzes hat ein Name Bedeutung', and recently has been elaborated by Ryle, who maintained that it is not correct to speak of using sentences, as it is correct and useful to speak of using words.[1]

In the *Tractatus*, Wittgenstein appropriated Frege's dictum partly to indicate how far Frege went wrong in supposing that, while words occur meaningfully in sentences, sentences themselves are just another kind of name. Unfortunately, it is not entirely clear whether Wittgenstein's '*Satz*' is best rendered as 'sentence' or 'assertion', though, on balance, 'assertion' seems the better choice. If he meant 'assertion', then, of course, he went slightly wrong, for words are used not only assertionally to make statements but also to ask questions, etc. But if Wittgenstein meant 'sentence', then he went slightly wrong again, but for quite a different reason. Single words will sometimes suffice to make statements. More generally, we may do without sentence contexts if other elements in the language situation secure that we shall succeed in accomplishing what we would accomplish with a full-fledged sentence. *The 'same thing' will have been said in two different utterances, though perhaps different word-uses are realized, if the same totality of conditions is indicated. Realizing the use of 'yes', for example, indicates that something else has been said and borrows from the conditions indicated in that other act.*

Ryle's formulation of the distinction is also inaccurate and probably inoperative. The fact is that we have yet to hit upon a generally workable formula for separating sentences from words. As we commonly employ 'word' and 'sentence', the distinction between them is far from clear and certainly not sharp; nor is it obvious that we can make the separation as precise as we would wish and still

[1]Frege, *Grundgesetze der Arithmetik*, v. 1, nos. 29–31, *Foundations of Arithmetic* (tr. by Austin), pp. x, 73 ff., 115; Wittgenstein, *Tractatus*, 3.3; Ryle, 'Ordinary Language', *Phil. Rev.*, April, 1953, pp.178 ff. See also Wittgenstein, *Philosophical Investigations*, Part II, 11. Strawson has challenged the thesis in his review of *Philosophical Investigations*, *Mind*, 1954, p. 73. Since this was first set down it has become quite a journal topic.

retain it as a useful philosophical tool. (Are we to say that 'yes' is a sentence or a word; or—as is more likely—is it both? Is 'gl' a word? No, but it has a sense, and so presumably a use, as in 'glisten'.) I do not deny there is this difference; I am sure there is. But I am confident that the distinction between word and sentence, for what it is worth, cannot be drawn except in terms of what one does with language. One might, for example, as a first approximation, want to say that a sentence is a total expression instantiated in the performance of a complete language act; a word might then be explained as an unbound expression (not, e.g. an affix) of some tongue which may, by the rules of that tongue, be employed in connexion with other expressions to complete language acts. This is inaccurate, and certainly not designed as a definition, but it is enough to indicate that we must make an upward reference to the use of language in order to draw the distinction between word and sentence. But let us anyway suppose that we have this distinction between a word and a sentence: what good will it do us? It seems pretty clear, as against Ryle, that one might occasionally wish to inquire whether a certain sentence were used, e.g., to make a statement or to give an order. It is, of course, true that in such a circumstance we would be doubtful, not about a use of words, but rather, about a use of language. All these observations indicate that Ryle comes on to the desiderated distinction from the wrong position, from expressions rather than from the uses they have; indeed, he draws the distinction at the wrong level, at the level of repeating expressions, when it must be drawn at the level of using language, e.g., making statements. It is this, I believe, which accounts for the resistance his doctrine has encountered in almost all quarters. Still, most of what Ryle says here seems to me to be substantially right.

To form a sentence and thereby perform a language act *is* to use words, and there is no further room to speak of using the sentence as a kind of complex word. Only that is a misleading brachylogy. More fully, putting sentences together on appropriate occasions so as to make statements, etc., *is* to use words. Ryle correctly observed that we learn the rules governing word-usage, and do not then need to learn new rules governing the usages of sentences. Learning how to construct meaningful sentences is involved in learning the rules for employing words.

*Though I would not retreat from the position maintained in this paper, that we should recognize a distinction between uses of language and uses of words, I am now inclined to think that the distinction is of less ultimate consequence for the theory of language than I supposed. What remains important is that we should not regard the elements of an utterance as small-scale utterances, or utterances as utterance elements.

My notion of a use of language corresponds to Austin's idea of an *illocutionary force*. A use of language is a *kind* of language action, the analogue in the realm of conventional action to an Aristotelian 'second substance' or 'substantial form'. I believe that the counterpart to Aristotle's thesis that every substance falls within a second substance holds for language: every language act falls within some one or several uses of language. This thesis, though hardly surprising, is of some significance, for I doubt that a comparable principle holds for entities of every kind, e.g., I doubt that every morsel of sand or every movement of a leaf is classifiable under some kind. Our everyday way of speaking of promising, conjecturing, etc., provides a rough and ready classification of conventional performances. While it is doubtful that we shall ever achieve a correct taxonomy of language by which language acts can be exhaustively classified within a finite set of independently defined exclusive categories, still, one can look forward to supplementing ordinary classification with more contrived, theoretically more manageable sorts, e.g., *asserting*.

A use of language, whether ordinary or contrived, is not itself a feature or property of language acts any more than the type *horse* is a feature or property of horses. Still, an animal may be a horse, in which case it has among other properties the property of being a horse. So too, a language act may be a promise, in which case it has, among others, the property of being a promise.

Word-uses, as I have introduced that idea, are not kinds of language act, but rather kinds of elements of language acts. Such elements may be 'realized in' language acts; thus one might realize a demonstrative referring element by uttering 'This' or 'Dies'. The elements in question may be in some measure specific to a language of family of languages, for they are assigned relative to a presumed morphological resolution of the sentences pertaining to such a language. Word-uses are theoretical contrivances introduced, as in classical grammatical theory, for purposes of semantically parsing sentences into their significant elements, but in a way which is meant to isolate the actual rules native speakers would have mastered in the course of learning the language. When, according to the glossary of classical grammar, we say that 'I' and 'Ich' are first person singular personal pronouns we at once classify the expressions as words and specify their common use. Any theory of language adequate to the

analysis of a particular language must provide machinery for semantically parsing utterances into word-uses.

Word-uses are not themselves features of language acts, though if
a certain word-use is contained in, viz., realized in, a language act,
then that act will have a certain feature.

Just as a substance will be classified as an acid only if it contains
a hydrogen ion, so it occasionally happens that language acts may
be classified within particular uses of language by virtue of
containing a certain word-use or connexion of word-uses. An act
may be classified as a conjecture just because it contains word-uses
realized by employing the expression, 'I conjecture', though it is
seldom so simple. We can, nevertheless, reasonably expect that our
language theory should enable us to determine the classifications
of the act from contributions made by various word-uses realized
in the act, just as chemical theory enables us to determine that
a substance is a sugar from the distribution of the hydrogen,
carbon and oxygen nuclei which it contains. A request may or may
not be marked by the occurrence of an expression equivalent in use
to, 'I would like you to'; but something about the deed must show
it to be a request.

In order to explain how that comes about, I must revert to a thesis
met above in my explanation of *word-uses*. The thesis is that in doing
a language act one must indicate all the conditions of success which
must be satisfied if the act is to succeed. I further suppose that we
shall want to explain uses of language by reference to certain of these
indicated 'conditions of success', and especially ones having to do with
the state and situation of the agent. An assertion, vaguely explained,
is a propounding or reporting of what the agent thinks he knows. A
characteristic condition of success for such an act is that the agent
could know that kind of thing. Again, a condition of success for giving
a command is that the agent has the authority. Now the indicated
conditions which fix the 'illocutionary force' may be indicated in a
package by the realization of a particular word-use (e.g., by an
'assertion sign'). But, more often, they may have to be collected from
the packages of conditions indicated by a number of expressions
having other uses, e.g., we may have to advert to some of the
conditions regularly indicated by the occurrence of the word 'is'.

It now should be clear that the ideas of a use of language and of
a use of words are theoretical contrivances which look ahead to the
provision of language theories presently available only in exiguous
form. But then it looks as if these theories are apt to be con-

currently absorbed into or subsumed under a still more general and abstract theory of 'conditions'. That is why I said that the distinction between uses of language and uses of words may be of less ultimate consequence than I originally supposed. But it still matters.*

II

I have been telling a modern version of an old story. It dates at least from Plato, and was a favourite of Cartesians and Idealists. I shall consider but one application, then detailing only a highly local case.

My argument shows that the distinction between stating and referring is not initially a distinction in referents, neither, *a fortiori*, is the distinction between predicating and referring a distinction in referents.

While we can represent a variety of predication by signs like 'is white' or '[] white' or 'white x', these do not have uses in the way in which 'white' or 'Polly' do. They schematize rather the ascription of the predicable *white* to objects, and thus a family of completed language acts. The distinction between predicating and referring is not a distinction between referents referred to in a single act of asserting and therefore not initially a distinction between kinds of objects such as material bodies, colours, numbers and, I add, assertions performed and statements made.

The many philosophers (Plato, Moore, Russell, Frege, Husserl, and Meinong among others) who have supposed that, when we make a statement about an object, we refer not to that object alone, but also necessarily to another object, like a proposition, truth-value, *Sachverhalt* or *Objektiv*, have simply failed to grasp the distinction between a use of words and a use of language. To give an extended illustration of the point, I shall now try to show that Frege's notorious difficulty over Concepts flows from the same source.[1]

Frege observed that it is never enough merely to refer to an object in order to say something about it; we must also say something about it. Expressions used to refer to Objects, Frege called '*Eigennamen*', which corresponds in a rough way to the more recent 'referring expressions', which I use here. Expressions used to talk about objects

[1]For Frege's theory see *Translations from the Philosophical Writings of Gottlob Frege*, ed. by Geach and Black, esp. 'Function and Concept', but also 'Concept and Object', 'What is a Function', and in other articles pp. x, 48 ff, 63 ff, 108; *Grundgesetze*, v. 1, nos. 1–4, 8, 19, 21–26, and 'Ueber die Grundlagen der Geometrie', *Jahresber. d. d. Mathematiker-Vereinigung*, v. 12, pp. 371 ff.

are properly included in the class of what Frege called '*Funktionnamen*', where this class seemed to comprise all meaningful signs not *Eigennamen*, exclusive (it would appear) of the assertion sign. One-place Fregian *Funktionnamen* I call 'predicates', and following Frege, shall think of them as written with a gap. Thus '[] blue' is a predicate. I shall restrict myself to predicates as they appear in acts of making statements.

*One may rightly demand, as Frege did, that a fully meaningful referring expression meaningfully employed must refer to an object.[1] Frege placed the referent-object as the *Bedeutung* of the referring expression, which latter we may now assume to be filling the gap of a predicate. What now is to be the *Bedeutung* of the predicate, for surely it must have one?[2] Frege answered that it was a Concept (*Begriff*), but was not long in deciding that Concepts must be very different from Objects, these last being the proper *Bedeutungen* of referring expressions.* I suppose his reasons are those we have observed before: we get no statement simply by calling off a list of names. In order to get a statement about an object we must refer to that object and predicate something of it. We have seen that predicating is indeed very different from referring; and one of the main reasons is that we must always predicate *of*. Frege accordingly thought that the *Bedeutung* of a predicate must directly embody this essentially predicate character, and held that this *Bedeutung*, like the predicate itself, must have a gap; as he put it, the Concept is '*ergänzungsbedürftig*' or '*ungesättigt*'.

[1] A referring expression may have a use and still lack a referent. In that event, one of the indicated conditions is not satisfied and the act must fail. If the act were an assertion, then no statement would be produced and, *a fortiori*, no question whether a produced statement were true or false could arise out of the act. Frege similarly allowed that expressions can have *Sinn* but lack *Bedeutung*. In that event, any sentence in which the expression appeared would also lack *Bedeutung*, viz., truth-value. My analysis of the situation carries Frege's conclusion on this disputed issue.

[2] I shall not argue the once-disputed question whether Frege would have held that Functions and, in particular, *Begriffe*, are *Sinne* or *Bedeutungen* or *Funktionnamen*. His distinction between Function and Object antedated that between *Sinn* and *Bedeutung*, though some of his later unpublished writings make it look as if he would have held that both Objects and Functions can be both *Sinne* and *Bedeutungen*. While I am convinced that that is the position he ought to have maintained, still it is interesting that Frege almost prohibits our raising for Functions the issues over identity which more than any other brought him to the contrast between *Sinn* and *Bedeutung*, for he expressly held that Function-names cannot meaningfully occur on either side of ' = '. It is also interesting if expected that all his examples of *Sinn* are objects. For our purposes it makes little difference whether some Functions are *Sinne*, as long as some *Begriffe* are *Bedeutungen*. I shall in effect be arguing that Functions *should* be regarded as neither *Sinne* nor *Bedeutungen* but rather as schematic language acts.

Frege's puzzle was then how it is that we can ever manage to talk meaningfully about Concepts. We can talk about something only by referring to it; that is, by using a referring expression; but what we refer to must always be an Object, and never a Concept, for Concepts are the *Bedeutungen* of predicates. The attempt to talk about Concepts is inevitably self-defeating, for we can talk only about things to which we might refer; and Concepts are excluded, almost by definition.[1]

Rightly taken, Frege was fully justified in insisting upon Concepts; rightly taken, he is telling us that we cannot get by without predicates; referring expressions are not enough. Making allowances for the fact that predicating is not the only species of stating, it is manifestly clear where predicates come from. A predicate is a piece of notational machinery employed to make or spoken of in connexion with making statements of a certain sort; if we employ the predicate under appropriate conditions, then we do make a statement of that sort. To employ a predicate is to put a name or other referring expression into one of the kinds of sentence contexts where it does assume reference. Indeed, rightly regarded, Frege's point is simple truth.

Difficulty comes not from the evasive physiognomy of Concepts, or from the ineptness of predicates, but from Frege's conception of a Concept. We are puzzled because we carry in the back of our minds the idea that a Concept—the alleged referent of a predicate—must be some queer kind of object. But what the argument shows is that a Concept is no kind of object at all, at least not a predicate-referent. Frege thought the Concept was something like an Object because he thought that the distinction between referring and predicating must be backed up by a referential distinction. From rightly noting that a meaningful word or combination of words is more than a mark and must also have a meaning or assemble a connexion of meanings, he erred in supposing that everything which has a meaning must also, at the very least, purport to indicate a *Bedeutung*. Apart from whether all uses are referring uses, we must distinguish carefully the connexion of meanings indicated by a

[1] Frege did, on the other hand, hold that Functions can be arguments of (higher order) Functions, and it is partly, I suspect, his demand that Functions resemble Objects in this *one* respect which left him prey to the puzzle just set forth. If we reinterpret Frege's idea of a Function in the way I suggest, then, taken with this theory of higher order quantification, we get the conclusion that higher order quantifiers are properly to be interpreted as ranging over assertions or statements or some similar kind of 'intensional object'.

predicate from the meaning which the various simple expressions in it might have. In our terms, the predicate itself has no use (of words), though the expressions embodied in it do. What it indicates is a range of complete language acts having features in common, and which differ in some one definite respect as is indicated by the ways in which we can fill in the predicate to get a proper sentence.

Frege wanted it both ways. In one mind he thought that all combinations of meaningful signs must work much the same; but in another mind, he saw an important difference between the roles of referring expressions and predicates. Frege went wrong and made the Concept into a queer thing, somehow like yet so unlike an Object, because he put predicating on the same level with referring; he made them somehow equal partners in the truth-value; to put it otherwise, he made referring expressions and predicates assume equal and simply complementary roles in the sentence. In fact, the predicate, if it *may* be said to have a use,[1] is used to predicate, i.e., to make a statement of a certain kind. Frege tried to compare two things which are not directly comparable: a use of words and a type of language act.

Concluding Note. It may be objected that this cannot be the correct analysis of Frege's difficulty, for he most certainly did allow that different 'propositional attitudes', such as questioning and asserting, might attach to the same *Gedanke*, as expressed by a sentence built of a referring expression and a predicate. But all this assumes what is highly questionable, namely the correctness of Frege's 'identical content' analysis of the relations between questions, statements, etc. In any case, while Frege does tell us what the *Bedeutung* of a statement-making sentence is, he never reveals what the *Bedeutung* of (say) a command is to be, and so we never know what would be the *Bedeutung* of a predicate employed to command. Frege seemed to think that the distinctions he made between *Sinn* and *Bedeutung*, *Gegenstand* and *Funktion*, and assertion and other 'propositional attitudes' were to be applied in tandem: first determine the *Sinn* of the expression; then determine whether its *Bedeutung* is an Object or a Function; then determine whether the expression is being used to assert, question, etc., or perhaps contributes to a mere *beurteilbare Inhalt*. Examination shows, in fact, that these distinctions cannot be related in this way. It is therefore no accident that Frege never succeeds in

---

[1] It is less confusing to speak about the use, not of the predicate, but of the occurring general-names, copulas, etc.

explaining the *Sinn* of expressions other than sentences and (perhaps) descriptive phrases, and that in the *Grundgesetze* he places the 'Thought' as the *Sinn* of a sentence (v. 1., No. 32), while in his last paper,[1] reverting to an idea intimated in the *Begriffsschrift*, he is inclined to cast the Thought as the complete 'content' of a judgement and, finally, he explains the *Bedeutung* of words only as they occur in statement-making uses of language. Not even Frege's celebrated rigour of mind sufficed to eliminate the uncertainty and incoherence which inevitably comes from trying to use too simple a system.

[1] See 'The Thought: A Logical Inquiry' (tr. by A. M. and Marcelle Quinton), *Mind*, 1956, e.g., p. 294. [Reprinted in *Philosophical Logic*, ed. P. F. Strawson, in the present series (1967). Ed.]

VII

MEANING AND USE

William P. Alston

THERE is a certain conviction about linguistic meaning which is widely shared today. This conviction might be expressed as follows. Somehow the concept of the meaning of a linguistic expression is to be elucidated in terms of the use of that expression, in terms of the way it is employed by the users of the language. To wit:

... to know what an expression means is to know how it may or may not be employed ...
Gilbert Ryle, 'The Theory of Meaning,' in *British Philosophy in the Mid-Century*, p. 255.

Elucidating the meaning of a word is explaining how the word is used.
Patrick Nowell-Smith, *Ethics*, p. 67

The meaning of a word is simply the rules which govern its use, and to ask for its meaning is to ask for the rules.
J. L. Evans, 'On Meaning and Verification,' *Mind*, LXII, p. 8

To give the meaning of an expression ... is to give general directions for its use to refer to or to mention particular objects or persons; to give the meaning of a sentence is to give general directions for its use in making true or false assertions.
P. F. Strawson, 'On Referring,' *Mind*, LXIX, p. 327.

... to know the meaning of a sentence is to know how to use it, to know in what circumstances its use is correct or incorrect ... A sentence is meaningful if it has a use; we know its meaning if we *know* its use.
G. J. Warnock. 'Verification and the Use of Language,' *Revue Internationale de Philosophie*, V, p. 318

And this conviction is not only held in the abstract. In the past fifteen years or so it has often been put into practice by way of

From *Philosophical Quarterly*, Vol. 13 (1963), pp. 107–24. Reprinted, with revisions and additions, by permission of the author and the *Philosophical Quarterly*.

investigating the use of one or another fundamental term, and a great deal of philosophical illumination has come out of these enterprises.

But despite the wide currency of the general conviction, and despite the numerous and wide-ranging investigations that have gone on under its aegis, no one has made a serious attempt to say, explicitly and in detail, what is to be meant by 'use' in these contexts, i.e., what is and what is not to count as revealing the *use* of a term. And still less has any serious attempt been made to say just how meaning is to be analyzed in terms of use, as so conceived. If we scrutinize attempts to spell out one or another feature of the use of a term, we shall find that a great many different sorts of facts about a term are mentioned. They include the conditions under which a sentence containing that word can or cannot be uttered, the circumstances which would make certain statements in which the word figures true or false, the sorts of sentential contexts into which the word can or cannot be inserted, the grammatical inflections of which it is or is not susceptible, the questions which can or cannot be asked concerning a particular application of the term, the responses which can or cannot appropriately be made to utterances in which it figures, the other expressions to which it is or is not equivalent, the sorts of performances which are typically carried out when the word (or a sentence containing the word) is uttered, the implications which sentences containing the word, or the utterance of such sentences, would have. And for each occurrence of such words as 'can' in the foregoing, we see a number of alternatives spread out before us— intelligibly, correctly, properly, appropriately—each of which raises a host of questions. It would be difficult to bring all such facts under a single rubric, and such incipient attempts as have been made are either patently inadequate or hopelessly sketchy or both. It does seem initially plausible to construe all this as the uncovering of various sorts of conditions for the *correct* use of the word in question, conditions having to do with either the linguistic or the extralinguistic environment of the word. (Cf. the quotation from Warnock above.) And since one is correct or incorrect as he does or does not follow certain rules, this could equally well be put in terms of getting at the rules which govern the use of the word. But such a formulation is not of much use unless we do something to separate the sort of rules and the sort of correctness which is involved in use in this sense, from the sorts which are not. For it is only too obvious that many sorts of rules which govern linguistic activity have nothing to do with use in any sense of that term in which meaning could conceivably be a function of use. For example, many speakers recognize rules forbidding them to use certain racy or obscene words in certain circumstances, or rules forbidding them to use crude or vernacular locutions in certain social circles; and such rules could be said to define a certain mode of correctness. And yet the consideration of such rules does nothing to bring out the meaning of these words.

In this essay I want to make a beginning at elucidating a suitable sense for 'use' and indicating the way in which meaning is to be understood as a function of use in this sense. I think it may serve to clear the air somewhat if I first indicate some directions from which no help is to be expected. In view of the apparently widespread impression that when one says that meaning is a function of use he is using 'use' in a quite ordinary sense, it may repay us to examine the most prominent contexts in which 'use' is used in a relatively unproblematical and unpuzzling way in connexion with linguistic expressions, in order to satisfy ourselves that none of them furnishes anything which will meet our present needs.

I

First consider the fact that the phrase, 'the use of "x"', as it is ordinarily used, fails to identify anything which an expression *has*, or which two expressions could be said to have in common. Ordinarily we speak of the use of a word, as of anything else, in the course of saying something about the fact of its employment—when, where, how frequent, etc.

The use of 'presumably' is inappropriate at this point.

The use of 'whom' at the beginning of a sentence is gradually dying out.

The use of 'by crackey' is largely confined to rustics.
Compare:

The use of sedatives is not indicated in his case.

The use of the hand plough is dying out all over Europe.

The use of automobiles in Russia is mostly limited to important officials.

It is clear that in such contexts 'The use of E' fails to designate anything which E has, and which it would share with any expression which had the same meaning, but fail to share with any expression which had a different meaning. If I were to ask one who had uttered the second sentence in the first list: 'What is the use of "whom" which is dying out, and what other expressions have the same use?', I would be missing the point of what he had said. In making that statement, he was not talking about something called 'the use of "whom"', which could then be looked for in other surroundings. He was simply saying that people are using 'whom' at the beginning of a sentence less and less. Nor is the question, 'What is the use of E?' any more fruitful. I suppose that 'What is the use of "sanguine"?' would mean, if anything, 'What is the point of using "sanguine"?', just as 'What is the use of a typewriter?' would ordinarily be understood, if at all, as an awkward way of asking 'What is the point of having (using) a typewriter?'; and this does not help.

Let us now look at some contexts in which we talk of the *way* an expression is used, or of *how* it is used. And let us consider what counts as a way of using an expression. Look at the adverbs we use to qualify 'A used E'.

A used 'Communist' effectively.

A used 'Yes sir' very insolently.

A uses 'Presumably' frequently.

Clearly none of these ways has an important bearing on meaning. The fact that two words are both used frequently, effectively, or insolently does nothing to show that they have the same meaning. Looking at the corresponding question, 'How is E used?', we might take anything which could serve as an answer to be a specification of a way of using E. It seems that such a question is normally concerned with the grammatical function of E. 'How is "albeit" used?' 'As a conjunction.' 'How is "Reverend" used?' 'As a title, not as a form of address.' 'How is "ce" used?' 'With forms of "être" under certain conditions.' Thus we could reasonably call 'as a conjunction', 'as a transitive verb', etc., ways of using expressions. But this won't do. Two words can both be used as a conjunction, or as a transitive verb, without having the same meaning.

We also speak of 'what E is used for', 'the use to which E is put', or 'the job E is used to perform'. But how do we specify what a word is used to do? It seems that the only cases in which we ordinarily make such specifications are of a rather special sort.

'And' is used to conjoin expressions of the same rank.

'Amen' is used to close a prayer.

'Ugh' is used to express disgust.
These are all cases in which it is impossible to teach someone the word by saying what it means, either because there is no approximately equivalent expression in the language ('and'), or because the exhibition of that expression would not be very helpful. (We might say '"Amen" means *so be it*', but this would be misleading at best; for it would give no hint as to the special circumstances in which 'Amen' is appropriately used.)

II

From this survey I draw the conclusion that in non-technical talk about using words we are most unlikely to discover a sense of 'use' which is even a plausible candidate for a fundamental role in semantics. And if so, a technical sense will have to be constructed. If we consider some of the arguments which have led, or might lead, people to embrace the use-analysis, they might contain some clue to a sense of 'use' which one could use in carrying out the analysis. I shall consider three such arguments.

(1) 'Since the meaning of a word is not a function of the physical properties of the word, and since a given pattern of sounds can have different meanings in different language-communities, or in the same language-community at different times, the meaning of a word must somehow be a function of the activity of language users, of what they do in their employments of the word.' This argument may well lead us to suppose that meaning is a function of use in some sense, but in itself it will not help us to pin down that sense.

(2) 'Specifications of meaning are commonly provided when we want to teach someone how to use the expression whose meaning we are specifying. Teaching someone how to use an expression is the native soil from which talk about meaning has grown. It is not, of course, the only sort of context in which one says what the meaning of a word is; there are also examinations, crossword puzzles, and many others. But it is the primary occasion for saying what a word means, and I would suppose that the other occasions are somehow derivative from it.' Now this does strongly suggest that in telling someone what a word means we are putting him in a position to be able to use it, hence that knowing what it means is being able to use it, and hence that the meaning of the word is a function of how it is used. But all this, I fear, goes on the assumption that we already have an adequate understanding of what is involved in how to use a word. I do not see

how we could derive such an understanding from these considerations.

(3) 'Ultimately a meaning-statement (a statement as to what a linguistic expression means) is to be tested by determining what people do in their employment of the expression in question. For in saying what the meaning of an expression is, what we do is not to designate some entity which could be called the meaning of the expression, but rather to exhibit another expression which has some sort of equivalence with the first.[1]

For example:

"Procrastinate" means *put things off.*[2]

"Prognosis" means *forecast of the course and termination of a disease.*

"Redundant" means *superfluous.*

"Notwithstanding" means *in spite of.*

If this is granted, the next question obviously is: what sort of equivalence must two expressions have in order that one can be thus exhibited in specifying the meaning of the other?[3] It seems plausible to say that it is equivalence in the way they are used that is crucial, for reasons similar to those put forward in the first argument. And this suggests that a meaning-statement is to be tested by examining people's employment of the expressions in question, to determine whether they are employed in the same way.'

From this line of thought we can at least derive a suggestion as to how meaning is related to use, whatever use might turn out to be.

[1]Arguments in support of this thesis are put forward in my essay, 'The Quest for Meanings', *Mind*, Volume LXXII, No. 285 (January 1963).

[2]I should say something in explanation of my notation. I italicise what follows 'means' in order to indicate that there is something special about this occurrence of the expression. This is clear from the fact that we are neither using 'put things off', e.g., in the ordinary way (it is not functioning as a verb), nor are we referring to it in a way that would be marked by enclosing it in quotes. (This latter point can be seen by noting that we could not expand the sentence into: '"Procrastinate" means the phrase, "put things off".') This type of occurrence, which I more or less arbitrarily call 'exhibiting', I take to be unique; and I believe that the only way to say what it is is to give the sort of elucidation of meaning-statements towards which I am working in this essay.

[3]'Having the same meaning' or 'synonomous' seems to me to be naturally employed wherever, as in the foregoing. I would speak of 'having the sort of equivalence which enables one to be exhibited in specifying the meaning of the other'. However one must be careful not to expect more from these phrases than they are intended to express. In using them I am not presupposing that I have specified, or can specify, something called 'a meaning' which they have in common. I shall freely avail myself of these phrases, but only as convenient and intuitively plausible abbreviations for the more cumbersome phrase.

We can sum up what has just been said in the following formula.

'x' means y (the meaning of 'x' is y) = df. 'x' and 'y' have the same use.[1] From this formula alone we get no help in trying to decide what meaning we should attach to 'use'. However if we could make explicit just what we would look for if we set out to determine whether two expressions are used in the same way, that might give us a clue as to a proper interpretation for 'use'.

Consider the statement, ' "Procrastinate" means *put things off*'. I can test this statement, at least for my speech, as follows.[2] I review cases in which I would say 'You're always procrastinating', and determine whether I would use the sentence 'You're always putting things off' to make just the same complaint. I think of cases in which I would say 'Please don't put things off so much' and determine whether I would use the sentence 'Please don't procrastinate so much' to make the same plea. I consider cases in which I say 'Is he still procrastinating all the time?' and I determine whether I would use the sentence 'Is he still putting things off all the time?' to ask the same question. And so on.

This suggests that a meaning-statement of the form, "x" means y' is to be tested by determining whether 'x' and 'y' can be substituted for each other in a wide variety of sentences without, in each case, changing the job(s) which the sentence is used to do, or, more precisely, without changing the suitability or potentiality of the sentence for performing whatever job(s) it was used to perform before the alteration. And since the 'suitability' or 'potentiality' of a sentence for the performance of a certain linguistic act is ultimately a function of the dispositions of the members of the community, a still more exact formulation would be this. The meaning-statement is justified to the extent that when 'x' is substituted for 'y' in a wide variety of sentences. and vice versa, the dispositions of members of the linguistic com-

---

[1] This formulation, and those on the next few pages, are vastly over-simplified by the pretence that each expression has only one use and only one meaning. This pretence has been adopted in order to enable us to concentrate on other problems first and will be dropped in due course.

[2] Here I limit myself to investigations of the meaning the investigator himself attaches to expressions, or the way the investigator himself uses expressions. This is not different in principle from what would happen in an investigation of the way other speakers use the expressions, but the initial description of the latter would be very much more complicated unless the checks were very rough indeed. I feel justified in allowing myself this simplification because I am bringing in testing procedures at this point for their suggestive value only. Of course ultimately we should have to consider how statements of meaning and use, as we shall have analyzed these terms, stand with respect to the possibility of inter-subjective testing.

munity with respect to employing sentences for the performance of linguistic actions is, in each case, roughly the same for the sentence produced by the alteration as for the sentence which was altered.

This in turn suggests the following way of conceiving use. First of all we shift our initial focus of attention from word-sized units to sentences. Even apart from the above considerations this is not an implausible move. The jobs which one might speak of using words to do, such as referring, denoting, and conjoining, have the status of incomplete aspects of actions, rather than of actions in their own right. One cannot, after bursting into a room, simply refer, denote, or conjoin, and then hastily depart. Referring or denoting is something one does in the course of performing a larger action-unit, such as making a request, admission, or prediction. It is therefore natural that we should begin the treatment of use with units the employment of each of which is sufficiently isolable to be treated as a complete action, i.e., with sentences.[1]

Having decided to begin with sentences, we can then define the notion of the use of a sentence as follows. ('s' and 't' will be used as sentence variables.)

> The use of 's' = df. the potentiality of 's' for the performance of one or more linguistic acts (more briefly, the linguistic act potential of 's').

Then if we recall the general formula relating meaning to use,

> IA. 'x' means y = df. 'x' and 'y' have the same use
>
> We can expand this for sentences, in terms of the above definition of the use of a sentence, as follows.
>
> IB. 's' means t = df. 's' and 't' have the same linguistic act potential.

For example, 'A haint caint haint a haint' means *it is impossible for one supernatural spirit to inhabit another supernatural spirit*. This is true because the sentences 'A haint caint haint a haint' and 'It is impossible for one supernatural spirit to inhabit another supernatural spirit' are usable to make the same assertion.

Some writers on this subject object to speaking of the meaning of a sentence.[2] They point out that sentences are not dictionary items, that one does not learn a new language sentence by sentence, etc. I

---

[1] Of course we have to take into account the fact that any linguistic element can function, for the nonce, as a sentence-surrogate, as in one-word answers to questions, e.g., 'John' in answer to 'Who was it that called?'

[2] See, e.g., Gilbert Ryle, 'Use, Usage and Meaning.' *Aristotelian Society Supplementary Volume*, Vol. xxxv (1961). [No. v (1) above.]

think they are being over-scrupulous. One can understand the in-frequency of talk about the meaning of sentences simply in terms of the fact that it is much more economical to present the semantics of a language in terms of word-sized units. And if this is the explanation, there is neither need nor justification for denying that talk about the meaning of a sentence makes sense on those, admittedly rare, occa-sions when it comes up. Incidentally the example given above is taken from one such occasion. A friend was playing for me a record of some Kentucky mountain ballads in which the sentence 'A haint caint haint a haint' occurred, and my friend asked whether I knew what *that* meant. However anyone who finds such talk distasteful can simply ignore the definition of sentential meaning. Nothing that is said about the mean-ing of words depends on it. (Although the discussion of word-meaning does depend on the notion of a sentence being used to perform a certain linguistic act.)

Returning to words and other meaningful sentence-components,[1] we shall not find ready at hand any way of specifying *what* the use of a given word is, just because, as pointed out above, sub-sentential linguistic elements are not the vehicles of the action units in terms of which our common-sense dissections of verbal behaviour are carried out. It would be a major task to develop a way of conceptualizing word-uses that is useful for semantics. (For a few brief remarks on this task see the last section.) Fortunately for the immediate purposes of this essay that will not be necessary. Since we are following out the suggestion that meaning-statements can be analyzed in terms of the notion of sameness of use of two expressions, it will be sufficient for that purpose to put forward a criterion for the sameness of use of two words. Following the lead of the testing procedures alluded to earlier, and exploiting our analysis of the notion of the use of a sentence, the following criterion emerges: (using 'u' and 'v' as variables for sen-tence-components)

> 'u' has the same use as 'v' = df. 'u' and 'v' can be substituted for each other in sentences without changing the linguistic act potential of each sentence.

Substituting into the initial meaning-use formula, we get

> IC. 'u' means v = df. 'u' and 'v' can be substituted for each other in sentences without changing the linguistic act potential of each sentence.

---

[1]For the sake of brevity I shall use the term 'word' alone, even where I intend what I am saying to apply to all meaningful sentence-components.

III

I must pause at this point to consider two objections to these formulations, the consideration of which will reveal important aspects of our subject-matter. First, it is possible for you to tell me that two expressions have the same use (or the same meaning) without thereby telling me what either of them means. For example, if I am ignorant of Japanese, you might tell me that two expressions in that language have the same use, without telling me what either of them means. And in that case I could know on authority that two expressions have the same use without knowing what either of them means. But then something is wrong with our formula, according to which to say that 'u' and 'v' have the same use *is* to say what 'u' means.

I do not believe that this objection is as formidable as it appears to be at first sight, although in order to meet it we shall have to sacrifice the classic simplicity of the analysis. It seems to me that when one tells someone what an expression means he is, in effect, telling him that two expressions have the same use; but he uses the meaning formulation only when he supposes that his hearer already knows how to use the second expression. Thus the meaning statement is subject to a presupposition which distinguishes it from the mere statement of equivalence of use. The ultimate reason for the presence of this presupposition is the fact, noted earlier, that specifications of meaning have the primary function of teaching someone how to use an expression. Pointing out that 'u' has the same use as 'v' will do nothing to help you master the use of 'u' unless you already know how to use 'v'. Once we make this complication explicit the difficulty vanishes. Rather than explicitly making this point on each occasion, I shall simply serve notice once for all that in each case the meaning-statement is to be taken to be equivalent to the use-statement only when the use-statement is subject to a presupposition than the hearer already knows how to use the second expression.

The second difficulty could be stated as follows. The sentences 'I have just been to dinner at the White House' and 'Heisenberg just asked me to write a preface to his latest book' are both usable to impress the hearer; but one certainly would not say that they have the same meaning, nor would one exhibit one of these sentences in order to say what the other means. Nor would the fact that 'call' can be substituted for 'dinner' in the first sentence without altering its suitability for being used to impress the hearer, do anything to show that 'call' and 'dinner' have, even in part, the same meaning.

In reflecting on this difficulty one comes to recognize a fundamental distinction between two sorts of acts one could be said to
perform by uttering a sentence (for the performance of which one
could utter a sentence), one of which is usable in our definitions, the
other of which is not. Consider the following lists.

I	II
report	bring x to learn that . . .
announce	persuade
predict	deceive
admit	encourage
opine	irritate
ask	frighten
reprimand	amuse
request	get x to do . . .
suggest	inspire
order	impress
propose	distract
express	get x to think about . . .
congratulate	relieve tension
promise	embarrass
thank	attract attention
exhort	bore

I am going to use the term 'illocutionary' to denote acts that
are naturally reported by the use of verbs like those in the first list
and 'perlocutionary' to denote acts that are naturally reported by the
use of verbs like those in the second list. I borrow these terms from
the late John Austin's *How To Do Things With Words*.[1] Austin chose
these terms because he thought of the first sort of act as done *in* uttering a sentence, the second sort as done *by* uttering a sentence. Although
I put less stock in this prepositional test than did Austin (who, indeed,
put it forward only with many qualifications), the terms seem felicitous.
However it will be clear to readers of Austin that my distinction does
not precisely parallel his; and it would be unfortunate if my termi-
nological appropriation should lead anyone to hold Austin responsible for the details of my analysis.

[1]Oxford: The Clarendon Press, 1962.

These two classes of acts seem to me to differ in the following important ways.

(1) It is a necessary condition for the performance of a perlocutionary, but not an illocutionary act, that the utterance have had a certain sort of result. I cannot be said to have brought you to learn something, to have moved you, frightened you, or irritated you, unless as a result of my utterance you have acquired some knowledge, have had certain feelings aroused, etc. But I could be said to have made a certain report, request, 'or admission, asked a certain question or offered congratulations to someone for something, no matter what resulted from my utterance. I have still asked a question whether you answer it or not, or for that matter, whether or not you pay any attention to me or understand me.[1]

(2) A perlocutionary, but not an illocutionary, act can be performed without the use of language, or any other conventional device. I can bring you to learn that my battery is dead by manœuvering you into trying to start the car yourself, and I can get you to pass the salt by simply looking around for it. But there is no way in which I can *report* that my battery is dead, or *request* you to pass the salt, without uttering a sentence or using some other conventional device, e.g., waving a flag according to a prearranged signal. This difference is closely connected with the first. It is because a perlocutionary act is logically dependent on the production of a state of affairs which is identifiable apart from the movements which produced it, that I can be said to perform that action whenever I do anything which results in that state of affairs. The result provides a sufficient distinguishing mark.

(3) Illocutionary acts are more fundamental than perlocutionary acts in the means-end hierarchy. I can request you to pass the salt in order to get you to pass the salt, or in order to irritate, distract, or amuse you. But I could hardly amuse you in order to request you to pass the salt, or get you to know that my battery is dead in order to report that my battery is dead.

A convenient rule-of-thumb (but no more than rule-of-thumb) is

---

[1]It may be an arguable point whether I can be said to have made a request of you if you have failed to understand what I said. But even if I am wrong in supposing that I can, there would still remain a sharp difference between the two sorts of actions with respect to effects. For even if that particular sort of effect is necessary for illocutionaries, it is a general blanket requirement that does nothing to distinguish between one illocutionary act and another. Whereas a perlocutionary act is made the particular kind of act it is by the condition that a certain sort of result has occurred. It is the specific character of the result that distinguishes it from other perlocutionary acts.

provided by the fact that an illocutionary, but not a perlocutionary, act can usually be naturally performed by the use of a sentence which includes a specification of the action performed. I can admit doing x by saying 'I admit doing x'. I can propose that we go to the concert by saying 'I propose that we go to the concert'. But perlocutionary acts resist this mould. In uttering 'You're fine, how am I?' I may be amusing you; but it would be odd, at best, to set out to amuse you by saying 'I amuse you that you're fine, how am I?'. If you were a fastidious and proud cook I might irritate you by saying 'Please pass the salt', but the sentence 'I irritate you to please pass the salt' would be an inept tool for this job.

The examples given earlier should make it clear that sameness of meaning cannot hang on sameness of perlocutionary act potential. On the other hand, I can find no cases in which sameness of meaning of sentences clearly does not hang on sameness of illocutionary act potential. I therefore propose that the generic term 'linguistic act' in our definitions be replaced by the more specific term 'illocutionary act'.

The notion of an illocutionary act is left in a rough state in this essay. It is obvious that if sameness of illocutionary act potential is such a crucial notion in my account, it is of the first importance that I have reliable criteria of identity for illocutionary acts. And to develop these I should have to go beyond the largely negative characterization so far provided and determine the sorts of conditions which must be satisfied if one is to be truly said to have performed a certain illocutionary act. Of all the loose threads left dangling in this essay, this one has the highest priority.[1]

IV

Having attained a measure of clarity concerning the sorts of acts involved, we can now turn to the task of correcting the oversimplification imposed on our definitions by the fiction that each expression has only one meaning and only one use. This is quite often not the case. 'Can you reach the salt?' sometimes means *please pass the salt*, sometimes *are you able to reach as far as the salt?*, and perhaps sometimes *I challenge you to try to reach as far as the salt*. 'Sound' has a great many different meanings—*audible phenomenon, in good condition, long stretch*

---

[1]For some further work on this problem, see my 'Linguistic Acts', *American Philosophical Quarterly*, Volume I (April, 1964), pp. 1–9; and Chapter 2 of my *Philosophy of Language*, Englewood Cliffs, New Jersey: Prentice-Hall, 1964.

of water, *measure the depth of*, etc. Moreover this unrealistic note in our definienda is reflected in the definientes. It is rarely the case that two sentences are used alike in every context, or that two expressions can be substituted for each other in every sentence without altering illocutionary act potentials. Thus corresponding to the above case of sentence-multivocality we have the fact that 'Can you reach the salt?' and 'Please pass the salt' are used to perform the same illocutionary act in many contexts but not in all. And corresponding to the case of word-multivocality cited above, we have the fact that 'sound' and 'audible phenomenon' can be substituted for each other in some sentential contexts without changing illocutionary act potentials, e.g., in 'Did you hear that . . .?', but not in others, e.g., in 'I've been sailing on the . . .'

Thus if our account is not to be largely irrelevant to the facts, we must provide definition-schemas for kinds of meaning-statements which reflect the fact of multivocality. First, note that we often say, loosely, ' "u" means *v*' where, although there are other meanings, this is the chief or most prominent one. I suggest that we take care of this sort of case as follows.

IIA. The chief meaning of 'x' is y = df. 'x' and 'y' usually have the same use.

The expanded version for sentences would run:

IIB. The chief meaning of 's' is t = df. in most contexts 's' and 't' have the same illocutionary act potential.

And the expanded version for words would run:

IIC. The chief meaning of 'u' is v = df. 'u' and 'v' can be substituted for each other in most sentences without changing the illocutionary act potential of each sentence.

I am afraid that the terms 'most sentences,' and 'most contexts,' which occur in these definitions, promise more than they can provide. They can be given no mathematical interpretation, not even one as unspecific as 'over half.' Since we have no classification of contexts of utterance, or even any way of determining whether we are confronted with the same context on two different occasions, we cannot begin to say how many distinguishable contexts there are, and hence no sense can be attached to talk of any definite proportion of contexts. As for 'most sentences,' no limit can be put on the number of sentence-types in a language, or even on the number of sentence-types in which a given word occurs; and so again there is no place for talk about a certain proportion of the total. I take it to be clear that it would not do to understand 'most sentences' to mean *most sentence-tokens which have actually occurred*; for this would make the results far too heavily influenced by the accidents of what has and has not happened to have been said. A similar point could be made for a similar proposal in the case of contexts. We might understand 'most sentences' to mean *over half the sentence-types which have actually been employed*; but then we should have to weigh these types in terms of the frequency with which tokens of each of them occur before we should be within hailing distance of what is needed. And the matter is further complicated by the fact that the prominence of a certain use is affected by factors other than the frequency of its occurrence, e.g., by how early in the course of learning the language it is generally acquired, or how important the topics are in respect to which it occurs. The most that can be said on this point is that the vagueness of the analysans nicely matches that of the analysandum.

This untidiness may well lead us to give up trying to introduce further refinements into the analysis of the notion of the chief meaning, and to concentrate instead on the notion of *a* meaning of an expression. In the light of the fact of multivocality this notion would seem to be the most fundamental one. *The* meaning of a univocal expression could be viewed as a limiting case, and talk of the chief meaning of a multivocal expression as a rough approximation which is good enough for certain working purposes. And with respect to the notion of *a* meaning it might seem that we could dispense with attempts to get at a suitable sense of 'most', and simply say that all that is required for it to be the case that a meaning of 'u' is *v* is that 'u' and 'v' sometimes have the same use. But unfortunately this will not do, since in specifying a meaning of 'u' we want to exhibit another expression with which the use in question is clearly connected. If our other expression, 'v', only exceptionally had this use, we would not clearly identify it by exhibiting 'v'. It would not quite do to say, 'A meaning of "manage" is *run*'; even though it is true that 'manage' and 'run' sometimes have the same use. Hence we have to introduce the more stringent requirement that the use which 'x' and 'y' have in common is a use which 'y' usually has. Thus:

IIIA. A meaning of 'x' is y = df. 'x' sometimes has the use which 'y' usually has.

Expanded for sentences this would read:

IIIB. A meaning of 's' is t = df. in some contexts 's' has the illocutionary act potential which 't' has in most contexts.

And expanded for words it would read:

IIIC. A meaning of 'u' is v = df. in most sentences in which 'v' occurs 'u' can be substituted for it without changing the illocutionary act potential of the sentence.

In this last definition the requirement that we choose a 'y' which usually has the meaning we wish to specify for 'x' is reflected in the specification of most of the sentences in which 'y' occurs. To say that 'u' sometimes, but not necessarily usually, has the use which 'v' usually has, is to say that 'u' can be substituted for 'v' in most 'v'-containing sentences, but not necessarily vice versa.

To say that 'x' has different meanings is to say that what is meant by 'x' on some occasions will differ from what is meant by 'x' on other occasions; in other words, it is to say that what the speaker means by 'x' on one occasion differs from what he meant by 'x' on another occasion. To round off the account I will suggest a pattern of analysis for such phrases.

> IVA. What A (the speaker) meant by 'x' on O (a particular occasion) was y (What was meant by 'x' on O was y) = df. 'y' usually has the use which 'x' had on O.

Again we guarantee that the meaning-statement does bring out the meaning by requiring that 'y' usually have the use which is in question. This can be expanded for sentences as follows:

> IVB. What A meant by 's' on O was t = df. the illocutionary act which A performed on O by uttering 's' is the illocutionary act which, in most contexts, would be performed by uttering 't'.

And for words the expanded version would be:

> IVC. What A meant by 'u' on O was v = df. if we substitute 'v' for 'u' in the sentence which A uttered on O, the resulting sentence would in most contexts be used to perform the illocutionary act which A was performing on O.

For example, 'When A said "He was so mean to me", what she meant by "mean" was cruel'. On our account this becomes: 'The sentence "He was so cruel to me" would usually be used to make the complaint which A was making in uttering "He was so mean to me".' Here the requirement that 'v' usually have the use to which we are trying to call attention cannot be reflected in an emphasis on substituting 'u' for 'v' rather than vice versa; for we are talking about a particular case in which 'u' rather than 'v' is being used, and so any substitution will have to be made into this context. Instead the requirement is reflected in the condition that the sentence resulting from the substitution of 'v' for 'u' be usually used to perform the act which is being performed on that occasion.

It seems that phrases like 'most contexts' and 'most sentences' are unavoidable in all these analyses. And so the chaotic state of these concepts is going to infect any meaning-talk.

It is worth noting that perlocutionary acts are even more obviously out of the picture when we are dealing with what A means by 'x' on O. Of course we have here an analogue of the point we made with respect to the general meaning-statement, ' "s" means *t*', viz., that there will be 't's which are often used to perform the perlocutionary act which 's' is being used to perform on O without it being possible to exhibit 't' in specifying what is meant by 's' on O. Consider a case where what I do (perlocutionary) in uttering 'The ultimate effects of thermonuclear explosions is a matter for conjecture' is to frighten my hearer. If someone who didn't understand asked 'What did he mean by that?', it would be misleading, to say the least, to reply, 'He meant *boo*'. Nor when in saying 'Can you reach the salt?' to a sensitive hostess who is also very touchy about the perfection of her cooking, I succeed in irritating her, would it be correct to say that what I meant was *you look ghastly this evening*. But here (with respect to what is meant on a particular occasion) the exclusion of the perlocutionary from the analysis of meaning can be justified in another way. With respect to the general notion of what an expression means, I do not believe that the converse of the above point holds, viz., that there will be sentences which have the same meaning but are not usually used to perform the same perlocutionary act(s). Such cases cannot be found because a sentence is normally employed to perform one or more perlocutionary acts because of what it means. 'Can you reach the salt?' is regularly used to get someone to pass some salt to the speaker just because of what the sentence means. But with reference to what one means by a sentence on a particular occasion, the converse does hold. One can find cases in which 't' can be exhibited to specify what was meant by 's' on O, without it being the case that 't' is usually used to perform the perlocutionary act(s) which 's' is used to perform on O. For example, in the second of the cases just mentioned, one could say that what the speaker meant was *please pass the salt*. But it is certainly not the case that 'Please pass the salt' is usually used to irritate a listener. Again where by saying to someone 'What's cooking lately?', I distract his attention from a conversation going on elsewhere in the room, (and to avoid raising other issues, let us assume that I had intended to produce this effect), one could correctly say that what I meant by 'What's cooking lately?' was *what have you been doing recently?* But this latter sentence is certainly not normally used to distract one's hearers.

F

As these examples suggest, it is in cases in which the perlocutionary use of a sentence is one which is non-standard for that sentence, dependent on peculiarities of the situation, that the inference from sameness of meaning to sameness of perlocutionary act breaks down. In specifying what was meant by 's' on O, we seek to exhibit another expression which normally has the same illocutionary use which was given to 's' on O. Where the perlocutionary use of 's' was one which normally goes with that illocutionary use, then naturally the 't' exhibited will normally have that perlocutionary use also. If the perlocutionary use of 'Can you reach the salt?' had been the one normally connected with its illocutionary use of requesting someone to pass some salt, viz., getting someone to pass some salt, then of course any sentence with the same illocutionary use would have had the same perlocutionary use as well. But where the perlocutionary use made on that occasion was non-standard, e.g., irritating the hearer, this use would be non-standard for the 't' as well. And it is also in these non-standard cases that sentences which usually have the perlocutionary use in question cannot be used to specify meaning.

The case of using the sentence 'What's cooking lately?' to distract the hearer's attention from a discussion, brings out another pertinent fact, viz., that there are perlocutionary acts for which no sentence is normally used. Where this is the case, we could not even attempt to say what was meant by exhibiting a sentence which normally has that perlocutionary use. There is no sentence which is normally used to distract. What will serve that purpose is entirely a function of the situation. Still less could there be any expression whose normal use is to deceive. If there were, it would obviously be useless for that purpose.

V

This is perhaps the best point at which to review the differences between meaning and use on our account. Some philosophers have talked as if a straight identification were possible. ('For a large class of cases—though not for all—in which we employ the word "meaning" it can be defined thus: the meaning of a word is its use in the language'. —L. Wittgenstein, *Philosophical Investigations*, I, 43.) But a moment's reflection shows that this will not do. The meaning of 'authentic' is *genuine*, but we could not specify the use of 'authentic' by saying that the use of 'authentic' is *genuine*. On the analysis presented here, meaning and use are about as closely connected as they could be short of an identification, but they differ in the following ways.

(1) Saying what the meaning of an expression is, is equivalent not to saying *what* its use is, but rather to saying that it has the same use as another expression. Of course if we knew what the use of 'u' was we would be in an ideal position to say what it means, for we would then be in a position to find another expression which has the same use, if there is one. But there is no guaranteed transition in the other direction, as is evidenced by the fact already brought out that, although we are often in a position to say what a word means (exhibit another expression that has the same use), we do not presently have in our conceptual repertoire adequate resources for saying what the use of a word is (in a semantically crucial sense of use).[1]

(2) Even if we compare the statement of meaning with a statement of sameness of use, rather than a statement as to what the use is, there is the difference that in the former, unlike the latter, we are not explicitly referring to two expressions, but rather referring to one and introducing the other in the very special way for which I have used the term 'exhibit'. This unique sort of occurrence might be thought to be merely a grammatical freak, which could be junked without interfering in any way with what is being said. However if we remember that a meaning-statement is to be distinguished from a statement of sameness of use by the presence of a presupposition to the effect that the hearer already knows how to use the second expression, we can see that this special mode of occurrence of the second expression is the grammatical sign of that presupposition and is by no means expendable.

It is worth noting that *sameness of meaning* (synonymity) cannot be distinguished from *sameness of use* in these ways. A statement of sameness of meaning carries no such presupposition as that just mentioned, nor is either expression 'exhibited' rather than just referred

[1] One may get the impression that to make ' "u" means *v*' equivalent to a certain kind of relation between 'u' and 'v' is to represent meaning as a wholly intralinguistic affair rather than as a matter of the relations between language and the (largely) non-linguistic world we use language to talk about. But this would be a mistake. As we have seen, the relation which 'u' must have to 'v' is equivalence of function in the performance of various illocutionary acts; and, although this point cannot be fully appreciated before the notion of an illocutionary act is subjected to a thorough scrutiny, it should be clear already that the performance of an illocutionary act involves relating oneself in various ways to extra-linguistic conditions and states of affairs. Hence if the meaning of an expression is a function of its contribution to the usability of sentences for performing illocutionary acts, its meaning will necessarily be a function of extra-linguistic conditions, though, to be sure, in a much more indirect way than is often supposed.

to. In fact, there would be no point in making any distinction between them if it were not for the grammatical connexion between the contrast of 'same meaning' and 'same use' and the contrast of 'meaning' and 'use', and if it were not for the fact that 'sameness of use', unlike 'sameness of meaning', is likely to lead us to look in what, according to the position of this essay, is the right direction.

VI

I now want to call attention to certain difficulties attaching to these definitions, difficulties that in various ways show the meaning idiom not to be completely adequate for the subject matter with which it is designed to deal.

(1) Consider the fact that multivocality is not enough to prevent a statement of the form ' "u" and "v" have the same use' from being wholly true. For it might be that even though 'u' has several different senses 'v' has just the same range of senses, distributed over its occurrences in the same pattern. In that case it would be unqualifiedly true, despite the multivocality of 'u,' to say that 'u' and 'v' could be substituted for each other in any sentence without altering the illocutionary act potentialities of that sentence. And yet it would not clearly be correct in this case to say unqualifiedly that 'u' means v. It is not that this would be clearly incorrect; it is rather that we would not know what meaning-statement to make. It would not seem quite right to say that 'u' has v as its only meaning, for that would seem to imply that 'u' has only one meaning. But on the other hand, it seems that nothing specific could be urged against that statement, for 'u' and 'v' are everywhere equivalent. The fact that meaning-talk is not forearmed against such a contingency suggests that underlying such talk there is an assumption that two expressions cannot be multivocal without diverging in their use at some point. And this assumption would seem to be justified; the fact that a given expression has a variety of senses makes it much more unlikely than it would have been otherwise that there should exist an exact synonym. The matching would have to be much more complex than it would if the expression were univocal. Hence I am not inclined to worry about this kind of discrepancy in our definition.

(2) The multivocality of 'u' is no more a necessary than it is a sufficient condition of the failure of universal adequacy of the statement, ' "u" and "v" have the same use'. And this fact provides some

actual cases of discrepancy between statements of this form and corresponding statements of the form, '"u" means v.' There are cases in which 'u' and 'v' are not everywhere intersubstitutable in the appropriate way, but where 'u' is not multivocal and where we would not be prepared to deny that 'u' has v as its only meaning. For example, '"wealthy" means—*rich*'. There are sentences in which a substitution of 'wealthy' for 'rich' will not leave illocutionary act potentialities unchanged, e.g., 'I like rich sauces'. And yet it seems that we should unhesitatingly affirm that the only (current) meaning of 'wealthy' is *rich*. Note that in this case 'rich' is multivocal, and that the failures in substitutability can be traced to that fact. Moreover the failures have to do only with the substitution of 'wealthy' for 'rich,' not the reverse. I am inclined to think that in any case in which substitutability fails even though 'u' is univocal these conditions will hold. But even so the fact remains that we would be prepared to make an unqualified meaning-statement in cases in which unrestricted substitution is not possible. Of course this difficulty could be handled very simply by modifying the definiens to make it require substitutability of 'u' for 'v' only in most cases. But I am not happy about this. Remember that meaning-statements are used primarily to help someone acquire mastery of the expression whose meaning is being given. That is, we find an expression, 'v', which, we suppose, he already knows how to use, and we tell him, in effect, to use 'u' in the same way. Now if in such cases we are interested, as it seems clear we are interested, both in teaching him to use 'u' correctly himself, and in teaching him to understand employments of 'u' by others, then for the first purpose we need to give him an expression he already knows how to use for which 'u' can be substituted, and for the second purpose we need to give him an expression he already understands which can be substituted for 'u'. And this means that the meaning-statement is a reliable device for the purposes for which it is intended only to the extent that unrestricted substitution in both directions are possible. Thus failures of substitutability in either direction should lead to a qualification of the meaning-statement. I think we can see why there is no modification when there are (minor) failures in substituting 'u' for 'v' only. Such failures indicate that there are uses of 'v' which 'u' does not have, but they do not necessarily indicate any plurality in the uses of 'u'. Therefore we do not want to say, on this basis, that v is only one of the meanings of 'u'. And this is the only qualification that is available, so long as we are restricted to the resources of ordinary meaning-talk. Here we seem to have a complication which the meaning idiom is incapable of expressing adequately.

(3) We have been talking as if whenever 'u' is substituted for 'v' in a sentence, the substitution either will or will not change the illocutionary act potentials. But if we remember that any sentence can be used to perform more than one illocutionary act, we will realize that a given substitution might conceivably alter the suitability of the sentence for performing some illocutionary acts but not others. And this complicates matters. Perhaps in most cases the alteration is an all or nothing affair. But there are cases of the mixed sort. If, e.g., we substitute 'place where alcoholic drinks are served' for 'bar' in 'I was admitted to the bar', we will leave unaffected the possibility that this sentence is used to report that one had been allowed to enter an establishment serving alcoholic beverages, but not the possibility that it is used to report that one has been granted the right to practise law. This complexity might be taken account of by modifying the definiens in each case to read 'without *substantially* altering the illocutionary act potentialities of the sentence in each case'. Of course there are various conceivable states of affairs in which this would not work. For example, it is conceivable, though it is not in fact the case, that in every sentence containing 'authentic,' or in most such sentences, the substitution of 'genuine' for 'authentic' would alter at least one important illocutionary act potential of the sentence, but leave at least one other important illocutionary act potential unaffected. In that case it would not be true to say that in most sentences in which 'authentic' occurs, 'genuine' could be substituted for it without substantially altering the illocutionary act potential of the sentence. And yet since a significant part of the illocutionary act potential of each of these sentences would be unchanged by such substitution, we might take this as indicating a significant overlap of meaning in the terms, and hence might want to say that one meaning of 'genuine' is *authentic*. I am not sure that this is a real possibility. But whether it is or not, it is noteworthy that here again we have certain complexities which cannot be adequately reflected in the meaning idiom.[1]

[1] It is maintained by some, e.g., by Paul Ziff in *Semantic Analysis*, Ithaca, New York: Cornell University Press, 1960, that there are cases in which at least rough equivalents of a word can be given, but in which it does not make sense to say that the word means so-and-so, e.g., 'tiger'. Ziff maintains that one would properly ask not 'What does "tiger" mean?', but rather 'What is a tiger?'. The class of cases for which this claim is made seems to roughly coincide with the class of terms which are such

The general trend of these considerations (to which should be added the difficulties mentioned above concerning such terms as 'most' and usually' in the definitions) is to exhibit various respects in which talk about meaning, as it actually goes on, is vague, rough, and lacking in resources for reflecting all the significant distinctions within its subject-matter. It is clear that meaning-statements are dealing with sameness and difference of use among expressions, but it should now also be clear that they are dealing with this topic in a relatively unsubtle fashion. If we want analyses of meaning-statements which closely reflect their actual use, we are not going to get anything very fine-grained. If we want to talk in a more precise way about the facts, the sameness-of-use idiom, as here developed, provides a more adequate instrument. In that idiom we can easily make such distinctions as that between failures of substitut-ability in the one direction or the other, and between the range of sentences in which substitution can be carried out and the extent to which substitution is possible in each of these sentences, distinctions which are obscured in the meaning idiom. We could then proceed to develop measures, along several different dimensions, of the extent to which two expressions have the same use.

Of course we could develop terms in the meaning idiom which would at least mark out segments of these dimensions and make that idiom more nearly adequate. But I doubt that the game is worth the candle. I fell that it is more fruitful to provide and refine analyses of meaning-statements just to the point at which it becomes clear what sort of claim is being made in meaning-statements, and then to pursue further refinements in the more supple sameness-of-use idiom. We should now be in a position to see that meaning talk is a practically convenient approximation of the theoretically more fundamental statement in terms of sameness of use. In helping some-one to learn to use an expression we find another which is approx-imately equivalent in use, and then, neglecting the various respects in which the two are more or less equivalent, we simply present the second expression as an equivalent, recognizing the complexity only to the extent of making some crude distinctions between *the* meaning, the chief meaning, and *a* meaning. It is clear that this is a useful procedure, but it is equally clear that the very complexities which

---

that no necessary and sufficient conditions for the application of the term can be given. The most plausible examples are all substantives. I do not wish to either accept or reject this position, though it seems plausible. I merely wish to point out that if it is justified it indicates still another limitation on the meaning idiom.

make the sameness-of-use idiom unsuitable for everyday language learning make it vastly superior for semantic theory.

However the sameness-of-use idiom has deficiencies of its own. For one thing, there are expressions for which, within the language, there are no synonyms, not even approximate ones, e.g., 'is' and 'and'. And this means that within the language we can neither say what they mean nor that they have the same use as some other expression. And yet we want to say that these words are meaningful or have a meaning; each of them plays an important and relatively consistent role in our talk, as much as other expressions which are not subject to this stability, e.g., 'albeit' or 'lid'. More generally, the presence or absence of an equivalent for a word in any given language seems to be an accident *vis à vis* the semantic status of that word; so that it should be possible to get at that semantic status without depending on such factors. This impression can be reinforced by considering the possibility of *inventing* an equivalent and, with luck, of getting it accepted into current use. In that case a meaning-statement, and a sameness-of-use statement would have become possible without any significant change having occurred in the semantic status of the word in question.

Second, it is an important defect of our analysis of 'same use' for words that it works only for intralingual equivalents. Remember that our analysis is in terms of substituting the two expressions for each other in a variety of sentences. This operation can be carried out only when the two words belong to the same language. If we try substituting 'eau' for 'water' in 'Give me some water', nothing happens; we draw a blank.

Both of these deficiencies would be remedied by developing a way of *specifying* the use which a given word has, as we have done for sentences, where, unlike our treatment of words, the criterion of sameness of use is based on a way of specifying *what* the use of a given sentence is. That would free us from any dependence on the existence of an approximate synonym in the language. Presumably it would be possible to specify (in English) the use(s) of 'and' or 'is', or any other expression which we would be inclined to call meaningful. And we could handle intralingual judgements of sameness of use by first separately specifying the use of each word and then basing assertions of (degrees of) equivalence of use on that. Thus for these reasons, and others,[1] the next major step in the direction pointed out by this

---

[1]One of the others is the following. It seems that we cannot give an adequate account

essay (after a thorough analysis of the notion of an illocutionary act) will be the development of a satisfactory way of identifying and describing the use(s) of a particular word. This is almost virgin territory. There are various terms in current use which might be thought to mark out large categories of such uses—'denote', 'connote', 'refer', 'qualify', 'conjoin', etc.; but although some, especially 'refer', have received a great deal of discussion, some of it quite subtle, virtually nothing has been done by way of developing a general method for identifying, classifying, and interrelating word-uses as a basis for semantic theory. At this point it can only be said that the difficulty of the enterprise is matched by its importance.

of knowing (or learning) the meaning of a word in terms of sameness of use. I can know (learn) the meaning of 'tree' without knowing (learning) that 'tree' has the same use as some other expression. But if we had an appropriate concept of the use of 'tree', we might well be able to show that what I know (learn) when I know (learn) the meaning of 'tree' is that it has a certain use.

VIII

MEANING AND ILLOCUTIONARY ACTS

David Holdcroft

I

IN the penultimate paragraph of J. O. Urmson's reconstruction of the late Professor Austin's William James Lectures, *How To Do Things With Words* (Oxford 1962), we read,

> I have as usual failed to leave enough time in which to say why what I have said is interesting. Just one example then. Philosophers have long been interested in the word 'good' and, quite recently, have begun to take the line of considering how we use it, what we use it to do. It has been suggested, for example, that we use it for expressing approval, for commending, or for grading. But we shall not get really clear about this word 'good' and what we use it to do until, ideally, we have a complete list of those illocutionary acts of which commending, grading, &c., are isolated specimens—until we know how many such acts there are and what are their relationships and inter-connexions.[1]

In this passage Austin obviously implies that there are a number of questions about the word 'good' which the theory of illocutionary acts (hereafter referred to by 'T.I.A.' for convenience) can be used to answer. Unfortunately he is not explicit about the precise nature and range of these questions, and merely contents himself with saying that they are questions about the use of the word. However, in view of what has been said in recent years about the connexion between, for example, the speech act of commending and the commendatory meaning of the word 'good', it seems possible that some of the questions about the word 'good' which Austin thought could be answered by the use of T.I.A., are questions about its meaning. And whether he did think this or not, it does seem worth considering whether in the case of any word or expression, T.I.A. could be used to answer any question that might be asked about the meaning of that word or expression. For while Hare's claim that the word 'good'

From *Ratio*, Vol. 6 (1964), pp. 128–43. Reprinted, with revisions, by permission of the author, *Ratio*, and Basil Blackwell.

[1] J. L. Austin, *How To Do Things With Words*, p. 162.

usually has commendatory meaning, and has it presumably as a result of the fact that it is usually used to commend, is but an isolated example of a claim that it is possible to explain the meaning of a word (or part of its meaning) by reference to the speech acts that are performed when it is uttered, some philosophers seem to have claimed, or at least written as though they believed, that it is possible to explain the meaning of any word by reference to the speech acts performed when uttering it.

Of course if T.I.A. can be used to explain the meaning of words in this way, then one would expect that it can also be used to answer questions about synonymity, and an interesting attempt to show that it can is to be found in a recent article by William P. Alston.[1] An informal statement of his position is contained in the following passage:

Consider the statement, ' "Procrastinate" means *put things off*'. I can test this statement, at least for my speech, as follows. I review cases in which I would say 'You're always procrastinating', and determine whether I would use the sentence 'You're always putting things off' to make just the same complaint. I think of cases in which I would say 'Please don't put things off so much' and determine whether I would use the sentence 'Please don't procrastinate so much' to make the same plea . . . . And so on.

This suggests that a meaning-statement of the form, ' "x" means *y*' is to be tested by determining whether 'x' and 'y' can be substituted for each other in a wide variety of sentences without, in each case, changing the job(s) which the sentence is used to do, or, more precisely, without changing the suitability or potentiality of the sentence for performing whatever job(s) it was used to perform before the alteration.[2]

In an attempt to work out his position in detail, Alston first defines the use of a sentence 's' as 'the potentiality of "s" for the performance of one or more linguistic acts (more briefly, the linguistic act potential of "s")'.[3] He continues,
. . . if we recall the general formula relating meaning to use,

IA. 'x' means y = df. 'x' and 'y' have the same use
we can expand this for sentences, in terms of the above definition of the use of a sentence, as follows.

[1] William P. Alston, 'Meaning and Use', *Philosophical Quarterly*, vol. 13, no. 51. [Holdcroft's article takes account of the changes made by Alston in 'Meaning and Use', pp. 141–165 above. Footnote references to the *Philosophical Quarterly* have been amended to refer to pages in this volume. Ed.]

[2] p. 147 above.

[3] p. 148 above.

IB. 's' means t = df. 's' and 't' have the same linguistic act potential.[1]

Introducing 'u' and 'v' as variables for sentence components, Alston introduces the following further definition.

'u' has the same use as 'v' = df. 'u' and 'v' can be substituted for each other in sentences without changing the linguistic act potential of each sentence.

And from this definition together with the original meaning formula (IA) we get, he claims, one further definition:

IC. 'u' means v = df. 'u' and 'v' can be substituted for each other in sentences without changing the linguistic act potential of each sentence.[2]

Presumably the linguistic act potential of a sentence is specified by reference to the set of linguistic acts it can be uttered to perform, so that if two sentences have the same linguistic act potential it will be possible to utter them to perform the same set of linguistic acts. Hence, in what follows, it is assumed that the question whether two sentences have the same linguistic act potential depends on the question whether they can be uttered to perform the same set of linguistic acts.

Later Alston places an important restriction on the kind of speech act to be considered in this context, a restriction which is designed to exclude all but illocutionary speech acts,[3] and, this restriction apart, he complicates his account considerably, a great deal of the complication being designed to deal with multivocality. These complications need not, however, concern us here, for in view of his explicit claim that he 'can find no cases in which sameness of meaning does not hang on sameness of illocutionary act potential',[4] there can be little doubt that he would defend the view that T.I.A. can be used to answer questions about sentence and word synonomy. And though he does not claim that T.I.A. can be used to explain the meaning of every word, he does seem to claim that it can be used to explain the meaning of some, namely words which have synonyms, or which are synonymous with longer expressions, in circumstances in which the meaning of the synonym or synonymous expression is understood already.

[1] p. 148 above.
[2] p. 149 above.
[3] Alston's use of 'illocutionary' is similar to Austin's, but not, he claims, in all respects the same.
[4] p. 153 above.

As far as I know, no other philosopher who has maintained that the meaning of a word is its use has explicitly equated the use of a sentence with the set of illocutionary acts that can be performed by uttering it, and as a consequence claimed that sameness of meaning 'hangs on sameness of illocutionary act potential'. Nevertheless, those philosophers who have maintained that the meaning of a word is its use, and who have treated the question 'What is the use of "w"?' as though in all important respects it is the same question as 'What jobs are performed by the utterance of "w"?'[1] have, I think, interpreted 'use' in a way broadly similar to Alston's, in that many of the examples of jobs done which are given involve the performance of an illocutionary act. And though it would clearly be wrong to foist on these philosophers the view that T.I.A. can be used to explain the meaning of every word, it is at least reasonable to maintain that if this view meets with serious difficulties, then so too will the claim that the meaning of a word is its use, so long as 'use' is interpreted in a way broadly similar to Alston's.

In what follows I shall be primarily concerned to argue that it is very doubtful whether T.I.A. could be used to explain the meaning of all (or most) words unless certain semantic information was used in such a way that the fact that it was used would make the claim an uninteresting one. I don't, however, think that it is very easy to show conclusively that this is so, and I certainly don't provide a rigorous proof that it is. All that I do is to offer a number of considerations which, taken together, indicate strongly that the claim that T.I.A. unsupplemented by semantic information can be used to explain the meaning of all (or most) words is false.

But first some explanation is perhaps called for of what I take to be involved in the claim in question and why it is I have chosen to discuss this particular claim. Using the expression 'T.I.A. alone' as a convenient abbreviation of the somewhat cumbersome expression 'T.I.A. unsupplemented by any semantic information', I take the substantiation of the claim that T.I.A. alone can be used to explain the meaning of every word of a language L to involve one in showing *at least* three things:

(1) That there is a class K of linguistic expressions of L, such that it is possible to explain the meaning of each member of K solely by reference to the illocutionary speech acts performed by uttering the expression.

---

[1] Cf, P. Nowell-Smith, *Ethics* (Pelican), p. 69.

(2) That in the case of each speech act referred to in explanation of the meaning of a member of K, there is a way of telling what speech act has been performed which does not involve making use of semantic information about L.

(3) The meaning of all words of L which are not members of K can be explained using only expressions which are members of K, or expressions which themselves are definable using only expressions which themselves are members of K, . . . , etc.

It seems to me that if all three things could be demonstrated, then interpreting 'use' in a way similar to that in which Alston does, the claim that the meaning of a word is its use would in some considerable measure be justified. Even if one could not establish (3), but could establish (1) and (2), and show that the meaning of the majority of words can be explained in terms of members of K, the result would still be an impressive one. But if one could not establish both (1) and (2), one would not have established anything that justifies the claim that the meaning of a word is its use (interpreting 'use' in the way Alston does, that is), for, at the very least, for this claim to be justified there must be cases in which it is possible to tell what the use of an expression is without making use of any semantic information about the language to which it belongs. And it is for this reason that the claim that T.I.A. can be used to explain the meaning of all (or most) words is uninteresting unless some restriction is placed on the use of semantic information in conjunction with T.I.A.

II

It would not of course be fair to criticize Alston's essay for failing to establish that T.I.A. alone can be used to explain the meaning of every word since, as I have said, it does not seem to have been his intention to establish that it can.

However, a discussion of Alston's position, and of his proposed definitions, will not be out of place here, since it will reveal, I hope, the difficulties in the way of supposing that T.I.A. alone could be used to explain the meaning of every word. For example, the difficulties in the way of supposing this would be formidable if his definition,

IB. 's' means t = df. 's' and 't' have the same linguistic act potential,

could be shown to be inadequate, because it is just false that any two sentences which can be uttered in the performance of the same set of illocutionary acts have the same meaning, and it could be shown also that if T.I.A. alone is to be used at all to explain the meaning of words it must be possible to use it *first* to explain the meaning of sentences. For that would mean that we had good reasons for supposing both that the success of the enterprise would depend on being able to explain the meaning of at least some sentences solely by reference to the illocutionary acts performed by their utterance, and that this could not be done.

But are there good reasons for supposing that if T.I.A. alone is to be used to explain the meaning of words, then it must be possible to use it first to explain the meaning of sentences? A brief consideration of Austin's general theory of speech acts, of which T.I.A. is but a part, will, I hope, show that there are.

The general theory is primarily a classification of the 'senses in which to say something may be to do something, or in saying something we do something'. Austin argues that to say something is always to do something, and that anyone who says something in the 'full normal sense' of saying something performs a kind of act which he calls a 'locutionary act'; the performance of an act of this kind *always* involves 'the utterance of certain noises, the utterance of certain words in a certain construction, and the utterance of them with a certain "meaning" in the favourite philosophical sense of that word, i.e. with a certain sense and with a certain reference'.[2] It is perhaps worth pointing out that in Austin's use of 'saying' it is not a necessary condition of someone's having said something that he should have made a statement. Thus if, for example in giving an order or asking a question, I utter certain words in a certain construction,[3] and with a certain meaning, then I have said something in Austin's sense of 'saying', even though I have said nothing which is either true or false.

Now it seems clear that usually if I perform a locutionary act (an act *of* saying something), I will also be doing something else as well; for example, I might be giving an order, making a suggestion, or giving a warning. And Austin seems to be right when he claims that the question whether on a particular occasion I was making a suggestion, or giving an order, etc., is one to which one may not know

[1] Austin, op. cit., p. 91.

[2] Ibid., p. 94.

[3] Presumably the construction will have to be of a certain kind, e.g., subject-predicate, so that saying something will involve uttering a sentence.

the answer, even though one knows what locutionary act has been performed. Thus, for example, it may be clear what locutionary act someone has performed using the sentence, 'Put on your life-jacket', clear, that is, what the words he used meant in the way in which he was using them, and yet it may not be clear whether he was giving an order, a warning, or merely making a suggestion. This seems to be a good enough reason for distinguishing the class of acts to which the last three mentioned belong from the class of locutionary acts, and this new class Austin calls the class of 'illocutionary acts'.

Now even with this intuitive characterization of an illocutionary act one thing seems clear, and that is that the performance of an illocutionary act will, in the vast majority of cases anyway, involve the utterance of a sentence. It is doubtless true that orders or warnings, etc., can be given without using any words at all, but in those cases in which in giving an order, or a warning, or asking a question, words are used, then a sentence will usually be involved. And this is hardly surprising, since presumably the main point of using language, for example, when giving an order, is to make clear what is being ordered, and to do this one needs to say what it is one is ordering someone to do and, very often, what it is one is ordering him to do it to. Furthermore, not only does the performance of an illocutionary act usually involve the utterance of a sentence, but if we select some arbitrary word occurring in a sentence uttered in the performance of an illocutionary act, and ask what illocutionary act was performed in uttering this word, the question does not seem to admit of an answer. Thus if you ask what illocutionary act I performed by uttering the word, 'Put', when I uttered the sentence 'Put on your life-jacket', I am going to be stumped for an answer—and in general if it is asked whether in uttering a sentence on a particular occasion I was giving an order, a warning, or giving advice, etc., while it may not be clear what the answer should be, at least it is usually clear enough that the question is appropriate, but if some arbitrary word is selected from the sentence uttered and it is asked whether in uttering that word I was giving an order, a warning, etc., then not only is it not clear what the answer should be, it is not clear that the question is appropriate.[1] This being so, it seems clear that if T.I.A. alone is to be used to explain the meaning of all (or most) words, it

---

[1] Suppose that I do use the sentence 'The film at the Plaza is a good one' to commend the film to someone: suppose now someone asks 'Were you using the word "good" to commend?' Obviously the answer is 'No': I used the whole sentence to commend,

must be possible to use it first to explain the meaning of at least some sentences. So we need to see whether this is in fact possible, and, clearly, whether it is or not is going to depend on the answer to the question, 'Is it true that no two sentences which differ in meaning can be uttered in the performance of all the same illocutionary acts?'

The answer to this question depends largely on how complicated the description of the act is supposed to be. Alston presumably has in mind a somewhat complicated description, for according to his definition 's' means t provided that 's' and 't' have in effect the same illocutionary act potential. And if attention is restricted to short descriptions of illocutionary acts such as 'making a statement', 'answering a question', 'making a comment on the weather', then it is far from clear that the sentences (a) 'It is raining', and (b) 'It is snowing' cannot be uttered to perform the same illocutionary acts, so that unless Alston has in mind more complicated descriptions of illocutionary acts than these, it is far from clear that his account can even get off the ground. However, since to prevent unwanted results consistent with his definition the description of the speech act must be a very full one,[1] a difficulty arises for anyone who wishes to say that T.I.A. alone can be used to explain the meaning of all or most sentences. For the only ways of lengthening the description of the speech act so that it will be true that no two sentences which differ in meaning can be used to perform all the same illocutionary acts, are such that the longer the description, the correspondingly greater is the uncertainty that there is a way of identifying the act so described which does not involve making use of semantic information about the language in question. (Such a way of telling will for convenience be called an 'independent way'.) Thus though both sentences (a) and (b) can be used to make a statement, or indeed a statement about the weather, or a comment on the weather, etc., only (a) can be used to make the statement that it is raining; so that if 'making the statement that it is raining'

and I used the word 'good' in commending. Maybe the utterance of the word plays a crucial role in the performance of the act, but it doesn't *constitute* the performance. Cf. Paul Ziff, *Semantic Analysis* (Cornell, 1960), p. 232.

[1] That Alston does have in mind lengthy descriptions of the speech act is indicated by the following passage, . . . ' "A haint caint haint a haint" means *it is impossible for one supernatural spirit to inhabit another supernatural spirit*. This is true because the sentences "A haint caint haint a haint" and "It is impossible for one supernatural spirit to inhabit another supernatural spirit" are usable to make the same assertion.' (p. 148 above.)

is allowed as a permissible description of an illocutionary act, then it will be plausible to maintain that (a) can be uttered in the performance of an illocutionary act which (b) can't. And, in general, if we make a rough distinction between short descriptions of illocutionary acts, the following being examples of such descriptions,

> giving a warning, giving an order,
> giving a verdict, asking a question,

and full descriptions which can be used not merely to report that someone has given, e.g. an order, but to report what order he gave as well, the following being examples of full descriptions,

> warning that the bull is about to charge,
> ordering that the door be closed,
> asking whether it is still raining,

then it is, I think, clear that only if we consider full descriptions of illocutionary acts is it at all plausible to suppose that if two sentences differ in meaning then there will be illocutionary acts which can be performed by uttering the one which can't be performed by uttering the other.[1] But where *full* descriptions of illocutionary acts are concerned, it is obviously less plausible to hold that there is an independent way of telling that an act, so described, has been performed than it is to hold that there is such a way of telling whether an illocutionary act falling under a short description has been performed. Yet if T.I.A. alone is to be used to explain the meaning of some sentences there must be such a way in both cases since, presumably, those illocutionary acts which can be performed only by uttering a given sentence, and any equi-significant sentence, will be the ones it is essential to refer to when using T.I.A. to explain its meaning—and if my argument is correct the vast majority of such acts will be ones falling under full descriptions.

It would be rash to assert that if we consider only full descriptions of illocutionary acts, there is no independent way of telling whether an act falling under one of these descriptions has been performed— though, of course, if there is not then T.I.A. alone cannot be used

---

[1] Of course even so, sentences which differ in meaning can be uttered in the performance of the same illocutionary act: I might order my child to fetch the newspaper by saying 'Fetch the newspaper', but if my wife had already *requested* him to fetch the newspaper I might *order* him to get it by saying 'Do what your mother asked you to do'. But the latter sentence can be used to perform illocutionary acts which the former cannot.

to explain the meaning of any sentence at all. However, it does seem that if one considers these illocutionary acts the performance of which involves what Professor Ziff has called a 'determinate' utterance, it is extremely implausible to suppose that there is any such way of telling what act has been performed under a full description. By a determinate utterance Ziff means 'an utterance that can be employed in making an assertion, or statement, etc., and such that if it is employed in making a statement precisely what statement is made is not dependent on the context in which the utterance is made'.[1] Thus, to use Ziff's own example, 'George K. crossed the Hudson at 2 a.m. on October 20th, 1943' is a determinate utterance, whilst 'He is in there', or 'It is over there', are clearly non-determinate. Now generally when someone uses a determinate utterance to make a statement, ask a question, etc., he does not do so in the presence of the persons, places, things, etc., which the statement is about. And this being so, it is difficult to see how if someone uses a determinate utterance in the performance of an illocutionary act, anyone who was not in possession of semantic information about the language used could identify the act performed under a full description. For if a determinate utterance is not uttered in the presence of the persons, places, etc., which the statement, or question, etc., is about, then there can be nothing in the context of the utterance with respect to which a hearer could formulate the hypothesis that this is what the statement, question, etc., is about, and consequently nothing at all to indicate what meaning the utterance has.

Of course where non-determinate utterances are concerned it might seem that the matter is otherwise. If when a non-determinate utterance is used to make a statement, ask a question, etc., precisely what statement is made or question asked is dependent on the context, then in many cases this is so presumably because the utterance is used to refer to situationally indicated objects or features in the context of utterance. And consequently it is quite plausible to suppose that the context of utterance is such that a person not in possession of semantic information about the language used might succeed in formulating a testable hypothesis as to what the statement was about, and thus go some way to gaining an understanding of what the utterance used meant. Whether a person could in fact identify an illocutionary act performed under a full description in this kind of way I don't of course know, and I have no wish to be

[1] P. Ziff, *Semantic Analysis* (Cornell, 1960), p. 126.

dogmatic on this point since whether he in fact could or not it does at least seem logically possible that he could.

Fortunately, however, I don't think it is necessary for me to show either that in fact he could, or that he could not. For even if he could, and I'll concede that it is logically possible that he could, there would still be reasons to doubt whether T.I.A. alone could be used to explain the meaning of some sentences and derivatively that of all or most words. And this despite the fact that to concede as much as I have now conceded might look like conceding that it is possible that my conditions (1) and (2) might both be satisfied. For having conceded that where full descriptions of illocutionary acts are concerned it is plausible to suppose that if two sentences differ in meaning they cannot be used to perform all the same illocutionary acts, and having conceded that in some cases it is possible that there is an independent way of telling what illocutionary act someone has performed under a full description, it looks as though I have gone some considerable way to granting that conditions (1) and (2) might be satisfied. What reason, it might be asked, is there for denying that the meaning of numerous sentences (i.e. all non-determinate ones) could be explained by referring to the illocutionary acts which can be both identified in the appropriate way, and performed only by uttering one of the sentences in question, or any equi-significant sentence?

Part of the answer to this question is that though it may be possible in some cases to independently identify an illocutionary act under a full description, the number of cases in which it is plausible to suppose that this is possible is very small. So that even if it were possible to explain the meaning of some sentences by referring to the acts in question, the number of sentences for which one could do this would be correspondingly small, with the result that the class K would be so small that it would be quite implausible to suppose that any set of operations could be specified on the members of K which would yield the meaning of all or most words of the language of which K was a subset of sentences.

I have already argued that it is not possible independently to identify an illocutionary act under a full description in those cases in which the performance of the act involves the utterance of a determinate sentence. It seems to me further that it is only those illocutionary acts which can be performed on some occasions by uttering a sentence but which, on other occasions, can be performed without using language at all that can plausibly be held to be independently identifiable under a full description.[1] Perhaps the simplest reason for supposing this is that if an act cannot be performed without uttering a sentence then it would seem to be practically impossible to show that it is not necessary to understand the sentence *first* to identify the act, and of course if it is necessary to understand the sentence first to identify the act under a full description, then any attempt to explain the meaning of the sentence by reference to the act would be circular. For example, if I cannot perform the act of stating that grass is green without using the sentence 'Grass is green' (or some equi-significant sentence, or some arbitrarily chosen symbol as in a code), then it is difficult to see how one could ever be sure that to be able to identify this act a person hasn't got first to know what the sentence I uttered meant—so that someone totally ignorant of the language I used would first have to arrive at a correct opinion as to what the sentence I uttered meant before he could identify the act I performed as the act of stating that grass is green. Indeed not only is it difficult to see that he wouldn't have to do this, but there is some reason to suppose that he would. For if there is no way of performing a given illocutionary act which does not involve uttering some sentence or other with a definite meaning, then the presumption is that the utterance of a sentence with that meaning is essential to the performance of the act. And if this is so then equally the presumption is that there is no way of identifying the act which does not involve making use of knowledge of the meaning of the sentence used or, at least, making use of information derived from someone who did know—as a Frenchman who spoke no English would be if told by a compatriot that I had just asserted that grass is green. Thus if I can only perform the act of stating that grass is green by uttering a sentence with a definite meaning then, I am suggesting, this act could only be identified by someone who knew, amongst other things, what this sentence meant, or who was making use of information obtained from someone who did know. Strictly speaking this would not mean that independent identification was impossible, in that to identify the act a person might not have to make use of any semantic information he *already* possessed, but it

[1] It might be objected here that by definition the performance of an illocutionary act involves uttering a sentence. Austin (op. cit., p. 113) writes 'to perform an illocutionary act is necessarily to perform a locutionary act', but he does not seem to be consistent on this point for on p. 118 he writes '. . .we can for example warn or appoint or protest or apologize by non-verbal means and these are illocutionary acts'. I see no objection to classing e.g. the giving of an order as an illocutionary act whether in giving it a sentence was uttered or not.

does mean that to identify the act such a person would *first* have to reach a correct opinion as to what the sentence uttered meant, so that it is reasonable to treat this case on a par with a case of non-independent identification, in that if this is so it would obviously be circular to attempt to explain the meaning of the sentence by referring to the act performed by uttering it.

It follows that the set of independently identifiable illocutionary acts can contain only those acts which can be performed both verbally and non-verbally and whose performance, when language is used, involves uttering only non-determinate sentences. Such a set is, I think, clearly only a small subset of the set of all illocutionary acts, and whilst the precise determination of its membership would be a matter of great difficulty I hope, in what follows, to indicate very briefly the reasons for supposing that its membership will be very restricted.

III

Using the classification of illocutionary acts proposed by Austin in Lecture XII of *How To Do Things With Words*, it is clear that at most very few members of his first and fifth classes will qualify for membership. Members of his first class he calls 'verdictives', and these ' . . . consist in the delivering of a finding, official or unofficial, upon evidence or reasons as to value or fact . . . .'[1] While it may be possible to perform some of the acts mentioned in this class without using any language at all, e.g. the acts of grading, or ranking, it seems to me so unclear that more than a few such acts could be independently identified under a full description that it is reasonable to ignore the members of this class for the rest of this discussion. His fifth class Austin calls 'expositives' and these 'are used in acts of exposition involving the expounding of views, the conducting of arguments, and the clarifying of usages and of references',[2] and the class includes such acts as stating, affirming, denying, questioning, answering and illustrating. In the nature of the case most of these cannot be performed without saying something, as Austin himself points out,[3] and though there are some marginal cases such as withdrawing, objecting or correcting, they are sufficiently few for

[1] Austin, op. cit., p. 152.

[2] Austin, op. cit., p. 160.

[3] Austin, op. cit., p. 119.

it to be reasonable for me to ignore all the members of this class also.

This leaves three classes. One of these, 'behabitives', is a rather heterogeneous class. In Austin's words 'Behabitives include the notion of reaction to other people's behaviour and fortunes and of attitudes and expressions of attitudes to someone else's past conduct or imminent conduct'. Examples of such acts are apologizing, thanking, deploring, congratulating and welcoming. There is no doubt that most, if not all, behabitives can be performed without saying anything. What is less clear is whether apart from very simple acts of this kind, e.g. welcoming, bidding someone farewell, applauding a performance, that many of these acts could be independently identified. Thus, if I congratulate you on your recent appointment by uttering the words 'Congratulations on your appointment' and clapping you on your back, the utterance of the words does seem to play a fairly crucial role in making it clear what it is I am congratulating you for and how the pat on the back is to be taken. It is true that this role cannot be described as essential. I could conceivably congratulate you on your appointment without uttering these or any other words. But then it does seem that the situation would have to be structured in a certain way and that the utterance of some sentence or other would play a crucial role in doing this: i.e. if you say 'I've got the job' and wordlessly I clap you on the back, then doubtless in most cases I will be taken to be congratulating you for getting the job. But someone who didn't understand the sentence 'I've got the job' could hardly be expected to realize that this was what I was doing—so even in this case an ability to understand a sentence seems to be necessary to identify the act performed. And it seems to me that the identification of the great majority of all but the most simple behabitives will involve the use of semantic information, either directly, as in the case in which it is necessary to understand the sentence I utter when clapping you on the back to know what it is I am congratulating you for, or indirectly, as in the case in which it is necessary to understand some sentence(s) either I or someone else has uttered previously to know that in clapping you on the back I am congratulating you on your appointment.

The situation seems to be somewhat similar when the remaining two of Austin's classes are considered; these are 'exercitives' and 'commissives'. An exercitive Austin describes as 'the giving of a decision in favour of or against a certain course of action, or advocacy of it. It is a decision that something is to be so, as distinct from a judgement that it is so',[1] while commissives are typically actions that commit one to a course of action. Doubtless the distinction between the two classes is not a very clear one since many acts Austin classes as exercitives obviously commit one to courses of action, though not all do. Typical examples of exercitives given by Austin are appointing, degrading, demoting, dismissing, naming, ordering and command-ing, while some typical examples of commissives are promising, covenanting, contracting and undertaking. It is clear, I think, that a large number of exercitives and an appreciable number of commis-sives can be performed without saying anything. Thus I can order you to leave by pointing, excommunicate you by making a ritual gesture, or warn you by flapping my arms; and I can embrace your cause by standing under your banner. However, once again apart from very simple acts of either kind it is very unclear that a large number could be independently identified—though in the case of exercitives it does seem likely that more relatively complex acts might be independently identified than in the case of any other classes, e.g. the acts of ordering (commanding) someone to shut the door, ordering (commanding) someone to leave the room, or warning someone that the bull is dangerous.

Two facts of importance emerge from this: firstly that the number of independently identifiable illocutionary acts is relatively small and, on the face of it, is not numerous enough to explain the meaning of more than a small number of sentences, so that the membership of K would be very small. Secondly since most independently identifiable acts will be relatively very simple ones, the sentences whose meaning could be explained by reference to these acts will from a grammatical point of view themselves be simple, e.g. such sentences as 'I apologize', 'I greet you', 'Congratulations!' and 'Leave the room'. So that K besides having only a very small membership will be a poor sample of the language in a different sense as well, in that it will contain only simple sentence-types. In this connexion the fact that very few, if any, expositives are independently identifiable is of special importance, since it means that illocutionary acts performed by uttering 'fact stating' or question sentences are not independently identifiable, with the result that there are no illocutionary acts by reference to which the meaning of sentences of either of these types could be explained. And if K contains either none, or just a few, sentences of either of these types then there is good reason to think that it will not be large

[1] Austin, op. cit., p. 154.

enough, or rich enough, to yield the meaning of all (or most) words of a language, no matter what set of operations is performed on its members.

NOTES ON THE CONTRIBUTORS

SIR ISAIAH BERLIN, formerly Chichele Professor of Social and Political Theory at Oxford, is now President of Wolfson College, Oxford. Among his publications are *The Hedgehog and the Fox* (1953) and *Karl Marx* (2nd edn., 1956).

FRIEDRICH WAISMANN, who died in 1958, was at one time associated with the 'Vienna Circle', but came to Oxford some years before the Second World War, where he held University appointments successively in the philosophy of mathematics and the philosophy of science. His *Introduction to Mathematical Thinking*, published in German in 1936, appeared in English translation in 1951, and his *Principles of Linguistic Philosophy* was published posthumously in 1965.

P. F. STRAWSON is a Fellow of University College, Oxford. His *Introduction to Logical Theory* was published in 1952, *Individuals: An Essay in Descriptive Metaphysics* in 1959, and *The Bounds of Sense* in 1966. He is the editor of *Philosophical Logic* in the present series.

W. HAAS is Professor in the Department of General Linguistics in the University of Manchester.

GILBERT RYLE is Wayneflete Professor of Metaphysical Philosophy at Oxford, and is the editor of *Mind*. Among his writings are *The Concept of Mind* (1949), *Dilemmas* (1954), and *Plato's Progress* (1966).

J. N. FINDLAY was until recently Professor of Philosophy at King's College, London. Among his writings are *Values and Intentions* (1961), *Language, Mind and Value* (1963), and *Meinong's Theory of Objects and Values* (2nd edn., 1963).

D. S. SHWAYDER, formerly a member of the Department of Philosophy of the University of California at Berkeley, is now at the University of Illinois. His book *Modes of Referring and the Problem of Universals* appeared in 1961, and *The Stratification of Behaviour* in 1965.

WILLIAM P. ALSTON is a member of the Department of Philosophy at the University of Michigan. His book *Philosophy of Language* appeared in 1964, and he has contributed many papers to philosophical periodicals.

DAVID HOLDCROFT, formerly a member of the Department of Philosophy in the University of Manchester, is now a member of the School of Philosophy in the University of Warwick.

BIBLIOGRAPHY

The items in this selective bibliography have been arranged in accordance with the classification of theories of meaning adopted in the introduction. The order of the items in each section is chronological; for convenience of reference, each item is numbered. When a book or article is concerned with more than one theory, a reference is included in each of the relevant sections; the item is given a number on its first appearance, and is afterwards referred to by this number.

DENOTATION THEORY

1. G. Frege, 'On Sense and Reference'. Frege's essay 'Über Sinn und Bedeutung' was first published in 1892. A translation by M. Black, entitled 'On Sense and Reference', is in *Frege: Philosophical Writings*, trans. by P. T. Geach and M. Black (Blackwell, Oxford, 1952), pp. 56 ff. A translation by H. Feigl, entitled 'On Sense and Nominatum', is contained in *Readings in Philosophical Analysis*, ed. by H. Feigl and W. Sellars (Appleton-Century-Crofts, New York, 1949), pp. 85 ff.

2. Bertrand Russell, 'On Denoting'. This essay, first published in *Mind* (1905), is contained in Feigl and Sellars, op. cit., pp. 103 ff., and in *Logic and Knowledge*, a collection of essays and lectures by Russell, ed. by R. C. Marsh (Allen & Unwin, London, 1956), pp. 39 ff.

3. G. Ryle, 'The Theory of Meaning', in *British Philosophy in the Mid-Century*, ed. by C. A. Mace (Allen & Unwin, London, 1957), pp. 244 ff.

4. N. E. Christensen, *On the Nature of Meanings* (2nd ed., Munksgaard, Copenhagen, 1965), Chap. 4.

5. E. J. Lemmon, 'Sentences, Statements and Propositions', in *British Analytical Philosophy*, ed. by B. Williams and A. Montefiore (Routledge, London, 1966), pp. 87 ff.
   Argues that Russell's theory of descriptions can be defended against Strawson ('On Referring'; cf. No. III) if it is seen, not as an analysis of ordinary usage, but as a logical tool.

IMAGE THEORY

6. B. Harrison, 'Meaning and Mental Images', *Proceedings of the Aristotelian Society*, (1962–3), pp. 237 ff.
   Discusses Price's account of image thinking in (11), Chaps. 8 and 9.
   F. Waismann, *The Principles of Linguistic Philosophy* (Macmillan, London, 1965), pp. 158 ff., 352 ff.

   Christensen (4), Chap. 5.

CAUSAL THEORY •

8. C. L. Stevenson, *Ethics and Language* (Yale U.P., 1945), Chap. 3.

9. J. Holloway, *Language and Intelligence* (Macmillan, London, 1951), Chap. 3.

10. H. L. A. Hart, 'Signs and Words', *Philosophical Quarterly* (1952), pp. 59 ff. A discussion of Holloway (9).

11. H. H. Price, *Thinking and Experience* (Hutchinson, London, 1953). Chaps. 6 and 7. Discusses the causal theory under the name of 'the inductive sign theory'.

12. H. P. Grice, 'Meaning', *Philosophical Review* (1957), pp. 377 ff. Contained in *Philosophical Logic*, ed. by P. F. Strawson, in this series.

13. J. Searle, 'What is a speech act?' in *Philosophy in America*, ed. by M. Black (Allen & Unwin, London, 1965), pp. 221 ff. Offers an emended version of Grice's analysis of meaning in (12). Waismann (7), Chap. 6.

PICTURE THEORY

14. L. Wittgenstein, *Tractatus Logico-Philosophicus*. 1st English edition, 1922; trans. by D. F. Pears and B. F. McGuiness (Routledge, London, 1961).

15. I. M. Copi, 'Objects, Properties and Relations in the *Tractatus*', *Mind*, (1958), pp. 145 ff.

16. E. Stenius, *Wittgenstein's Tractatus* (Blackwell, Oxford, 1960), pp. 88 ff., 157 ff. Besides expounding Wittgenstein's picture theory, defends a modified form of the theory.

17. M. Black, *A Companion to Wittgenstein's 'Tractatus'* (C.U.P., Cambridge, 1964), pp. 72 ff.

18. J. Griffin, *Wittgenstein's Logical Atomism* (Clarendon Press, Oxford, 1965), pp. 87 ff.

19. G. Pitcher, *The Philosophy of Wittgenstein* (Prentice-Hall, Englewood Cliffs, New Jersey, 1964), pp. 75 ff.

Waismann (7), pp. 307 ff.

VERIFICATION PRINCIPLE

20. A. J. Ayer, *Language, Truth and Logic* (2nd ed., Gollancz, London, 1946). The preface contains (pp. 5 ff.) a revised version of an earlier attempt (pp. 35 ff.) at formulating the verification principle.

21. A. Church, Review of (20), *Journal of Symbolic Logic* (1949), pp. 52–3.

22. D. J. O'Connor, 'Some Consequences of Prof. Ayer's Verification Principle', *Analysis* (1949–50), pp. 67 ff. Modifies the verification principle as stated in Ayer (20).

23. R. Brown and J. Watling, 'Amending the Verification Principle', *Analysis* (1950–51), pp. 87 ff., 114.

Comments on O'Connor (22). and offers another version of the verification principle.

24. C. Hempel, 'The Empiricist Criterion of Meaning', *Revue Internationale de Philosophie* (1950). Reprinted in *Logical Positivism*, ed. by A. J. Ayer (Allen & Unwin, London, 1959), pp. 108 ff., with a postcript (1958) by the author.

25. C. Hempel, 'The Concept of Cognitive Significance: A Reconsideration', *Proceedings of the American Academy of Arts and Sciences*, Vol. 80 (1951–4), pp. 61 ff.
An extension of (24). Hempel argues that cognitive significance (by which is meant both empirical meaning and purely logical meaning) belongs not to sentences, but to systems as wholes, and is a matter of degree.

26. K. R. Popper, 'Philosophy of Science: A Personal Report', in *British Philosophy in the Mid-Century*, pp. 155 ff.
A short account by Popper of what he meant by his criterion of falsifiability. It should be noted that this paper is not contained in the second edition (1966) of *British Philosophy in the Mid-Century*.

27. P. Nidditch, 'A Defence of Ayer's Verifiability Principle against Church's criticism', *Mind* (1961), pp. 88–9.
Comments on Church (21).

28. J. O. Wisdom, 'Metamorphoses of the Verifiability Theory of Meaning', *Mind* (1963), pp. 335 ff.
Concerns what is called here the 'verification principle'.

29. D. Makinson, 'Nidditch's Definition of Verifiability', *Mind* (1965), pp. 240 ff.
Criticizes Nidditch (27), and offers another formulation of the verification principle.

30. C. Hempel, 'Empiricist Criteria of Cognitive Significance: Problems and Changes', in Hempel, *Aspects of Scientific Explanation* (Collier-Macmillan, London, 1965), pp. 101 ff.
Combines 'with certain omissions and some other changes' the contents of Hempel (24) and (25).

VERIFICATION THEORY

31. M. Schlick, 'Meaning and Verification', *Philosophical Review* (1936). Page references in the introduction are to the article as printed in Feigl and Sellars, op. cit., pp. 146 ff.

32. J. L. Evans, 'On Meaning and Verification', *Mind* (1953), pp. 1 ff. Primarily concerned with the verification theory, but discusses the verification principle also. In the context of a discussion of meaning, argues (p. 9) that 'whereas we can properly speak of the rules governing the use of words, we should not speak of the rules governing the use of sentences'. Cf. Ryle (36).

33. A. R. White, 'A Note on Meaning and Verification', *Mind* (1954), pp. 66 ff.
    Comments on Evans (32).

34. R. W. Ashby, 'Use and Verification', *Proceedings of the Aristotelian Society* (1955–6), pp. 149 ff.
    Waismann (7), Chap. 16.

USE THEORY

35. L. Wittgenstein, *Philosophical Investigations* (Blackwell, Oxford, 1953), especially pars. 1–43.

36. G. Ryle, 'Ordinary Language', *Philosophical Review* (1953), pp. 167 ff.
    Argues (pp. 178 ff.) that one should not speak of the meaning of sentences as their use, a view developed in No. v above.

37. G. E. Moore, 'Wittgenstein's Lectures in 1930–33', *Mind* (1954), pp. 5 ff.
    Also in Moore, *Philosophical Papers* (Allen and Unwin, London, 1959), pp. 257 ff.

38. L. J. Cohen, 'On the use of "The use of"', *Philosophy* (1955), pp. 7 ff.
    Criticizes Ryle's analogy in (36) between the use of words and the use of instruments or implements.

39. C. K. Grant, 'On using language', *Philosophical Quarterly* (1956), pp. 327 ff.
    In a discussion which is complementary to (38), considers the senses in which it may be said that sentences are 'used' to make statements.

40. A. R. White, 'The Use of Sentences', *Analysis* (1956–7), pp. 1 ff. A criticism of Ryle (36).
    Ryle (3).

41. R. Brown, 'Meaning and Rules of Use', *Mind* (1962), pp. 494 ff. Argues that (p. 511) 'the class of meaning rules is only a sub-class of those rules which regulate the use of a word'.

42. W. P. Alston, 'The Quest for Meanings', *Mind* (1963), pp. 79 ff. An article which is in effect complementary to No. VII above; criticizes the view that a meaning is a kind of entity.

Pitcher (19), Chap. 10.
Christensen (4), pp. 149 ff.
Waismann (7), Chaps. 5 and 8.

INDEX OF NAMES

(not including authors mentioned only in the Bibliography)